Teacher For Early Years

TEACHER FOR EARLY YEARS

Supporting educators and parents through the Early Years curriculum

Antonyms, partitioning, onomatopoeia... oh my!

When it's been some time since these words have been in your vocabulary, it can seem daunting supporting children with their learning. As Early Years teachers and tutors with over twenty years experience, the question we are asked most by parents is:

"How can I help my child at home?"

Teacher for Early Years started out as a resource to help tutors, but has since become so much more. It is a specialised guide to help ANYONE working with children in the Early Years: **teachers, tutors, teacher aides, parents** and **graduates**. It can help you plan lessons; support students who are falling behind; and even help you differentiate for those working at a different level to their cohort.

Research indicates that the Early Years are a crucial time for brain development; gaps in these years may lead to children struggling as they move through school.

This all-in-one resource breaks down all the important areas of Literacy and Numeracy curriculum expectations, giving you the confidence and inspiration to plan practical and engaging activities.

Teacher for Early Years is an absolute must for all Early Years teachers and parents!

HOW TO USE THIS BOOK

Stuck for ideas? Sick of thinking on your feet?

This book takes the guesswork out of creating appropriate learning experiences using tried and tested ideas. It has been divided into twelve different areas of support, with each section providing learning goals and activities designed for *children up to eight years old.*

It has been divided into twelve sections:

 Getting Started
 Holistic Support
 Speaking and Listening
 Reading
 Writing
 Book by Book

 Numbers and Algebra
 Supporting Your Mathematician
 Problem Solving
 Activities with Dice, Cards, and Grids
 Assessment
Appendix

We hope this resource helps you to plan engaging, challenging and fun lessons to help accelerate your little superstar!

Enjoy!

Jen and *Kelly*

HOW THIS BOOK WORKS

For Myla and Milky,
Our little cherubs, who drive us crazy but inspire us daily ♡

Copyright © 2021 by Kelly Quilter and Jen Tunney
ISBN 978-0-9954057-5-2

Contact: kelly@teacherforaday.com
Illustrations: trishrubiano@gmail.com
Layout: jewelrubiano@hotmail.com

All rights reserved. This book or any portion thereof may not be reproduced or used in any manner whatsoever without the express written permission of the copy owner except for the use of brief quotations in a book review.

Please note:

> The Early Years of school is also a time when we begin to not only see learning gaps, but also learning difficulties may start to present themselves. This book does not aim to specifically support substantial learning difficulties, however if you have tried and tried with these activities, and you still aren't seeing results, it might be time to talk to a paediatrician, teacher or support teacher for inclusive education. Using this book may facilitate educators and parents to identify learning difficulties earlier, potentially leading to more funding and support at school. **Remember to follow your instincts, if you are not reassured after the first specialist, be sure to get a second opinion**

TEACHER FOR EARLY YEARS

A holistic approach to teaching Literacy and Numeracy in the Early Years

Specialised Edition

By Kelly Quilter and Jen Tunney

Illustrations by
Isabela Beatriz Rubiano
Jewel Rubiano

CONTENTS

TABLE OF CONTENTS

Getting Started

12	What Are They Learning?
13	Engaging Your Learner
	Getting To Know Your Learner
14	Getting Started: The First Session
16	What A Learning Session May Look Like
17	Session Learning Focus
18	My Learning Goals
20	Helping Your Child To Focus
	Brain Breaks
21	Reflecting on Learning
22	In Your Toolkit
23	Apps and Websites

Holistic Support

26	**Motor Skills and Crossing The Midline**
27	Activities To Support Crossing The Midline
28	Gross Motor Activities
30	Fine Motor Activities
32	Developmental Red Flags
33	Having A Positive Mindset
34	Making The Most of Learning Opportunities

Speaking and Listening

38	**English: Speaking and Listening in the Early Years**
	Supporting Speaking and Listening
	Active Listening
40	Get Exploring
	Super Speaking
42	Questioning Games
	Use Your Body
44	**Oral Language Screener**

Reading

48	**English: Reading in the Early Years**
	Learning Letters and Sounds
49	An Example of Exploring the Letter Aa
50	Confusing Letters

Specialised Edition

Reading

51	**Supporting Your Reader**
	0-4 Years
52	Foundation
54	Year 1
55	Year 2
56	Reading and Comprehension Skills
57	Comprehension Strategies To Promote Reading Success
58	Decoding Strategies
59	Learning High-Frequency/Sight Words
60	Sample List of High-Frequency/Sight Words
61	Learning to Read Words
64	A Sample List of Rich Texts For the Early Years

Writing

70	**English: Reading in the Early Years**
	Supporting Your Writer
	0-4 Years
71	Foundation
72	Year 1
73	A Few Spelling Rules For Year 1
74	Year 2
75	A Few Spelling Rules For Year 2
76	What To Do if You Can't Spell a Word
77	Check Your Sentence
78	Working Together To Check Your Writing
79	Writing Goal Checklist
80	Let's Start Writing
81	Pre-Writing Line Development
82	**Some Suggested Activities to Support Writing**
	Foundation
84	Year 1
86	Year 2
90	Generic Early Years English Activities

Book By Book

94	Book by Book Introduction	102	There's A Sea In My Bedroom
95	Brown Bear, Brown Bear, What Do You See?		Koala Lou
96	Dear Zoo	103	A Day At The Zoo
97	Wombat Stew		
98	The Very Hungry Caterpillar		
99	The Magic Hat		
	Pig The Pug		
100	Goldilocks and The Three Bears		
	Possum Magic		
101	Don't Let The Pigeon Drive The Bus		

TABLE OF CONTENTS

Teacher For Early Years

Numbers and Algebra

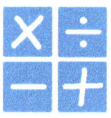

106	**Beginning Mathematical Processes**
	Determining Attributes
	Matching
107	Sorting
	Comparing
108	Ordering
	Patterning
109	**Pattern Formations**

Supporting Your Mathematician

112	**Supporting Your Mathematician**
	0-4 Years
115	Foundation
124	Year 1
142	Year 2

Problem Solving

152	**Addition and Subtraction Strategies for Foundation to Year 2**
153	Draw A Picture
154	Word Problems
155	Count On
156	Use One Five or Ten Frame
157	Use Two Ten Frames
	Number Lines
158	Addition To Ten/Rainbow Facts
159	Think Big, Count Small
160	Doubles
161	Extending Addition to Ten/Rainbow Facts
	Near Doubles
162	Look for Friendly Pairs
163	Use a 100 Grid to Solve Problems
164	Finding The Difference
165	Extending Doubles Using Multiples of Ten
166	Fact Families/Inverse Operations
167	Bridging Through Ten
168	Bridging Through Ten Using Multiples of Ten
169	Partitioning
170	Split Strategy
171	Jump Strategy
	Rounding Up or Down
172	Compensation Strategy
173	Vertical Addition and Subtraction (no regrouping)
174	Vertical Addition and Subtraction (with trading/regrouping)

176	**Multiplication and Division Strategies**	180	Arrays
		181	Number Lines
	Repeated Addition	182	Number Sentences
178	Drawing or Making Equal Groups	183	Fact Families/Inverse Operations

Activities With Dice, Cards, and Grids

186	**Activities Using Dice and Cards**
	Foundation
188	Year 1
190	Year 2
192	**Activities Using the Hundred Grid**
	Year 1
196	Year 2
198	**Extra Important Mathematical Learning in F – 2**
200	Shape

Assessment

204	**Foundation Assessment Overview**
205	Beginning of Year: Number and Algebra
206	End of Year: Number and Algebra
207	**Year 1 Assessment Overview**
208	Beginning of Year: Number and Algebra
209	End of Year: Number
210	End of Year: Algebra
211	**Year 2 Assessment Overview**
212	Beginning of Year: Number
213	Beginning of Year: Algebra
214	End of Year: Number
215	End of Year: Algebra

Appendix

English

218	Letter Flashcards
224	Concepts of Print
225	Letter/Sound Checklist
226	Letter/Word/Sentence Sort
227	Editing A Sentence
228	Sentence Boundaries
229	Grammar and Punctuation
236	Mnemonic Spelling Tricks
237	Mnemonic Posters
238	**Structure and Features**
239	The Writing Process
240	Recount/Journal
242	Letter/Email
244	Procedure
246	Narrative - A Story
250	Exposition/Persuasive
256	Information Report

Math

260	Numeral Rhymes
262	Number Flashcards
266	Cookies for Addition and Subtraction
267	Five Frame
	Ten Frame
	Foundation Pattern Assessment
268	Numbers to 10 Thinkboard
269	Numbers to 20 Thinkboard
270	Hundred Grid
	Blank Hundred Grid
271	MAB or Base 10 Blocks
272	Two-Digit Place Value Chart
273	Three-Digit Place Value Chart
274	Lily pads and Frogs
276	Number of The Day Year 1
277	Number of The Day Year 2
278	**Glossary of Terms**

WHAT ARE THEY LEARNING?

Ask the teacher for a curriculum overview (learning intentions) at the beginning of each term. If they don't have a paper or digital copy, arrange a meeting to allow you to gain further information.

CREATING A LEARNER:
Students need to know or expect that learning should be difficult, If it's too easy, they probably aren't learning anything new. They need to understand that all learners, no matter what age, will come across unavoidable challenges when learning. More information about having a Positive Mindset can be found on **page 33.**

Children learn best by being active learners, rather than passive. Their knowledge will have a better chance of becoming embedded if they have the opportunity to put into practise what they have learnt and are given the chance to teach and share their understanding with others.

It is imperative that you are able to monitor your little learner and ensure you don't push them so hard that they grow to resent homework and learning. **Our goal is to cultivate curious minds and develop a lifelong love of learning.**

GOOD LEARNERS:

- **Use what they have learnt.**
- **Know that their brain needs to be exercised.**
- **Build on their learning.**
- **Make mistakes work for them, not against them.**
- **Apply multiple ways to solve a problem.**
- **Keep learning.**
- **Make knowledge their own.**
- **Gather information from a variety of sources.**
- **Know the power of the word 'YET'.**

Specialised Edition

ENGAGING AND SUPPORTING YOUR LEARNER

- ✓ Build on your child's interests, strengths and skills.
- ✓ Create a positive, supportive environment.
- ✓ Maintain high expectations.
- ✓ Provide engaging and relevant activities.
- ✓ Give explicit instructions where necessary.
- ✓ Take the time to observe, wait and listen to children.

 # GETTING TO KNOW YOUR LEARNER

Does your child tell you that they did nothing or they can't remember what they did? Find out more by varying your questions each day. Instead of the popular "How was your day?" or "What did you do today?"

ASK

What did your teacher say today that really stood out for you?

Did your teacher say or teach anything today that you didn't understand?

If your teacher was here now, how would he/she describe your day?

What can you tell me about your maths lesson?

What did you write about today?

Can you teach me how you... *(practise spelling words/ write a letter/ count to --).*
    Ask the teacher for direct curriculum links or good questions to focus on.

Was there anything you found challenging/easy today?

What superpower could have helped make today even better?

Did you make any mistakes today? What could you do differently next time?

What was the best/worst part of today?

Did you learn anything new or interesting? Tell me about it.

Did you do anything today that you are proud of?

Who put a smile on your face?

Did anything funny or weird happen today?

What's something you're looking forward to at school?

Did you hear anyone say anything nice today?

Who is a good learner in your classroom? How do you know? What qualities do they have that makes them a good learner?

How do you know when you are learning something new?

What can you do when you find something too difficult to do on your own?

Did you help anyone today?

GETTING STARTED

GETTING STARTED: THE FIRST SESSION

This is the time to start building a rapport with your learner – the more you get along, the better the results!

- [ ] Introduce yourself – tell the child (and parent) some information about yourself and your interests.

    "I am studying to be a teacher and I am so excited to put my training into action/I have been teaching for X years and love seeing those lightbulb moments when children are making connections and learning something new."

- [ ] Talk with the child to identify their interests, strengths, needs and goals. Do they know what they are good at and what they need to work on?

    What do you like to do in your spare time? What are you finding difficult/ easy at school? What do you want to get better at?

    Complete **Two stars and a Wish** to help them identify their strengths and weaknesses in their learning **(see explanation on page 21)**.

- [ ] Assure them that you are there to help them and that today you will be just asking some questions to identify goals and to plan for the next session.

ENGLISH FOCUS – This may take more than one session:

- [ ] **Assess letter/sound awareness** for students in Foundation or if they are really struggling in Year One/Two. (Be sure to check upper and lowercase formation). This takes a long time, so they will most likely need a brain break **(See brain break ideas on page 20, alphabet flashcards on page 218-224 and letter/sound assessment on page 225).**

- [ ] Collect a **writing sample for Foundation – Year Two students**. Depending on child's age and ability, this might be just squiggles, their name, a few familiar words or a recount of their day. Observe pencil grip, writing conventions (left to right, top to bottom, spaces between words), letter formation, spelling, sequence of ideas, punctuation, etc., and use this to focus on for the next session.

- [ ] Use a picture book to **assess print concepts for Foundation – Year Two students**, to identify what they know about books and early print conventions (see checklist on **page 224**). If you are supporting reading, read the book and then ask child to complete a retell storyboard (Use template in the appendix – easy version on **page 248** or harder version on **page 249** to assess comprehension skills). This could also be used as a writing sample to identify writing goals (see above).

- [ ] Complete a **simple reading assessment** for children who know most letters/sounds– use the **High-Frequency/Sight words** lists on **page 60** to create some simple sentences (see supporting images for underlined words **on page 59**) from each list. Print out the list and tick off words as they are read.

    E.g.,   List 1 – I can see a <u>dog</u>. I like my <u>mum</u>.
    List 2 – Here is the little <u>cat</u>. Come and look at the little cat.
    List 3 – That man said "Yes!" He went to the <u>shop</u>.
    List 4 & 5 – We have all had a play on the <u>swing</u>, but not dad.

> If this is too easy, use online books from Speld SA website (go to Resources, Phonics Books) to identify reading ability using decodable texts. These can be downloaded and printed prior to the session or read online if you can get internet access.

MATHS FOCUS

- [ ] Assess the student's mathematical understanding using the sample assessments F – 2 on **page 204–215**. Use this to identify goals and plan for the future.

AFTER THE SESSION

- Check in with parents, let them know that you were able to gather some useful information to identify needs and plan for the next session. Ask the parent for curriculum information from the school (most school's share this with parents) or ask for the teacher's contact details to email them directly.

- Start thinking about short-term and long-term learning goals, remember these for the follow up session. Ideally, these will be written at the start of session two, with the student's input, so they feel ownership over their goals.

SESSION TIPS

- Sit side by side in a communal area with minimal distractions.
- Keep track of what was covered in each session – parents could ask for this at any time.
- Organise each child's work neatly in their book, keep worksheets in folders or books for easy access. Provide or request a document wallet to store homework resources they may need to work on between sessions.
- Be prepared – have a list of learning goals and focus activities before you arrive for each session.
- Plan for movement/brain breaks, most five-year-old children can only sit and concentrate for ten minutes at a time.
- Praise the student on their effort, not the end result **(see Positive Mindset information on page 33)**. You will see greater achievements if you praise the process, not the product.
- Ease their nerves and remind them that you are right there beside them to help.
- Share learning with parents after each session – Today, we focused on... Over the next week, it would be great if you could practise/revise...

WHAT A LEARNING SESSION MAY LOOK LIKE

FOLLOW UP SESSION SAMPLE	Introduce the learning for the session, make links to previous learning. Get children interested in the topic.
Orientation Up to five mins (Depending on age F – Year Two)	After explaining learning goals, you may wish to complete one of the following suggestions: • Introduce new sight words that they will come across in the text. • Use the book: If your focus is reading, you might do a picture walk (use the pictures to tell the story). If your focus is writing, read the book. • Watch a video on YouTube linked to the topic (ensure you have checked all video content before showing to children). • Make direct links to previous learning including challenges that were faced. • Model new letter/sound and practise formation. • Introduce new language that you will be exploring during the session. • Count aloud forwards and backwards using a number line or grid. • Play a problem-solving game, revising previous strategy taught (e.g., how many of these problems can you solve in one minute?). 🔥 Be transparent with your learning goals, as children will experience more success if they know what they are working towards. Learning Focus goals should be written at the start of each session, plus the child should have short- and long-term goals that they are working on. See page 18, 19 for Learning Goals posters.
Enhancing 10 – 20mins (Depending on age F – Year Two)	This is the learning focus of the session – building on prior knowledge and making connections with new learning. E.g. You may wish to complete one of the following suggestions: • Writing task – respond to the text or a stimulus. See writing suggestions on page 82–89. Go through checklists on page 77–79. • Reading skills - Use posters on pages 57-58 to support decoding and comprehension skills. See reading suggestions on page 51–55. • Complete Book by Book suggestions on page 94–103. • English – See a range of activities on page 90–91 to complement texts. • Number - Use Number sections for each year level page 112–149. • Complete hundreds grid activities on page 192–197. • Explore problem solving on page 152–183 or dice and card games on page 186–191. **Please see corresponding sections for many more activity ideas.**
Synthesising Up to five mins (Depending on age F – Year Two)	This is your chance to check in with your littler learner and gauge how they are going. E.g., you may wish to complete one of the following suggestions: • Revise/discuss learning using Reflecting on Learning strategies listed on page 21 as a way for students to share learning and educator to assess understanding. • Give feedback on student's short and long-term goals and adjust accordingly.

Please note – this is a guide only, the suggested times will depend on the child's age and the specific learning goal.

Specialised Edition

Learning Focus Goals

Use ONE of these to write goals together at the start of each <u>session</u>.

Today we are learning to:

This will help us to:

E.g., **Today we are learning to:**
Count on from any given number.
This will help us to:
Add numbers together and solve problems.

Today we are learning to:

Today I am looking for:

E.g., **Today we are learning to:**
Write complete sentences.
Today I am looking for:
A capital letter to start the sentence and a full stop to end the sentence.

My Learning Goals

Name: **Date:**

MY SHORT-TERM GOALS

In the next four weeks, I am working on...

CHECK IN after four weeks

How am I going so far?

☐ I can't do these... YET   ☐ I am on track   ☐ I have achieved these goals

MY LONG-TERM GOALS

In the next four months, I am working on...

CHECK IN after four months

How am I going so far?

☐ I can't do these... YET   ☐ I am on track   ☐ I have achieved these goals

To achieve my goals, I need to:

Specialised Edition

My Learning Goals

Name:	Date:

MY SHORT-TERM GOALS	MY LONG-TERM GOALS
• • •	• • •
REVIEW after four weeks	**REVIEW after four months**
←———┼———┼———→ I can't do it… yet / I am on track / Achieved! Ready for new goals	←———┼———┼———→ I can't do it… yet / I am on track / Achieved! Ready for new goals
REFLECTION	**REFLECTION**
Let's celebrate! Give yourself two stars for the progress you have made and one wish for future goals. ⭐ ⭐ ✨🪄	Let's celebrate! Give yourself two stars for the progress you have made and one wish for future goals. ⭐ ⭐ ✨🪄
MY PLAN! To achieve my goals, I will…	**MY PLAN! To achieve my goals, I will…**

GETTING STARTED

 HELPING YOUR CHILD TO FOCUS

Stay calm, even when the child may be frustrated. Let the child know that while it is tricky, you are there to help and guide them.

Use an animated voice.

Use *First... Then...* statements. E.g., First we will do some writing, then you can have a quick run.

Remember to give them a brain break if they need it, as a quick activity may help them to re-focus. See below for ideas.

 BRAIN BREAK IDEAS

Have a piece of fruit.	Ten star jumps, high knees, kick backs.	8,4,2,1 *(stand up, shake your hands 8 times, shake your legs 8 times, shake your hands 4 times, shake your legs 4 times and so on).*
Just Dance! / Go Noodle! Available online.	Jump on the trampoline for two minutes.	Run on the spot as fast as you can for 10 seconds.
Go for a quick run around the yard.	Do ten push ups on the ground or on the chair.	Go for three laps around the room and touch each wall.

Specialised Edition

 # REFLECTING ON LEARNING

It is really important that children are given the opportunity at the end of each session to discuss and reflect on their learning. This is also a great chance for the educator to access and assess their level of understanding. Be sure to use a variety of these strategies as they will strengthen children's understanding and assist you with future planning. This should be brief and link back to the learning.

General discussion and purposeful questioning – identify new learning or goals achieved.

Be a teacher – go and teach ---- about... OR teach me about...

Reflect – discuss the information learnt.

Two stars and a wish – students identify two things they feel confident in and one area they wish to improve on.

Show me how you feel – give yourself a thumbs up/down/midway to identify how you're going with your work.

Create a visual – this could be a co-created poster, a labelled diagram or an illustration by the learner.

Fast five – tell me five things you learnt about...

Comprehension – use **Comprehension questions** on page 56.

Educator feedback – observations of the sessions.

Create a rubric/bingo game – children can highlight learning goals as they are achieved using the 3x3 grid with the words *I can...*

Journal it – write down some learning reflections.

Exit pass – before you leave today, tell me what you learnt...

TODAY I READ/LEARNT

Retell – information learnt or stories in sequence. Use storyboards on pages 248-249.

Goal setting – co-create goals for the next session.

Student feedback – student leads the conversation *(Tell me how you went today and why? How are you going with this learning and why?)*.

Feedback Sandwich – educator starts with positive feedback, followed by an area needing improvement, followed by another positive comment.

Teacher's view – ask the student to assess their own work from the teacher's perspective.

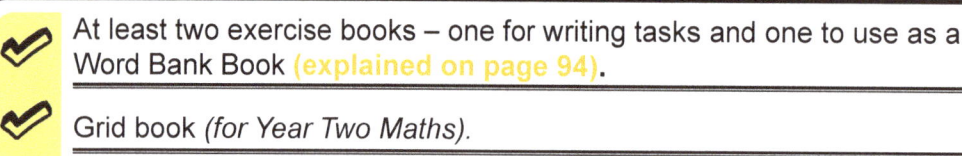 IN YOUR TOOLKIT

- ✓ At least two exercise books – one for writing tasks and one to use as a Word Bank Book *(explained on page 94)*.
- ✓ Grid book *(for Year Two Maths)*.
- ✓ Writing, cutting, gluing materials.
- ✓ Alphabet letter cards *(see appendix page 218-224)*.
- ✓ 100's grid (see *page 270* for hard copy or search online for an interactive 100's grid).
- ✓ Number cards to 100 *(make or buy)*.
- ✓ Snap lock bags to store flashcards.
- ✓ Whiteboard or clear plastic sleeves with blank paper inside.
- ✓ Whiteboard marker and cloth rubber *(a tissue will work just fine)*.
- ✓ Deck of cards.
- ✓ Dice: a few 6-sided and 10-sided (available online).

In addition:

Play money for Year One and Two.

Access to picture books.

A variety of hands on resources to practice letters and numbers including playdough, shaving foam, sand etc.

Laminator (if possible).

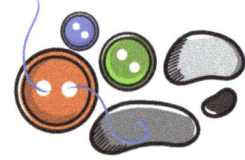

Counting materials - counters, buttons, pebbles, etc.

Specialised Edition

📱 APPS AND WEBSITES

APPS FOR CREATING
– Sharing Learning

Use these apps to create presentations and posters, take and label photos, record audio (insert audio or use dictation – speech to text), sketch/draw, practise typing as well as learning the appropriate use of digital technology.

- Book Creator
- Keynote/PowerPoint
- Sketches School
- Clips
- iMovie
- Notes

APPS FOR PRACTISING
– Learning Through Repetition

- ABC Reading Eggs, Eggy Words, Eggy Numbers, Eggy Vocabulary
- Khan Academy Kids
- Nessy Learning
- Touch and Write
- Teach Your Monster to Read
- Mathletics
- RAZ Kids – Kids A-Z
- Literacy Planet
- Maths Seeds

SOME USEFUL WEBSITES

YouTube Kids	Videos on most topics.
Study Ladder	Set tailored Literacy and Numeracy tasks for students.
Pobble 365 and Literacy Shed	Themed film clips and lessons to support Literacy.
Starfall ABC	Supports early Literacy skills.
Go Noodle	Movement breaks and mindfulness.
Cosmic Kids Yoga	Yoga immersed in stories.
Nat Geo Kids	Research topics using kid-friendly information.
Pevan And Sarah	Catchy songs and worksheets.
Cool Math 4 Kids & Math Playground	Interactive games.
Kiddle Encyclopaedia	Safe internet search results.
ABCYa	A website (and app) to support Literacy and Numeracy.
Topmarks	Interactive Literacy and Numeracy games.
SPELD SA Phonic Books	Free decodable readers available to print or read online.
Learning Games For Kids	Educational games for most subject areas.

GETTING STARTED

Supporting the Whole Child

Teacher For Early Years

MOTOR SKILLS AND CROSSING THE MIDLINE

To support children's learning, we must also promote their ability to cross the midline and provide activities for them to develop their fine and gross motor skills.

Crossing the midline activities will support children to activate both sides of their brain. This action is where children are able to cross over their body to perform a task, such as reaching for something with their right hand when it is on the left side of their body or even sitting cross-legged on the floor. Crossing the body's midline helps with many everyday tasks such as writing, getting dressed, and playing sports, and can impact a child's development and learning.

Gross motor is the physical skills we all need in order to crawl, stand, sit, walk, run, hop, skip, jump, ride, swim, catch, throw, kick and do all of the active tasks in our daily lives. Gross motor skills can affect balance and movement as it involves using the core stabilising muscles needed to sit and learn.

Fine motor means *"small muscles"* and these skills refer to the refined ability to manoeuvre the muscles in your fingers, thumbs and hands. It is an important skill to aid in tasks such as writing, cutting, gluing, feeding, doing up buttons and zips, tying shoelaces and many other self-help tasks. Children's hands need to build up strength in order to accomplish many everyday duties and we can help develop this through fun activities and play.

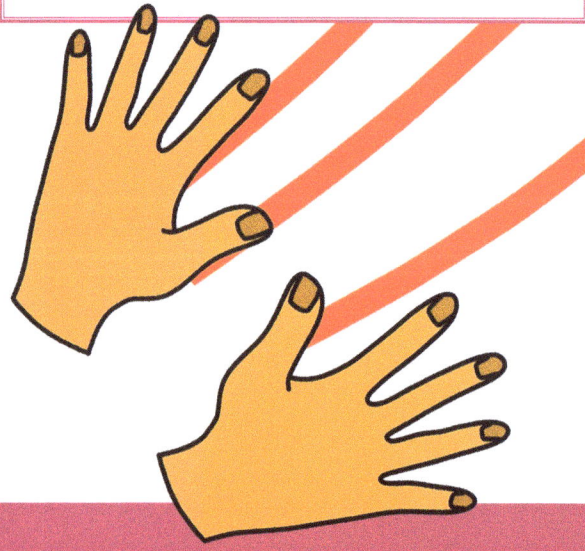

Without decent gross motor skills, children will not be able to sit and listen for long, and without fine motor skills, they will struggle to write. Children need support to work on their muscular strength (small and big muscles) and endurance, timing and control, body awareness and coordination and ability to cross the midline.

CROSSING THE MIDLINE

Crossing the midline happens when your child moves their arm or leg across the imaginary line down the middle of their body. If a child is having difficulty crossing the midline, this may mean they are finding it difficult to use both sides of the body together. This can result in difficulties in a variety of educational experiences including but not limited to writing, cutting, and tracking words on a page. It can also affect gross motor skills including crawling and reaching, skipping, and kicking a ball.

Activities to support crossing the midline:

- Touch your left shoulder/ear/foot with your right hand and vice versa.
- Sit cross-legged on the ground and pass a tennis ball around the body.
- Stand up, legs together, and pass a tennis ball around the waist and knees.
- Open legs, pass tennis ball between legs in a figure-eight motion.
- Sit cross-legged on the ground, back-to-back with child, pass a soccer ball around to each other using two hands on the ball.
- Brush teeth and hair.
- Participate in dancing and yoga.

- Sit and use dancing streamers, waving them all around the body.
- Climb rock walls.
- Use hula hoops.
- Kick a ball at a target with an inner foot, sideways kick.
- Ask the child to kneel on the floor, throw a ball to them standing slightly to the side so they have to reach across their own body to catch.
- Play Simon Says and make sure the movement instructions cross the midline.
- Stand in the middle of the coffee table, trace finger from one end to the other, repeat with the other hand.

- Cross over walking: lay a rope on the ground or draw a line with chalk. Let the children walk with their left foot on the right side of the rope and their right foot should only land on the left side of the rope.
- Stand up straight, touch right elbow on lifted left knee and vice versa.
- Learn the Nutbush or Macarena dance.
- Alternate hands when completing tables activities such as puzzles, sticking and removing stickers, eating with cutlery.
- Put left glove on with right hand and vice versa.
- Crawling, marching and monkey walking.
- Skipping with and without a rope (five + years).

Gross Motor Activities

Obstacle Course
Use a variety of equipment including climbing frames, slides, tunnels, hoops, stepping blocks, balls, skipping ropes, bikes, monkey bars (supervise), and balance beams. If you don't have any equipment, draw instructions in chalk on the ground.

Explore:
two-foot jumping, hopping, tip toeing, balancing, crawling, crab walking, monkey walking, frog jumps, leaping, galloping, running and rolling.

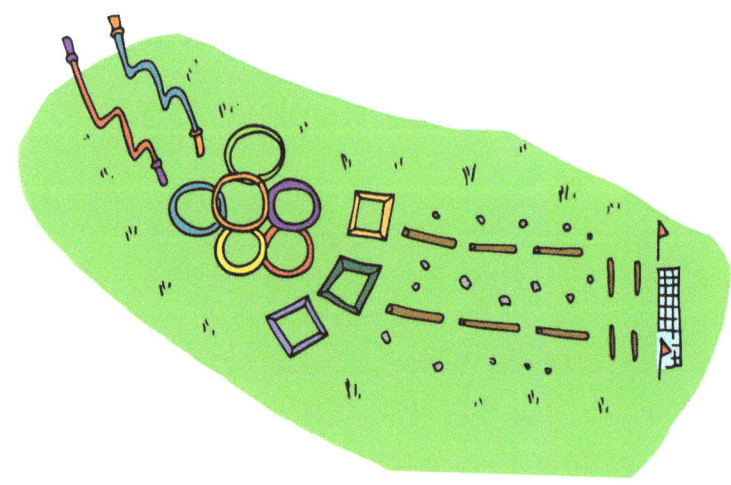

Skipping Rope
A skipping rope can be used in the traditional way, but it is a tricky skill to master for the young ones. Some other ways to use it are:

- To spin it slow and low around in circles and get the children to jump over it.

- Wobble the rope like a snake in the grass and get children to jump over it.

- Hold it up at both ends and play limbo with it.

- Two people hold it at each end and swing it around and the children need to run through without getting hit. The more advanced can try jumping on their way through.

- Place it on the ground in different shapes and get children to balance on it like a tight rope.

- Tie two ropes together and two people holding the ropes with their legs (like the game Elastics). Students can then practise jumping over and between the rope. Move the rope higher up the legs for more of a challenge.

Specialised Edition

Yoga
Yoga is a great skill for stretching, calming and promoting mindfulness. Practise Downward Dog, Cat and Cow Pose, Child's Pose, Standing Tree Pose, Star Pose, Warrior Pose, Cobra (with the tongue out), etc. Improvise a rocket launching into space, the sun rising, butterflies opening their wings and trees swaying side to side.

Climbing
Climbing frames and ladders are the best and safest way for children to practise this skill. Ensure that they are safely positioned and that they are changed regularly to encourage an interest in the activity.

Ball Skills
Catching, throwing, kicking and bouncing are important skills to help develop eye/hand and eye/foot coordination.

- Throwing the ball up in the air to themselves and catching it.
- Dribbling a bouncy ball by hitting it repeatedly.
- Kicking a ball from the ground then progressing to kicking it from your hands.
- Keep a balloon in the air by hitting it repeatedly.
- Throwing and catching with someone else.
- Throwing a beanbag, ball or soft object to a target e.g. in a hoop on the ground, through a basketball hoop, into a bucket etc.
- Bouncing the ball and catching it.
- Kicking or throwing a ball to a wall. You could make a target on the wall for more of a challenge.
- Kicking, catching and chasing the ball with someone else.

Teacher For Early Years

Fine Motor Activities

Feely Bags
Put random items into a bag and get children to touch, feel and grab to guess what it is. Older children can match their findings to a clue card and cross off their findings.

Dress Ups
Provide dress-up clothes with different fasteners such as buttons, zips, press studs, buckles, etc.

Grab It
Pick up cotton balls, pom poms, shells, rocks or gems using tweezers/tongs or pegs. Hide these items in foam, rice or cooked spaghetti, etc. for an added element.

Box Collage
Give children access to craft with scissors, sticky tape and colours, and go crazy!

Magnets
Magnets can be used to explore how they attract and resist as well as move metal objects around.

Carpentry
Use nails, hammers and wood to get the children "working" on their hand skills.

Lego
Lego is great for getting those fingers working and developing fine motor skills.

Messy Play
Water, slime, wet sand, shaving foam, goop, and clay are all fun ways to explore with their fingers and hands.

Tracing
Give students a black-lined colouring in picture and some tracing paper or baking paper and get them to copy the picture underneath.

Washing Babies
Give children baby dolls, baths, towels, clothes, a clothesline and pegs, and let them play and develop their fine motor skills in a real-world setting.

Tactile Picture
Place buttons/tokens/pasta on to a patterned picture, e.g., ladybug or leopard spots, rays of a sun using pasta, a caterpillar's body using buttons.

Play Dough
Play dough has many benefits for developing fine motor skills. Children can hide small objects such as marbles in them.

Specialised Edition

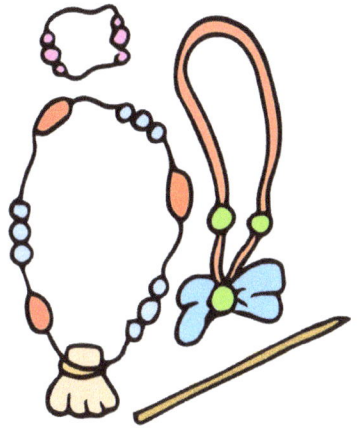  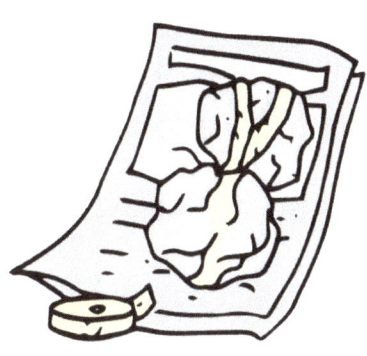

Threading
Using string, wool, pipe cleaners, a stick or kebab stick, get children to practise their threading. You could use pasta, fruit loops, beads, small hair ties, cut-up straws, paper with holes punched in them or anything you can find with a hole in it! Necklaces and bracelets are always a hit with this activity.

Drawing
Using different writing materials to draw with is a great way to work on their fine motor and pre-writing skills. Chalk, wax crayons and oil pastels are great as children have to apply more pressure for them to work effectively.

Paper Ball Toss
Give the children newspaper, magazine or brochures to scrunch into balls. They can then use tape to wrap around and secure it into a ball. Using the ball, they can play a game by shooting it into a basket or container.

Cutting
Cutting with scissors is an important skill to develop and requires strength in their fingers and hands. Any cutting activities will help with this. This will need to be supervised.

Some ideas are-
- Cutting up pictures from magazines or brochures and sticking them on paper. They can create a birthday or Christmas shopping list or decorate a card for someone with pictures they might like.
- Cutting play dough with scissors. Practise rolling it into a snake, then cutting it.
- Cutting around a given shape or along a line. Draw a straight, wavy, zigzag line for them to cut along.
- Cut up cooked spaghetti.
- Cut up craft items for collage such as wool, feathers, patty pans, ribbon, etc.
- Cut the grass or trim a bush.

Developmental Red Flags

Teacher For Early Years

As educators, it is important that we are observing children and ensuring they are meeting their milestones. Often, parents rely on our opinions as they aren't sure what is regarded as 'normal' or 'abnormal' development. Early intervention is key; therefore, advise your paediatrician if you notice a child not meeting their normal milestones.

Here are some Red Flags to look out for-

	6 months	9 months	12 months	18 months	2 years	3 years	4 years	5 years	Red Flags at any stage
Social/Emotional	Does not smile or squeal in response to people	Not sharing enjoyment with others using eye contact or facial expression	Does not notice someone new; Does not play early turn-taking games (e.g., peekaboo, rolling a ball)	Lacks interest in playing and interacting with others	When playing with toys tends to bang, drop, or throw them rather than use them for their purpose (e.g., cuddle doll, build blocks)	No interest in pretend play or other children; Difficulties in noticing and understanding feelings in themselves and others (e.g., happy, sad)	Unwilling/unable to play cooperatively	Play is different than their friends	Not achieving indicated developmental milestones; Strong parent concerns; Significant loss of skills; Lack of response to sound or visual stimuli; Poor interaction with adults or other children; Difference between right and left sides of body in strength, movement or tone; Loose and floppy movements (low tone) or stiff and tense (high tone)
Communication	Not starting to babble (e.g., adah; oogoo)	No gestures (e.g., pointing, showing, waving); Not using 2 part babble (e.g., gaga, arma)	No babbled phrases that sound like talking; No response to familiar words	No clear words; Cannot understand short requests e.g., 'Where is the ball?'	Does not have at least 50 words; Not putting words together e.g., 'push car'; Most of what is said is not easily understood	Speech difficult to understand; Not using simple sentences e.g., big car go	Speech difficult to understand; Unable to follow directions with 2 steps	Difficulty telling a parent what is wrong; Cannot answer questions in a simple conversation	
Fine Motor and Cognition	Not reaching for and holding (grasping) toys; Hands frequently clenched	Unable to hold and/or release toys; Cannot move toy from one hand to another	Nutrition is largely liquid/puree; Cannot chew solid food; Unable to pick up small items using index finger and thumb	Not holding or scribbling with a crayon; Does not attempt to tower blocks	No interest in self care skills e.g., feeding, dressing	Difficulty helping with self care skills (e.g., feeding, dressing); Difficulty manipulating small objects e.g., threading beads	Not toilet trained by day; Unable to draw lines and circles	Concerns from teacher about school readiness; Not independent with eating and dressing; Cannot draw simple pictures (e.g. stick person)	
Gross Motor	Not rolling; Not holding head and shoulders up when on tummy	Not sitting without support; Not moving e.g., creeping or crawling motion; Does not take weight well on legs when held by an adult	Not crawling or bottom shuffling; Not pulling to stand; Not standing holding on to furniture	Not attempting to walk without support; Not standing alone	Unable to run; Unable to use stairs holding on; Unable to throw a ball	Not running well; Cannot walk up and down stairs; Cannot kick or throw a ball; Cannot jump with 2 feet together	Cannot pedal a tricycle; Cannot catch, throw or kick a ball; Cannot balance well standing on one leg	Awkward when walking, running, climbing and using stairs; Ball skills are very different from their peers; Unable to hop 5 times on each foot	

Lack of limited eye contact

Parents - If there are Red Flags call your Family Doctor or Child Health Nurse
Professionals - REFER EARLY – DO NOT WAIT

Article from: https://www.health.qld.gov.au/__data/assets/pdf_file/0015/160701/red-flag-a3-poster-banana.pdf

HOLISTIC SUPPORT

HAVING A POSITIVE MINDSET

Children need to understand that being healthy is not only about eating nutritious food and exercising regularly but also about thinking positive thoughts. Teach students that a marathon runner could have an amazing diet and exercise every day but without a positive mindset, they would not be as healthy as they could be.

We must support children's thinking and their belief in themselves. Many children believe that others are just born talented. Children need to see that hard work and practice will improve their skills and abilities.

The Power of Positive!
Encourage children to use this language:

- My brain is like a muscle, I have to exercise it!
- This is hard, but I will keep trying!
- I could give up now or I could keep practising and hopefully improve.
- No one is good at everything straight away – it takes times and practise!
- Mistakes are good, they help me learn!

Supporting Children to Have a Positive Mindset

- Learn the power of the word **YET...** Make a list of **Things We Can't Do** *YET...*
- Learn about training regimes of tennis players, musicians or Olympic swimmers – look how hard they work!
- Watch videos or read stories where characters could have given up but instead, they persisted and succeeded (Try **Pixar short film – Piper**).
- Tell stories about wanting to give up, but persisting (*Learning to drive a car was so hard for me but I persisted. If I had not kept trying, I would be taking the bus today*).
- Develop an understanding that our brain needs to be trained.
- Help children to see and understand that their learning and intelligence can grow with time and experience.
- When supporting children with their learning, praise the effort and process – not always the outcome or product. Acknowledge and make comments on persistence, effort, hard work, focus, and strategies used.

Remember: Our goal is to cultivate curious minds and develop a lifelong love of learning.

Teacher For Early Years

MAKING THE MOST OF LEARNING OPPORTUNITIES

Do you have a spare few minutes?

Play games or have a conversation using the ideas listed below. Encourage parents to explore these when children are in the car or the bath. These suggestions are great for **Foundation to Year Two students.**

Guess My Word – Give your child clues about the word you are thinking of: it rhymes with, it starts with, it is the colour blue, it could be used to describe, a synonym is (word with the same meaning), an antonym is (word having the opposite meaning).

Other Words For – Pick a word *(e.g., small)*, make a list of synonyms. Other suggestions for overused words - said, went, put, then, big, nice, etc. This is explained in more detail on **page 90**.

Flash Cards – Make high-frequency/sight word flashcards by cutting up cardboard and keeping a set in the car and/or around the house. Do the same with new vocabulary words they have learnt and written in their Word Bank books or spelling words.

Rhyme It, Syllable Count, Odd One Out, Give Me Five, Count My Words, Tongue Twisters, Twenty Questions – all explained in the **Speaking and Listening section** on **pages 38-43**.

Licence Plates – Use licence plates and race each other to find all the letters of the alphabet, in order, or all the numbers from zero to nine.

How Many – How many words can you think of that start with **/s/**? or **/ch/**? How many animals can you list that are carnivores? (meat-eaters). How many shop names can you think of?

True or False – Using a variety of questions *(e.g., A horse has a tail? Boys are always taller than girls? A tiger has spots?)*.

Eye Spy – Can be adapted in a variety of ways. Using initial letter (it starts with the letter **t**), initial sound (it starts with the sound **/t/**), starting to blend letters (using two letters – It starts with the blend **/dr/**), or end sounds, (it ends with the sound **/t/**).

 **Measurement Game** – What is larger than, weighs less than, wider than, narrower than? *E.g., what is heavier than an elephant?*

Sing it – Sing nursery rhymes, alphabet song, days of the week, months of the year and songs on the radio.

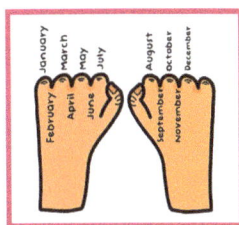 **Months of the Year** – Learn the number of days in each month by practising the rhyme – 30 days has September, April, June, and November... Explained further on **page 198**.

Count forwards and backwards to and from 20, 100, 1000 depending on your child's age and ability. Practise starting counting from different starting points.

Silly Stories – Make up silly stories with your child by adding a sentence or a few words in turn.
One sunny day…
An alien climbed into his spaceship…
So that he could visit…
The planet Jango…
He shot off into space, and when he arrived…

What is the Chance? – Use the language of chance to answer – likely, unlikely, certain, impossible, equal chance *(e.g., What is the chance you will see a dragon today? What is the chance you will drink water today? What is the chance you will get chicken nuggets for dinner?)*.

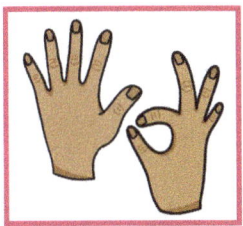 **Number Fingers** – Call out numbers less than ten for children to make using their fingers. Encourage them to make the same amount in multiple ways. *E.g., Can you show me 8 fingers in two different ways?*

Maths Games – For Year 1 and 2, practise instant recall of addition to ten (e.g., 3 + ___ = 10), extend to multiples of ten if too easy (e.g., 30 + ___ = 100), doubles facts to ten (double 4 or 4 + 4 =, double 7 or 7 + 7 =) increase this to multiples of ten if too easy (double 40, double 70).

 **Does It Need a Capital (Year 1 +)** – List off proper and common nouns (Tip - names of places, brands, days of the week, religions, months of the year, titles of books, movies, songs, people, etc. all need to be capital).

Skip Count – Count in twos, fives, tens and threes to 20, 100 or 1000 depending on the age of your child.

ENGLISH: SPEAKING AND LISTENING IN THE EARLY YEARS

Speaking and listening is the fundamental part of all English, yet we sometimes forget to take the time to teach skills in these areas and expect children to just 'pick it up'. Ask your child's teacher or the schools' inclusive education teacher if you're worried about your child's speech. They may recommend a speech therapist.

Use the Oral Language Screener on pages 44-45 to identify areas of need.
Remember, they can't write it if they can't say it.

SUPPORTING SPEAKING AND LISTENING

ACTIVE LISTENING

Follow Instructions
Follow instructions with an increasing number of parts. By Year Two, students should be able to follow three-step instructions.

e.g.
Take off your shoes, put them on the shelf, then hang up your jacket.

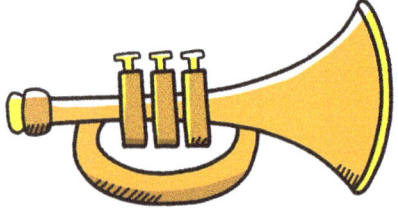

Sound Discrimination
Identify sounds in nature or outside in general (animals/vehicles), musical instruments, voices, etc.
Did you hear that vehicle, what do you think it was? Whose voice can we hear now?
You can also find specific apps with varying sounds to help them with listening and deciphering.

Barrier Games
Draw a simple picture using 2D shapes *(squares, triangles, circles)* then describe it for your child, keeping it well hidden from them using a barrier. Compare pictures. Start with something simple like a house on a sunny day –.

e.g.
Draw a square in the middle of your page, draw a triangle on top of the square. In the top left-hand corner, draw a yellow circle. Next to the square, draw a pink flower, etc.

Syllable Count
Count syllables in words – each syllable will have a vowel sound in it *(not necessarily a vowel when written, but a vowel sound)*. A way to practise identifying syllables is by placing your hand palm side down under the chin and see how many times your chin hits your hand when you say a word.
e.g.
Start with their name
   <u>Jen-es-sa</u>   <u>Pau-line</u>

Rhyme it
Identify rhyme in songs and stories and play **'What rhymes with...?'** Remind students that the end sound will remain the same whilst the initial sound will change.

Segmentation
Orally break words apart into segments and ask your child to blend them back together.

e.g. **What word am I saying?**
   c–a–t,   r–ai–n,   f–r–e–sh

Odd one out
Play odd one out games. You can start with objects for younger children and work your way up to letter patterns with older students and they need to determine the odd word/object.

e.g.
Easy: triangle, dog, square
Harder: sip, tap, flap

I went shopping...
Play 'I went shopping,' take turns to add items.

e.g.
Player 1 – I went shopping and I bought a hat.
Player 2 – I went shopping and I bought a hat and some gloves.
Player 1 – I went shopping and I bought a hat, some gloves and a rabbit.

Keep playing until someone forgets the list. A fun twist is to list items in alphabetical order.

SPEAKING AND LISTENING

GET EXPLORING

Tons of Texts
Read and have students listening to lots of different text types and exploring new vocabulary. Use big books, picture books, non-fiction books, websites, magazines, newspapers, letters, posters, postcards, brochures, cartoons, cereal boxes, etc.

World Around Us
Use everyday events to immerse your child in relevant and rich vocabulary, such as chickens hatching and the cycle of life, progress of construction sites, a trip to the zoo, etc.

SUPER SPEAKING

Poetry
Learn a poem to recite in front of family members (Ken Nesbitt and Bruce Lansky have some good choices for the early years). Otherwise, learn nursery rhymes, search on the internet or in poetry books.

Give Me Five
Say five words and ask them to repeat back.

Count my words
Say a sentence then ask, *"How many words did I say?"*

Varied Voices
Read texts, sing songs and nursery rhymes and talk using different voices *(loud, soft, scary voice, high pitched, whisper, etc.)*.

Say it like...
Say this sentence like a... *(man, woman, baby, king, queen, opera singer, rapper, teacher, etc.)*.

Cat got your tongue
Practise using non-verbal cues such as facial expressions and gestures to answer questions.

e.g.,
Do you like ice-cream? *(Child could smile, raise eyebrows excitedly and lick their lips)*
How do you feel about theme park rides? *(Child may grimace with a scared face, or jump up excitedly)*.

Tongue Twisters
Learn and say tongue twisters – *She sells seashells by the sea shore, Peter Piper, How much wood would a woodchuck chuck if a woodchuck could chuck wood?*

QUESTIONING GAMES

Celebrity heads
The child is given a famous person or character to guess. Questions can only be **"yes"** or **"no"** answers.

Twenty Questions
Pick a mystery object according to a category (food/animal/place etc.). One player to ask up to 20 questions and the answer can only be 'yes' or 'no'.

Guess Who? Boardgame
This game provides lots of opportunities for questioning, speaking and critical thinking. Recommended for 6+.

Questions, commands and statements
These sentence types need to be explicitly taught. **Questions** are when we are asking something, **commands** order or advise someone to do something and **statements** tell us something.

Question Dice
Use labels to turn a dice into a **5W's + H** question cube to use after each story or event.

1 = Who, 2 = When, 3 = What, 4 = Where, 5 = Why, 6 = How questions

USE YOUR BODY

Body Language Detective
Explore different ways of expressing emotions, including body language and facial expressions. Take turns to guess what emotion the other person is trying to relay without speaking.

Sign Language
Learn some sign language, make up your own secret hand signals.

Specialised Edition

SPEAKING AND LISTENING

Mime
Practise miming by playing charades or acting out an animal, action or story.

Copycat
Copy a series of actions (to encourage focus) – clap, clap, slap, slap, shake, shake.

Props
Create prop boxes with dress ups or use hand puppets and felt boards to act out stories.

IMPORTANT REMINDER

Listen, check and gently correct pronunciation of commonly mispronounced words.

SOME DIFFICULT TO PRONOUNCE WORDS:

Spaghetti, drink, animal, teeth, yellow, hospital, hippopotamus, thumb, three, threw, feather, weather, strawberry, hamburger, caterpillar, crocodile, drink, cucumber, toothpaste

Gently correct mispronunciations – many young children will replace a harder sound with an easier one.

e.g.
tar for car.

Teach students tongue placement.
e.g.
"When I make the /f/ sound, I place my teeth on my bottom lip and I push the sound out, I should even feel some hot air on my hand if I place it in front of my mouth. When I make the /th/ sound, I stick out my tongue and rest it under my top teeth." – (this is one of the last sounds to master and is easily confused with /f/ or /v/).

Use a mirror to practise making sounds and discussing what the different parts of their mouth are doing. **What happens to your mouth when you make the /m/ sound? What about /n/?**

SPEAKING AND LISTENING

EARLY YEARS ORAL LANGUAGE SCREENER

Take the time each day to really listen to and observe your little learner, use this screener for goals to work towards **by the end of Year Two.**

Vocabulary: DOES YOUR CHILD...	With support	Independently
Use a variety of words to express ideas		
Recall words and ideas readily		
Speak clearly with appropriate volume and vocabulary		
Use correct pronoun (he/she)		
Use correct plural and tense (past, present, future)		
Match pictures or items with appropriate words		
Use new vocabulary learnt from texts and conversations		
Sentence conventions / expression: DOES YOUR CHILD...		
Form lengthy, well-constructed sentences		
Use correct prepositions (positional words - under/next to/behind, etc.)		
Use correct grammar, saying words in the correct order		
Accurately repeat sentences that were heard		
Receptive language: DOES YOUR CHILD...		
Correctly follow two or more spoken instructions		
Recall information, keeping track of the ideas mentioned in a story they heard		
Respond to a story, demonstrating understanding of the sequence of events and main characters		
Respond with answers that fit with the topic or story (literal and inferential comprehension). See **page 56** for sample questions.		

SPEAKING AND LISTENING

Articulation, phonemic expression, speech and speaking patterns: DOES YOUR CHILD...		
Speak fluently without hesitation or displaying stuttering or stammering		
Speak at an acceptable pace – neither excessively slowly or rapidly		
Easily find words to express what they want to say		
Pronounce/articulate sounds or words accurately		
Using language to achieve purposes: DOES YOUR CHILD...		
Use language in a range of ways, for example, to express feelings		
Understand what other people say and mean		
Use the words most appropriate to a context, *e.g., to be polite*		
Use the rules of conversation, *e.g., initiating conversation with peers, taking turns, know when to stop, or respond to social cues from the audience*		
Follow a conversation without going off the topic or forgetting what has been said		
Understand that language changes depending on the audience		
Perceiving and attending to spoken language: DOES YOUR CHILD...		
Maintain focus and is not easily distracted especially when background noise is present		
Understand most auditory information without the need for visual cues		
Follow instructions without one on one repetition of information		

ENGLISH: READING IN THE EARLY YEARS

🔊 LEARNING LETTERS AND SOUNDS

Children learn phonics (sounds) through listening to and reading picture books, singing songs and rhymes, playing games, using word walls, reading letter/sound books, sounding out words and writing meaningful texts. Some schools may be using a phonics program, it's a good idea to contact your child's teacher to find out what and how they are learning phonics at school to facilitate your ability to reinforce this learning at home.

When teaching letters and sounds, try to link this learning to the text you are exploring.

For a hands-on approach to learning letters and sounds, use the ideas suggested for learning high-frequency/sight words on pages 61-63.

Explore a variety of texts and take the time to point out phonics in context. There are many texts you can use for each letter of the alphabet.

Some suggestions for exploring the letter **/Aa/** include:

> **Cat On The Mat** – Brian Wildsmith
> **Ten Apples Up On Top** – Dr Seuss
> **The Ants Go Marching** – Dan Crisp
> **Ten Red Apples** – Pat Hutchins
> **The Cat on the Mat is Flat** – Andy Griffiths

While it's important to teach the main sound that each letter makes, students need to know that many letters can make a number of sounds. Let's look at the letter **Aa**. Students mostly learn that /a/ says /ă/ as in '**ánt**'. But /a/ can also make the sound:

> /or/ as in '**water**'
> /ar/ as in '**pa**'
> /ə/ as in '**about**'
> /ā/ as in '**bake**'
> /ŏ/ as in '**what**'

An example of exploring the letter Aa

> *This is the letter **Aa**, it's the first letter in the alphabet (show capital and lowercase letter and remind students that each letter in the alphabet has an upper and lowercase version).*
>
> *We can hear this sound at the start of the word **apple** and **ant**.*
> *Can you tell me the sound that you can hear at the start of those words? (may need to do extra explicit teaching here to ensure child knows the meaning of the beginning/middle/end of a word)*
>
> *Can you think of any more words that start with the sound /a/?*

Show one of the books listed on page 48. Examine the title.

> *Can you find a word that starts with the letter **Aa** or has an /a/ in it?*

Read the story, emphasizing the /a/ sound.

> *I saw the letter **Aa** written in that book so many times! Let's practise writing the lowercase letter a.*

Show your child how to write it, verbalising your thought process.

> *We start with the c shape, close it up and draw a line down the side.*

Do a few more examples then draw some **dotted a**'s for your child to copy. Encourage them to do their own, ensure they are sitting on top of the line as they get better at formation. Challenge them to write it with their eyes closed. Add some correctly spelt words beginning with **Aa** to their Word Bank book (explained on page 94). Remember to expose children to a variety of fonts (e.g., a *and* ɑ).

Not only do we need to teach individual letters and sounds, but also **blends** *(two or more letters making separate sounds)* **digraphs** *(two letters making one sound)* and **trigraphs** *(three letters making one sound)*. Once your child knows some letters and sounds, they can start learning to blend letters together to make words.

Suggested order of learning letters and sounds

s, a, t, p, i, n *(use this knowledge to start writing 2 and 3 letter words – sat, is etc).*
c, k, e, h, r, m, d
g, o, u, l, f, b
ai, j, oa, ie, ee, or
z, w, ng, v, oo *(long sound as in 'boot')*, **oo** *(short sound as in 'book')*
y, x, ch, sh, th, *(soft sound as in 'thong')*, **th** *(hard sound, as in 'this')*, **wh**
qu, ou, oi, ue, er, ar

Some examples of blends:

bl, cl, pl, gl, sl, br, cr, dr, fr, tr, mp, ld, nd, squ, spr, str

Some examples of digraphs and trigraphs:

sh, ch, th, wh, qu, ph, oo, ng, oa, ee, ea, au, igh, ore, air, ear, tch

Confusing Letters

Many letters in the English alphabet look similar. A large number of children will struggle to distinguish the difference between these confusing letters. They must be given the opportunity to explore same and different by comparing, sorting, and matching objects. More information can be found about this in **Beginning Mathematical Processes** starting on page 106. Confusing letters include b/d, p/q, m/w, i/j, f/t and u/n. Please remember that letter reversals are age-appropriate in Foundation but by Year Two, children should be writing most letters in the correct direction and formation.

SUPPORTING YOUR YOUNG READER: 0-4 YEARS

When books are read over and over again, young children will begin to recall the words and 'read' from memory. This is the beginning of reading.

Read to your child daily and let them see you reading.

Model reading top to bottom and left to right by tracking words with your finger.

Point out the title, author and illustrator. Read the blurb and make predictions about the ending together.

Read My First Word books – one word and one picture.

Point out words, letters, numbers and images, and discuss how words go together to make sentences.

Re-read the same texts over and over and ask your child to retell the story to you. This will also allow them to see that the text remains the same every time.

Talk about the stories you read, discuss how characters are represented, make links to their own experiences, discuss familiar characters and settings from texts.

Read rhyming stories and nursery rhymes.

Begin to explore letters in the world, sing the alphabet frequently, point to each letter individually as they are said *(make sure they slow down at l,m,n,o,p)*.

Watch YouTube clips on letter formation and the alphabet. Jack Hartmann has some good clips for learning letters and numbers. They may also enjoy Numberjacks and Alphablocks clips on Youtube.

Visit the library, bookstore, Museum, Sciencentre, Planetarium, etc.

Students will ideally be able to recognise their own name before beginning school. Being able to write it is even better!

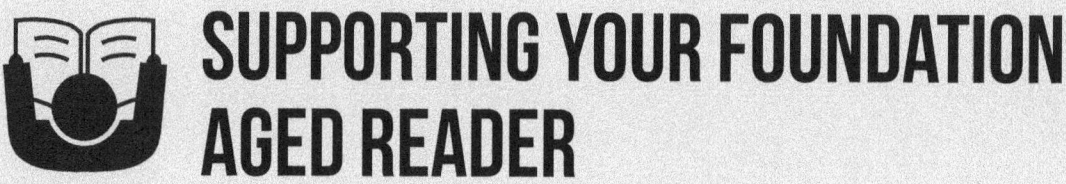

SUPPORTING YOUR FOUNDATION AGED READER

(Continue to build on all skills listed earlier)

Explicitly teach left to right directionality for reading both words and sentences.

Identify letter names and their most common sound *(use flashcards, stick letter cards on the floor/fridge/toilet door, read licence plates and signs)*. Remind them that there are 26 letters in the alphabet and each letter has capital and lowercase formation. Order alphabet cards, matching upper and lowercase letters **(see pages 218-224)**.

As children start to learn letters and sounds, explicitly model how to blend sounds together to make words.

Assist your child in understanding that some letters make more than one sound **(see explanation on page 48)**.

Explore the difference between letters, words, numbers and sentences **(see page 226)**.

Learn high frequency/sight words, ask your child's teacher for a copy of the program they are using, or pull words directly from the text and practise 5-10 words at a time (depending on your child). **See page 60 for a sample list and pages 61-63 for activity ideas** to support this learning.

Search for high frequency/sight words in the print environment and when reading books.

Ask simple comprehension questions **(see page 56 for generic questions)**.

Predict the story ending using the front cover or blurb, or stop at pivotal points and ask your child to predict what might happen next.

Scan pictures for clues to give meaning to the text – remind students that images give information too.

Encourage your child to read short, predictable texts with familiar vocabulary and supportive images *(e.g., 'I see a ... I can see a...)*.

Let your child see you reading a range of texts *(e.g., Tonight, I am reading a recipe. It is telling me the steps for how to make dinner)*.

Model self-reflection when you come to a tricky word – *(Woah, that word was so tricky! I had to sound out all of the letters carefully and then use the picture for clues)*. Remind students that not all words can be 'sounded out' and we need to learn some words by sight.

Hang words around the house – *(fridge, door, bedroom, etc.)* to encourage reading.

Examine beginning, middle, end of fictional stories. Explore problem and solution, identify if there was a goodie/baddie.

Track words carefully by pointing to each word as you say it.

Acknowledge and discuss basic punctuation marks including full stop, exclamation mark and question mark. **Discuss each mark** – a **full stop** looks like a dot and tells us to breathe An **exclamation mark** looks like a number 1 with a dot under it, it tells us to use emotion. A **question mark** looks like the start of a number 2 with a dot under it. Point out **commas** as a *'pause'* mark.

Assess understanding of print conventions – **see page 224.**

Identify beginning, middle and end sounds in words using consonant/vowel/consonant words (CVC) *e.g., nap – stretch it out and segment it.*
n-a-p, what sound did you hear at the end of the word?

Read decodable words and sentences *(e.g., A man sat on a mat)* using sounds they know.

Explicitly teach rhyme, read lots of rhyming stories and nursery rhymes, remind students that rhyming words sound the same at the END of the word but the beginning sound will change.

Make real-life connections with other texts and their own experiences.
e.g., Have you ever read another story with this problem?
Have you read another story with a bear as the main character?
What would you do if...?
This character has lost her teddy, have you ever lost a teddy?
Does this text remind you of anything from the past or something you have seen on the news?
Has your friend ever treated you like this?
Do you have any friends who have had this problem?

Discuss likes and dislikes about characters, events and stories.

Explore and discuss fiction and non-fiction texts. How are they different?

SUPPORTING YOUR YEAR 1 READER

(Check that they have mastered all the skills mentioned previously and continue to build on these)

Help children understand that texts serve different purposes *(to entertain, to inform)* and that this affects how they are structured or organised **(see pages 238-259)**.

Describe differences between texts including fiction/non-fiction and identify some language features used *(e.g., the language and punctuation used in a narrative would be different to an information report)*.

Discuss texts – express opinions about characters, settings and events, retell information in sequence.

Continue to identify the role of the author and illustrator.

Make connections between texts and life– **see Foundation level for ideas page 53**.

Discuss the ways that different characters are represented *(clothing, facial expressions, actions)*. Learn about inner and outer character traits **(see page 101)**.

Recognise a larger number of high-frequency/sight words (see ideas on **pages 60-63**).

Model one to one correspondence between spoken and written words *(e.g., I read one word, I say one word)*.

Verbalise your thinking when reading tricky words – learn decoding strategies **(page 58)**.

Build vocabulary by creating a list of new and interesting words and revise them frequently – add new words to Word Bank book (exercise book, discussed on **page 94**).

Discuss favourite parts/words/sentences from the text.

Acknowledge and discuss punctuation marks including capital letters, question marks, full stops, exclamation marks and how they can be used to signify different types of sentences such as statements, commands or questions.

Explore print concepts including table of contents, index, headings and diagrams.

Point out and discuss nouns, verbs and adjectives.

Identify basic conjunctions *(and, because)* and explain how they assist with joining ideas in sentences.

Visualisation strategies, read a rich text such as **Owl Moon** by **Jane Yolen** or **Australia At The Beach** by **Max Fatchen and Tom Jellett** and have your child illustrate their mental imagery.

Retell fictional texts in sequence or key points from information learnt.

Make up a new title page for your favourite book.

Specialised Edition

 SUPPORTING YOUR YEAR 2 READER

(Check that they have mastered all the skills mentioned previously and continue to build on these)

Answer direct/literal *(information straight from the text)* and inferential *(using clues from the text and their own prior knowledge)* comprehension questions **(see page 56 for ideas)**.

Retell texts using correct sequence, vocabulary from the text and characters' names.

Help them to make connections between texts and their own experiences **(see page 53)**.

Fluently read a wider variety of texts *(poems, jokes, letters, procedures, information reports, expositions, narratives)*.

Discuss the structure *(how it is written)*, features *(vocabulary)* and purpose *(reason for writing)* and intended audience of a variety of texts. See structure and features of some familiar texts in the appendix – **page 240-259**.

Compare texts – read a variety of texts *(narrative/information report/recipe)* about the same topic and compare them for similarities and differences. For example, **Tiddalik The Frog** *(narrative)*, **Poison Dart Frogs** *(information report)* and **Frog's Legs Soup** *(procedure)* and compare their structure and features.

Identify quotation *(speech)* marks, commas, brackets, apostrophes, ellipses *(...)* as well as other basic punctuation marks and discuss purpose.

Compare similarities and differences between characters and different texts on a similar topic using **Venn Diagrams (see page 232)**.

Make possible predictions for alternative choices the characters could have made.

Point out, discuss, explore nouns, verbs, adjectives, adverbs and conjunctions.

Expand vocabulary using dictionaries and thesaurus' and add new words to Word Bank Book.

Explore print concepts including table of contents, index, headings, subheadings, glossary, tables and diagrams.

Discuss and identify figurative language **(see page 86)** and character development as a strategy that authors use to make their writing more exciting.

Use a range of decoding strategies independently **(see poster on page 58).**

Learn to summarise and take notes about key facts learnt after reading non-fiction texts.

Explore opinion vs fact, *e.g., Zebras are cute* vs *zebras are a four legged creature*.

Use a variety of comprehension strategies such as visualising an unseen text, using graphic organisers, summarising key info, retelling, making predictions, inferring, making connections **(see pages 56-58)**.

READING AND COMPREHENSION SKILLS

Visualise: Read books, without showing the images. Ask child what they pictured for the main character/s, setting, etc. Show and discuss.

Make Connections: Make connections between the text and their own life; the text and other texts; the text and the world. Have you read another book with similar characters/ problem? See more question samples on page 53.

Predict: Read the title/blurb and ask questions about how the story might end, stop at pivotal points, and ask what the character might do next?

Summarise: Use storyboards to retell what was heard or read in fictional texts. Play **Fast Five**, after reading non-fiction texts – *Tell me five things you learnt about ...*

Monitor Meaning and Expand Vocabulary: Readers should always understand what they are reading, otherwise it is just words on a page. Find meaning through discussion, dictionary definitions and internet searches.

Discuss and Answer Questions: Ask and answer literal and inferential comprehension questions to check for understanding (see sample questions below).

Literal Comprehension Questions
(answers are straight from the text)

Was this text fiction or non-fiction? How do you know?

What type of text is this? (narrative/informative/procedure, etc).

What was the main characters name? Supporting characters/Who else was in the story?

Where was the story set? How do you know/what were the clues to tell you this?

What would be another good title for this book?

Who do you think the intended audience is? (e.g., kids? chefs? scientists?)

5 W's + H questions (Who, what, when, where, why, how?).

Inferential Comprehension Questions
(answers are found using clues in the text and by building on prior knowledge)

Why do you think ... was feeling...?

Why do you think the character said/did that?

Why do you think ... finds this so challenging/funny/scary?

Why do you think ... is going ...?

Why do you think ... happened?

What do you think ... could be used for?

What do you think his house would look like? Where do you think it could be?

Remember not to overload children with questions. Two-three questions are enough for Foundation age students and up to five questions for Year Two.

COMPREHENSION STRATEGIES TO PROMOTE READING SUCCESS

Visualise

I can listen to the text and form a mental image.

Predict

I can make valid guesses about the text I am reading or viewing.

Make Connections

I can make connections with my own life, with other stories/information and with the world around me.

Summarise

I can retell the text in sequence. I can recall key information using topic vocabulary.

Monitor Meaning and Explore New Vocabulary

I can listen carefully to check if the text makes sense. I can discuss and use new words from the text.

Discuss

I can ask and answer questions about the text. I know that some answers will be written in the text and some answers, I will have to infer.

DECODING STRATEGIES TO PROMOTE READING SUCCESS

Sound It Out

I can sound out from left to right, then blend the sounds to read the word (d-o-g)

Chunk It

I can break words into parts using chunks such as blends and digraphs. I can look for smaller words inside larger words.

Syllabify It

re-mem-ber

I can chop words into syllables. I know that each syllable will have a vowel sound.

Flip The Vowel

Did Superman wear a red cap or a red cape?

I can try using the long or short vowel sound to see if the word makes sense.

Make Links

If d-o-g spells dog, then l-o-g must spell log. If l-o-g spells log, then logg-i-ng must spell logging.

I can use my knowledge of similar words and rhyming words. I can cover prefixes and suffixes to focus on the base word.

un-friend-ly/care-ful

Makes Sense

Does it make sense? Does it sound right?

Does it match the image?

I can listen to myself and monitor meaning as I read. I can re-read if needed, to check it makes sense.

LEARNING HIGH-FREQUENCY/ SIGHT WORDS

Initially, it may be best to approach teachers to find out the program they are using. That said, many schools are now moving away from programs, and only teaching words that are linked directly to the context of the classroom or the text being read. This means that if the text of the week was **"Where Is the Green Sheep"** by **Mem Fox and Judy Horacek**, the high frequency/sight words learnt would be - *where, here, is, the, but, a*. The teacher may also use this text to explore *rhyme, repetition and spelling patterns, digraph* **'ee'**.

Definitions:

High-frequency words
– Words occurring frequently in books and early readers.

Sight words
– words that must be memorised by sight. These can not be decoded as they do not fit standard phonemic practise. These are also called 'heart' words as we learn them by heart.

Some children will see a word once and immediately commit it to long-term memory, but for most children, this won't be the case. These children may need to be exposed to the same word at least 30 times before they remember it. That is why we strongly believe that a balanced approach to teaching sight words in context, as well as immersing children in words through hands-on activities, will get the best results. Please see **pages 61-63** for engaging ways to learn high-frequency/sight words.

List 1 – I can see a <u>dog</u>. I like my <u>mum</u>.

List 2 – Here is the little <u>cat</u>. Come and look at the little cat.

List 3 – That man said "Yes!" He went to the <u>shop</u>.

List 4 & 5 – We have all had a play on the <u>swing</u>, but not dad.

On the following pages, you will find a list of high-frequency/sight words. This has been created based on words that we know children will come across in readers as well as words they may want to write. Each list contains ten words; however, some children would benefit from focusing on only five words at a time.

Sample List of High-Frequency/Sight Words

LIST 1
see	can	I	a	my
like	and	the	to	it

LIST 2
in	is	on	we	little
was	went	here	come	look

LIST 3
at	am	no	you	said
yes	of	be	that	he

LIST 4
mum	all	up	are	play
as	for	had	too	dad

LIST 5
have	not	so	they	but
go	book	his	if	her

LIST 6
happy	me	with	big	park
want	got	what	or	this

LIST 7
when	there	day	where	then
who	saw	back	about	live

LIST 8
came	look	asleep	boy	because
very	would	could	shout	girl

LIST 9
again	into	get	now	some
house	off	going	goes	away

LIST 10
after	thank	today	make	walk
school	laugh	inside	friend	read

LIST 11
birthday	weekend	playground	dear	do
put	found	good	thing	children

LIST 12
one	two	three	four	five
six	seven	eight	nine	ten

Specialised Edition

Learning to Read Words

Hands On

Make words with glitter glue/wool/string/dough, trace the letters while saying the letter name and then the word (c-a-n: can), write words in sand/shaving foam/rice.

Hopscotch

Make a hopscotch game with chalk on concrete, writing words in each box.

Bulls Eye

Write words on flashcards and stick them to the wall, play target practise games using bean bags/balls/nerf guns.

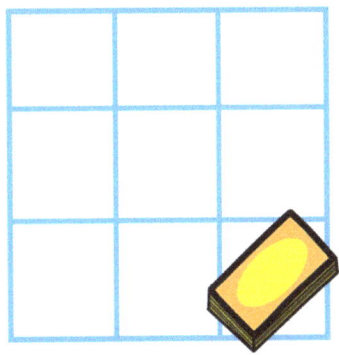

Bingo

Make 3 x 3 grids. Choose 12-15 words and write them on flashcards. Keep them face up, each player chooses 9 to write on their game board. Place cards face down in a pile. Flip over one card at a time, read and cross off words. First to cover their board is the winner.

Light Them Up

Write words on sticky notes and stick them to the wall. Turn down the lights and give your child a torch. Shine the torch and read each word.

Colour Time

Write words in large bubble writing. Colour them in.

Chop Them Up

Write words on card, then chop up each word into pieces to make a puzzle.

61

READING

Snap

Print/write out two copies of a number of sight words, shuffle, split the deck between two players. Take turns to place a card face up in a pile and snap when you see a pair. You can also play Memory/Concentration with these cards.

Hide and Seek

Hide words around the room/house/garden, read words as they find them.

Carpark

Draw a carpark on paper and have your child park their toy cars on the word you call out.

e.g. Can you park your red car on the word 'here?'

Ten Pin Bowling

Stick a word on each pin. Read them as you knock them down.

Letter Tiles

Use magnetic letters, scrabble tiles or foam bath letters to spell words.

Whack!

Write words on bug shapes or post-it notes, then give your child a clean fly swat to smack the words with! This is a great two-player game.

Read My Back

Write words on the child's back – *Can they guess the word?* Swap places. Can use fingers or pencil and paper.

Specialised Edition

Musical Words

(Musical chairs) Write words on A4 pieces of paper. Play music, when the music stops, children must stand on a piece of paper and read the word aloud. Great group game.

Catch A Word

Tape strips of masking tape to each section of a beach ball, write words on each strip. Students read the word closest to them as they catch the ball.

Erase The Word

Write words on whiteboards *(or clear plastic sleeves with blank paper inside)*. Give your child the board and an eraser. Call out one word at a time and have your child rub out the matching word until all are gone.

(Challenge: write some words twice — once with the correct spelling and once with incorrect spelling. See if they spot the difference).

Change Your Voice

Read flash cards using funny voices.

Storytime

Find words in storybooks – **Where Is The Green Sheep by Mem Fox and Jody Horacek** is full of repeated high-frequency words.

Technology

Use an internet search to find online games/activities and use iPad apps.

READING

A SAMPLE LIST OF RICH TEXTS FOR THE EARLY YEARS

(ORGANISED BY SUGGESTED FOCUS)

Nothing beats the hard copy of a good book, but if you can't access it, most of these are available to view on YouTube.

Rhyme, Repetition and Vocabulary

- Any picture books – Julia Donaldson
- Edward The Emu, Edwina The Emu – Sheena Knowles and Rod Clement
- Olga The Brolga – Rod Clement
- Fancy Nancy series – Jane O'Connor
- How Do Dinosaurs series – Jane Yolen and Mark Teague
- Thelma The Unicorn and Pig The Pug series – Aaron Blabey
- The Bear series, The Wrong Book - Nick Bland
- Brown Bear, Brown Bear, What Do You See? – Eric Carle
- The Magic Hat, Where Is The Green Sheep, Time For Bed – Mem Fox
- Good quality fairy tales
- There's A Sea In My Bedroom, Lucy Goosey – Margaret Wild
- Banjo And Ruby Red – Libby Gleeson
- Who's In The Shed – Brenda Parkes
- Grandpa and Thomas, Mr McGee, The Pear In The Pear Tree – Pamela Allen
- Duck In A Truck – Jez Alborough
- Aliens/Dinosaurs Love Underpants – Claire Freedman and Ben Cort
- We're Going on a Bear Hunt – Michael Rosen and Helen Oxenbury

Recount

- Diary Of A Wombat – Jackie French
- Sebastian Lives In a Hat – Thelma Catterwell
- Alexander and the Terrible, Horrible, No Good, Very Bad Day – Judith Viorst
- Wilfrid Gordon McDonald Partridge – Mem Fox
- Are We There Yet? – Alison Lester
- Just Another Ordinary Day – Rod Clements

Specialised Edition

Persuasive

- The Day the Crayons Quit series – Drew Daywalt
- Don't Let The Pigeon Drive the Bus series – Mo Willems
- I Wanna Iguana/ I Wanna New Room – Karen Kaufman Orloff
- Hey, Little Ant! – Hannah Hoose
- The Great Kapok Tree – Lynne Cherry
- The Perfect Pet – Margie Palatini and Bruce Whatley

Procedures

- The Very Blue Thingamajig – Narelle Oliver
- Wombat Stew – Marcia Vaughn
- How To Sneak Your Monster into School - Chris Francis
- Feathers For Pheobe – Rod Clement
- George's Marvellous Medicine – Roald Dahl
- The Little Red Hen – varying authors
- How To Catch A Monster – Adam Wallace
- Recipes/Science experiments/instructions for games

Letter Writing

- Dear Zoo – Rod Campbell
- The Jolly Postman and Other People's Letters – Janet and Allan Ahlberg
- Dear Mrs LaRue – Mark Teague
- A Monster Wrote Me A letter – Nick Bland
- Can I Be Your Dog? – Troy Cummings
- Dear Teacher – Amy Husband

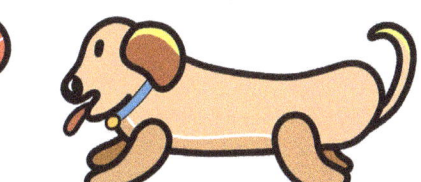

Text Innovation

(change perspective, characters, setting, vocabulary, etc.)

- The Three Little Pigs – multiple authors
- The True Story of the Three Little Pigs – John Scieszka
- The Three Little Wolves and the Big Bad Pig – Eugene Trivizas and Helen Oxenbury
- The Boy Who Cried Wolf – multiple authors (links to honesty for personal/social)
- The Wolf Who Cried Boy – Bob Hartman
- The Cocky Who Cried Dingo – Yvonne Morrison and Heath McKenzie
- The Three Billy Goats Gruff – multiple authors

Personal/Social Development

- I Like Myself – Karen Beaumont *(celebrates being unique)*
- The Rainbow Fish – Marcus Pfister *(sharing and friendship)*
- Only One You – Linda Kranz *(being unique)*
- Giraffes Can't Dance – Giles Andreae and Guy Parker-Rees *(persistence)*
- The Girl Who Never Made Mistakes – Mark Pett and Gary Rubinstein
- It's OK to make Mistakes/It's Ok to be Different – Todd Parr *(acceptance)*
- Beautiful Oops – Barney Saltzberg *(turning mistakes into masterpieces)*
- OK Book - Amy Krouse Rosenthal *(feelings)*
- Misery Moo – Jeanne Willis and Tony Ross *(emotions)*
- Elmer series – David Mckee *(being unique)*
- Koala Lou – Mem Fox *(determination, jealousy)*
- The Fabulous Friend Machine – Nick Bland *(changes in feelings)*

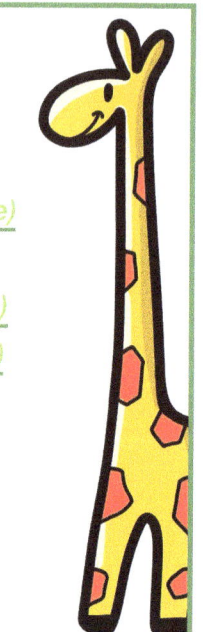

Math Links

- The Very Hungry Caterpillar/The Bad Tempered Ladybird – Eric Carle
- Ten Terrible Dinosaurs – Paul Stickland
- One, Two, Three – Tom Slaughter
- One Is a Snail, Ten is a Crab – April Pulley Sayre
- Ten Apples Up on Top/ Wacky Wednesday – Dr Seuss
- Rosie's Walk – Pat Hutchins
- One Odd Day/My Even Day – Doris Fisher and Dani Sneed
- Counting On Frank – Rod Clement
- Mouse Count – Ellen Stoll Walsh
- What's The Time, Mr Wolf – Debi Gliori
- One White Wishing Stone – Doris Gayzagian
- Uno's Garden – Graeme Base
- Who Sank The Boat/ Mr Archimedes' Bath – Pamela Allen
- Ten Black Dots – Donald Crews
- Teddy Bear Patterns – Barbara Barbieri McGrath
- A Pair Of Socks – Stuart J Murphy
- Sort It Out! – Barbara Mariconda
- Ten Seeds – Ruth Brown
- Pattern Bugs or Pattern Fish – Trudy Harris

Science and Environmental focus

- **The Tiny Seed** – Eric Carle *(life cyles)*
- **Where the Forest Meets the Sea, The Window** – Jeannie Baker *(human impact on the environment)*
- **Possum Magic** – Mem Fox *(Australian bush)*
- **Handa's surprise** – Eileen Brown *(culture)*
- **Where the Wild Things Are** – Maurice Sendak *(explore habitats and features)*
- **Stellaluna** – Janell Cannon *(animal study)*
- **Non-fiction topic books**
- **Seagull** – Danny Snell *(human impact on animals)*
- **Big Rain Coming** – Katrina Germein and Bronywn Bancroft *(weather and seasons)*
- **The Curious Garden** – Peter Brown *(caring for places)*
- *Cat and Fish* – Neil Curtis and Joan Grant *(features of different places)*
- **Tom Tom** – Rosemary Sullivan and Dee Huxley *(special places)*
- **Speak Chinese, Fang Fang!** – Sally Ripin *(celebrating cultural diversity)*
- **The Lost Girl** – Ambelin Kwaymullina and Leanne Tobin *(representations of locations)*
- **Drought/Flood** - Jackie French *(weather)*

Novels

High quality literature (to read with your child)

- **Any books** – Roald Dahl
- **The Secret Garden** – Frances Hodgson Burnett
- **Charlotte's Web and Stuart Little** – E.B. White
- **Narnia** – C.S. Lewis
- **Peter Pan** – J.M. Barrie
- **The Hobbit** – J.R.R Tolkien
- **Black Beauty** – Anna Sewell
- **Diary of A Wimpy Kid** – Jeff Kinney
- **Harry Potter Series** – J.K.Rowling
- **Choose Your Own Adventure books** – Edward Packard (and other authors)
- **Paul Jennings short stories**
- **The Complete Tales of Winnie the Pooh** – A.A. Milne
- **The Wind in the Willows** – Kenneth Grahame

ENGLISH: WRITING IN THE EARLY YEARS

Young writers need explicit instruction to complete writing tasks. Please take the time to teach correct pencil grip and letter formation as these become very difficult to correct by the time students are in Year Two. It is also important that you take the time to model the generic structure and features of different text types. These can be found in the appendix **(pages 238-259)**.

SUPPORTING YOUR YOUNG WRITER: 0-4 YEARS

Explore manipulative activities, *e.g., cutting (safe scissors), gluing, dough, construction, Lego, duplo, kinetic sand, pegs, eating utensils, threading, plastic tweezers, etc.*

Encourage children to use a variety of mark-making materials including crayons, chalk, textas, paint brushes and pencils.

Model writing for your child – speak aloud about what you are writing and why.

Play with push and pull toys.

Complete fine motor activities suggested on **pages 30-31**.

Celebrate children *'having a go'* at mark making.

Explore sound discrimination – Sounds in nature *(animals, traffic, etc.)*, instrumental sounds *(voice & musical instruments) (links to speaking and listening)*.

Explore words – count words in sentences, clap to signal words, orally identify and compare long words and short words.

Syllables – Clap and count syllables in words, say syllables slowly and children identify the word by blending the syllables together to re-make the word *(ha-ppy)*.

Rhyme – sing nursery rhymes, listen to rhyming stories, sing songs and create rhymes.

Support active play – using gross motor skills will support fine motor skills needed for writing. Get children running, jumping, climbing, hanging, swinging and sliding. See **pages 28-29** for more ideas.

SUPPORTING YOUR FOUNDATION AGED WRITER

(Continue to build on all skills listed earlier)

Use triangular shaped pencils or pencil grips to support correct grasp (page 80).

Model writing left to right, top to bottom. Verbalise writing conventions. *'I start the sentence on the left of the line, I always use a capital letter at the start of the sentence and leave a space between each word. I end each sentence with a mark which can be a full stop, question mark or exclamation mark.'*

Practise writing their name and other important words at every opportunity.

Use letter cards to play snap, memory, Go Fish or create Bingo games (see pages 218-224).

Encourage children to independently create short texts to communicate ideas.

Explicitly teach rhyme – words that sound the same at the end of the word (but are not necessarily spelt the same).

Copy words and sentences from favourite books.

Model leaving spaces between words *(sometimes a concrete object can support this such as a popsicle stick).*

Point out and discuss punctuation marks and their purpose.

Hang important words around their desk/room so they can easily access them *(mum/dad/pet's name, etc).* Encourage children to start labelling their pictures.

Always support students to read their writing aloud. Make a few corrections at this age but don't go over the top or students may become reluctant to have a go.

Buy write on/wipe off books from stores or make your own whiteboard using a blank piece of paper in a clear plastic sleeve. Write their name/sight words on the paper for them to trace over. Remind children that all lowercase letters start from the top and go down, apart from 'e' and 'd' as they start in the middle of the letter.

Encourage students to write for enjoyment and experiment with letters they know.

Play iPad games and type words using word processing programs (see page 23).

Explore the difference between capital and lowercase letters.

Explicitly teach and play with all 44 sounds exploring one or a few at a time.

SPELL decodable words using known sounds through games and structured activities (e.g., it, is, sit) as they learn more and more letters and sounds (see pages 48-50).

Segment sounds in words (sit = /s/ /i/ /t/).

Blend sounds in words (/h/ /a/ /t/ = hat).

SUPPORTING YOUR YEAR 1 WRITER

(Check that they have mastered all the skills mentioned previously and continue to build on these)

Explore confusing letters such as **b/d**, **p/q**, **i/j**, **a/u** and make your own posters to hang above their desk (there are lots of ideas online).

Encourage students to write a variety of meaningful texts such as information reports, narratives *(stories)*, poems, lists, letters, recipes and instructions. Take time to discuss that different texts are written for different purposes and audiences *(see pages 238-259)*.

Focus on conjunctions and how they help us to connect words and ideas in sentences *(and, but, or, yet, so, because, if, since, unless, until, etc.)*.

Explore time words and discuss how they help us connect and sequence ideas *(first, next, later on, after that, etc.)*.

Practise editing simple sentences, checking spelling and using the correct punctuation.

Improve sentences – practise making sentences sizzle by adding in **adjectives** *(to describe nouns)*, **adverbs** *(to describe verbs)* *(see examples in appendix pages 229-231)*.

Write out the alphabet, using a different coloured pencil for the vowels. Check letter formation and direction.

Model and encourage children to use correct pencil grasp *(see page 80)*.

Play iPad games and type words using word processing programs *(see page 23)*.

Take the time to practise letter formation and handwriting. Purchase handwriting books from stores/find sheets online/practise writing in exercise books.

Learn about nouns, verbs and adjectives – ask them to write their favourite sentence from a book and use coloured pencils to find and colour capitals, punctuation marks, nouns, verbs etc.

Display/publish your child's writing (make sure it is their best copy).

Learn about vowels and consonants. Note that the letter 'y' is often called **the sixth vowel**.

Manipulate/delete sounds (dig without the /d/ sound makes 'ig'). Swap letters to make new words – *dig – d = ig + p = pig*.

Learn to spell high-frequency/sight words.

Revise CV (**C** - *consonant*, **V** - *vowel*) and VC words (to, on, us, it).
Revise CVC words (cat, dog).
Revise and teach CCVC words (flip, stop).
Revise and teach CVCC words (fist, jump).
Teach CCVCC words (blank, stink),.
Teach the following digraphs through stories, games and play. **'sh'** *(ship)*, **'ch'***(chop)*, **'th'** *(thin)*, **'th'** *(this)*, **'ck'** *(kick)*, **'wh'** *(what)*, **'ng'** *(king)*, **'qu'** *(queen)*, **'ee'** *(week)*, **'oo'** *(food)*, **'oo'** *(book)*

A FEW SPELLING RULES FOR YEAR 1

Explicitly teach the following spelling rules but remind children that not every rule works for every word:

- **Bossy 'e' rule** – The **'e'** is silent and is attached to the other vowel separated by a consonant *(cake, bite)*. This is often called **'silent e'** or **'magic e'**.

- **'k'** precedes the vowels **'i'** or **'e'** *(e.g., kite or kettle)* & **'c'** precedes other vowel sounds *(e.g., cat or cone)*.

- When two vowels go walking, the first one does the talking. We generally hear the long or short sound of the first vowel.

- Writing plural nouns by adding **-s** and **-es**.

- Two syllable words ending in **'y'**, such as *'happy'* and *'puppy'*.

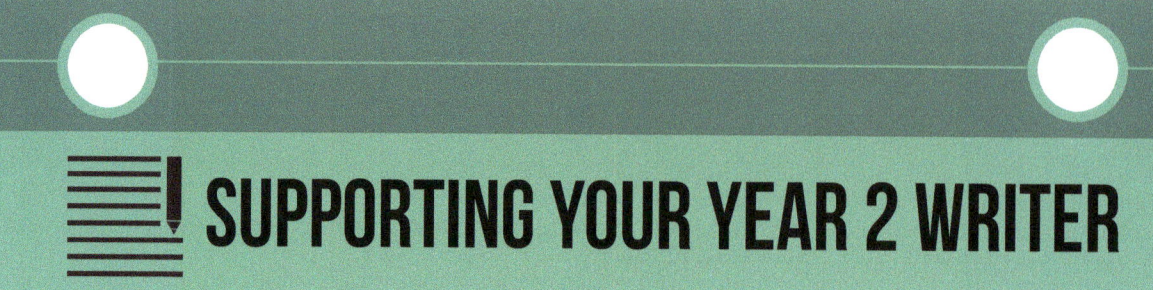

SUPPORTING YOUR YEAR 2 WRITER

(Continue to build on all skills listed earlier)

Revise and teach nouns, verbs, adjectives, adverbs, conjunctions, connectives and figurative language (see Glossary on pages 278-280 and activities on pages 229-231).

Learn some spelling rules (see page 75).

Use the 5W's + H questions to enhance writing – Tell me about your trip to the beach:
Who, what, when, where, why, how?
Write using all of the senses: At the beach, what did you see? Hear? Smell? Taste? Touch?

Explore a wide range of punctuation marks – including exclamation marks, question marks, quotation marks, apostrophes, ellipses, commas. See Glossary on page 278-280 and resources in appendix page 227-228, 234-235.

Revise and edit writing to make improvements. See The Writing Process on page 239.

Learn about prefixes, suffixes and silent letters.

Buy handwriting books to practise pre-cursive writing.

Publish and display their best work.

Revise vowels and vowel sounds and explain why they are important.

Explore compound words (butter + fly = butterfly).

Learn about synonyms and antonyms – create lists and explain that these lists will help improve our writing.

Put words in alphabetical order.

Write a range of texts including narrative, information reports, procedures, explanations expositions, poems, recounts etc. See appendix 240-259 for the generic structure and features of these texts.

Innovate on favourite texts – change 'The Boy Who Cried Wolf' to 'The Girl Who cried Shark' and re-write the story. Other ideas include changing the main character from female to male, changing the mean wolf to a kind wolf, changing the setting, etc.

Re-write sentences from texts into workbooks and use the Check Your Sentence poster on page 77 to find and colour coordinate the parts of the sentence e.g., capital letters = green, end mark = pink etc. When children are confident with this, they should be encouraged to colour code their own, original sentences.

A FEW SPELLING RULES FOR YEAR 2

- **Adding suffixes 'ed' and 'ing'**
  If a word ends in two consonants, just add the suffix.
  walk = walking, jump = jumped

  If a word ends in a vowel and then a consonant, double the final consonant before adding the suffix.
  hop = hopped, skip = skipping

  For words that end in 'e,' just add 'd' for 'ed,' and drop the 'e' before adding 'ing'.
  hope = hoped, hoping

- **Contractions** – words where an apostrophe takes the place of missing letters after two words have been contracted.
  do not = don't, I am = I'm, can not = can't

- Teach the **spelling of irregular high frequency words** including:
  said, have, like, some, come, were, there

- Teach **homophones** (words that sound the same but are spelt differently) of high frequency words including:
  there, they're, there; two, to, too

- Words containing **'ph'** such as tele**ph**one and silent letters *(knife, gnome)*.

- **c/k rules**
  When the /k/ sound comes after another consonant, we usually use the letter **k**:
  task, silk, drink, dark.

  When the /k/ sound comes straight after a short vowel sound we usually spell it **ck**:
  pack, deck, clock, luck

  But ... words ending with the sound /ik/ have an *extra rule*:
  At the end of a **one-syllable word**, use **ick**:
  lick, stick, click.
  In words of **more than one syllable**, use only **ic**:
  panic, electric, traffic

- Explore **soft 'c'** *(mice)* and **soft 'g'** *(cage)*. Often, but not always, when 'c' or 'g' meets e, i, or y, its sound is soft.

What to do if you can't spell a word...

RECOGNISE Put a circle around the word and check the spelling later.

WRITE as much of the word as you can, then fill in the details later.

SYLLABIFY Tap out the syllables, saying them quietly, then write the word part by part.

WRITE the word several ways and choose the one that looks right.

ASK SOMEONE.

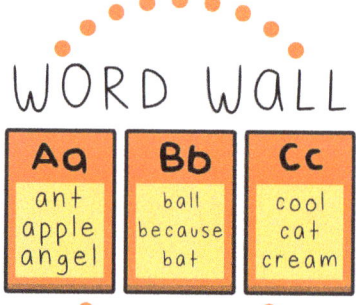

REFER to books, class lists, charts and words around the room.

USE a dictionary or a thesaurus.

CHECK YOUR SENTENCE

Sentence writing needs to be explicitly taught and modelled. Print this checklist out and have it next to your child as they are working. By the end of Year 2, they should be able to check that they have included all these parts.

☐ **Capital Letters** A B C

☐ **End Mark** . ?

☐ **Noun**

☐ **Verb**

☐ **Spaces between words**

☐ **Neat Writing**

☐ **Correct Spelling**

☐ **Does it make sense?**

☐ **Interesting words**

WORKING TOGETHER TO CHECK YOUR WRITING

Use this as an oral checklist to go through after your child has finished their writing and has read their writing aloud.

QUESTIONS TO ASK

- Does it make sense?
- Are the ideas in order? Does the text flow?
- Do we need/have all the words?
- Is more information needed?
- Is the punctuation appropriate?
- Have we used varied and appropriate vocabulary?

WRITING GOAL CHECKLIST

Use this checklist to help set future writing goals. This checklist is designed for Year 2 students: thus, the indicators and language would need to be adapted for younger children.

I am working on...

- ☐ Letter formation / cursive writing
- ☐ Size of letters
- ☐ Letter direction
- ☐ Writing left to right, using the whole line
- ☐ Correctly utilising the red and blue lines
- ☐ Re-reading my writing to ensure it make sense
- ☐ Leaving spaces between words
- ☐ Using capital letters for proper nouns and at the start of sentences
- ☐ Using punctuation marks accurately
- ☐ Sounding out a wider range of words confidently
- ☐ Extending my writing through complex and compound sentences
- ☐ Accurately spelling high frequency words
- ☐ Persisting, even when it seems difficult
- ☐ Exploring a wider range of punctuation marks (. ! , ? ... ")

Teacher For Early Years

 # LET'S START WRITING

Support early writing by encouraging lots of mark making, scribbles, tracing or copying shapes, doodles, painting, drawing and colouring.

Start modelling letters explicitly once your child shows an interest in letters or once they start formal schooling. Start with the letters in their name, teaching correct upper and lowercase formation. Some children might start to show an awareness of letters from two years old, some not until much later.

There are many programs available to support learning letters and sounds (e.g., *Soundwaves, Little Learners Love Literacy*). 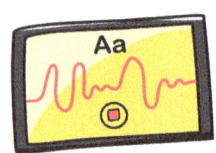 Many of these programs incorporate letters, images and a chant to support multiple learning styles.

Use the fine motor support suggestions on **pages 30-31** to promote hand dexterity and get little hands ready for writing. Most children will need to be shown how to hold a pencil correctly.

Remember **all children are different**, some children will take a week to learn a new letter, some more than a week and some less.

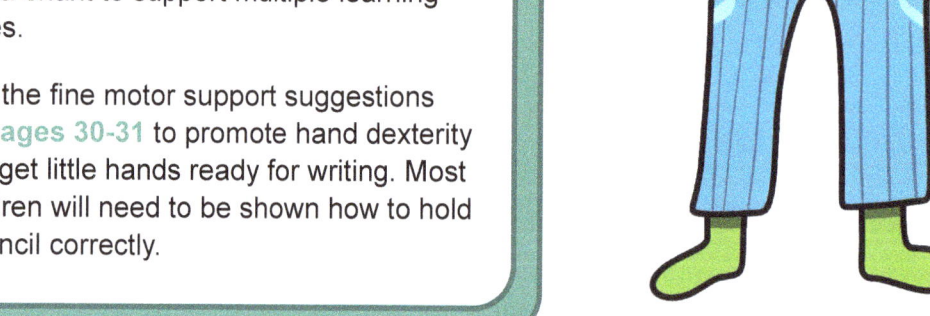

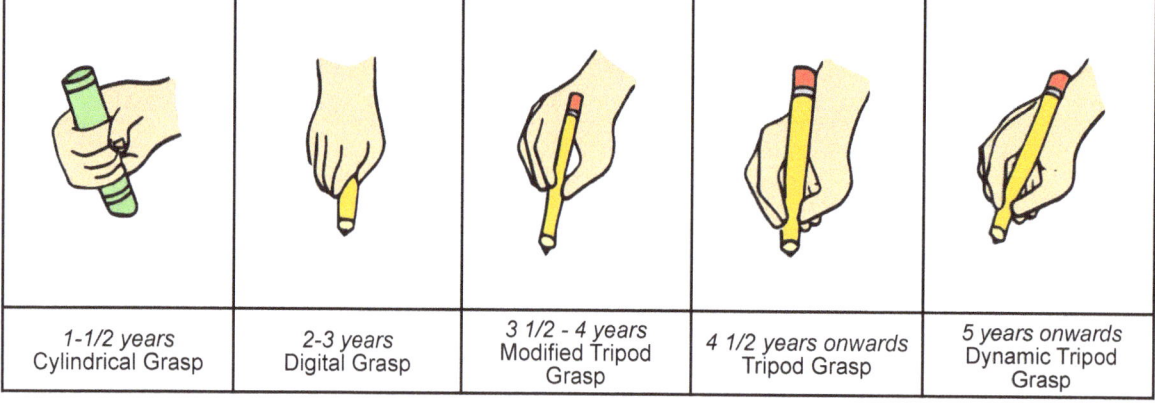

| 1-1/2 years Cylindrical Grasp | 2-3 years Digital Grasp | 3 1/2 - 4 years Modified Tripod Grasp | 4 1/2 years onwards Tripod Grasp | 5 years onwards Dynamic Tripod Grasp |

Specialised Edition

PRE-WRITING LINE DEVELOPMENT

Before attempting to write letters, children should master these shapes first. Ask them to draw or trace lines and shapes relevant to their age and skills. The ages are a developmental guideline of mastery.

3 years

4 years

5 years

The following pages are a sample of writing activities to explore, starting from letter formation to writing words, to replicating the generic structure of a variety of texts. Please see generic structure posters **on pages 238-259 and templates in the appendix** to support this learning.

For each age group, children will need extensive modelling and scaffolding to experience success with their writing. This will include exposing them to a range of sample pieces, using templates to simplify tasks, co-writing and scribing when needed, and using a combination of technology and handwriting to keep writing tasks stimulating.

From an early age, children must be explicitly taught the difference between letters, numbers, words, and sentences. Write a sample of each on a whiteboard or paper and ask students to point to/rub out each as you call them out. Alternatively, create a cut and paste activity with a chart for them to cut, sort and paste. See **Letter/Word/Sentence Sort on page 226.**

WRITING

SOME SUGGESTED ACTIVITIES TO SUPPORT WRITING

FOUNDATION

LETTERS/SOUNDS

Complete **letter/sound assessment on page 225**, Show alphabet cards **(pages 218-224)** and ask students to identify the letter, most common sound, and a word beginning with that sound. Use this to guide learning.

Encourage writing, observe letter formation, this needs to be explicitly taught and modelled. All letters are formed from the top down, except for letters **'d'** and **'e',** which start in the middle.

Explore letters in the world around them. **Refer to page 50** for the suggested order of learning letters and sounds.

WORDS

Create a Word Bank Book **(Explained on page 94).**

Hang new words around the house and encourage them to use this vocabulary.

(e.g., Today, I learnt the word 'gliding,' what does it mean? How can I use it in a sentence?).

Create word family and rhyming word lists.

Break words into syllables. | Practise spelling **high-frequency/sight words.**

SENTENCES

Use a simple checklist **(adjust the one on page 77),** to check for basic writing conventions.

Write sentences using **high-frequency/sight words**: I can see a ... This is a ... I went to... I like... The - is red... We are going to the ...

Use the **'I Can Illustrate my Sentence'** sheet **(see appendix page 233).**

Complete the **letter/word/sentence sort (see appendix page 226).**

LISTS

Write lists using classmates/friend's names, favourite toys/animals/colours/foods/games/activities, birthday and Christmas wish lists.

Link lists to stories heard or read (e.g., all the animals the boy saw on the farm).

Specialised Edition

LETTERS

Write a letter to Santa/Tooth Fairy/Easter Bunny/a relative/a friend/the Zoo.

Write a letter pretending to be a character in a book (e.g., Goldilocks apologising to the three bears).

Write postcards to a loved one.

OPINIONS

Write opinions on different topics:

- Do you prefer cats or dogs? Horses or zebras and why?
- What character/game/food do you like or dislike?
- What is the best dinner/book/movie/animal in the world and why?

RECOUNT

Write about the weekend/holidays – give a sentence starter *(At the weekend, I ...)*.

Write about an event/excursion.

Retell a familiar story (recount what you heard or read).

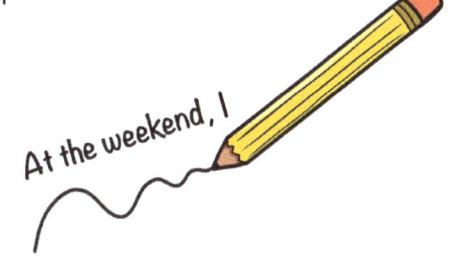

NARRATIVES

Use story boards and story maps to retell a familiar story.

Re-write familiar stories.

Write original stories, give character, setting and problem as a stimulus.

(e.g., An elephant got lost in the jungle).

POEMS

Use rhyming words to create simple poems.

Innovate on familiar nursery rhymes.

I SAW A............, SITTING ON A............WEARING A............, HE WAS VERY...............

HICKORY, DICKORY...............
A MOUSE RAN UP THE...............

WRITING

YEAR 1

WORDS

Learn spelling rules and how to spell **high-frequency/ sight words.**

Play word assosciation games: write 'flower' on the board and give children 30 seconds to write as many alternatives or adjectives as they can. e.g., *sunflower, daffodil, beautiful.*

Recognise compound words. **(see Glossary page 278).**

Build on vocabulary by adding new words to the Word Bank book and be sure to use these words in your everyday conversations. Model how to use a thesaurus.

Read and write sentences from books. Identify and colour common nouns, proper nouns, verbs.

Write adjectives to describe characters. **(See sample in appendix page 229).**

small brave friendly

Rewrite nouns as plural and change tense of verbs (past or present).

SENTENCES

Explore the difference between questions and statements.

Focus on punctuation marks and their purpose (capital letters, full stops, exclamation marks, question marks).

Practice using full stops and capital letters to write a sentence **(see page 227).**

Practise ending a sentence, refer to **Editing Sentences: What mark do I need? (see page 228).**

Learn to write simple and compound sentences.

Compose Bump it Up sentences **(see appendix page 231).**

Make connections between other texts and their own lives using sentence starters such as – *This text reminds me of... I felt like this when... I saw this at...*

LISTS

Write a list of animals you know, children in your class, favourite dinners, items to pack in school bag or for a day at the beach, birthday/Christmas wish lists, shopping list, favourite items etc.

Write a list of all the emotion words you know.

LETTER

Pretend to be one character, writing a letter to another character.

Write emails and letters to friends and family.

Write to mum/dad/grandparents to thank them for all they do.

Adult to leave notes for children and encourage them to write back.

OPINIONS

Write about the world's best pet, animal or playground.

What are the positives and negatives of being famous?

How do you feel about grocery shopping? What about spiders? *"In my opinion..."*

PROCEDURES

Write instructions for a game, how to cook an egg, how to be a good mum, how to plant a bean seed, how to ride a bike. Use generic structure on **pages 244-245**.

EXPLANATIONS

Draw a timeline of events *(how does an orange at a farm become juice at my home?)*.

Explain a better material for the three little pigs to build a house from.

REPORTS

Write animal fact sentences about their favourite animal under headings such as diet, habitat, appearance, interesting information, etc. Do the same with any of their interests using appropriate headings.

POEMS

Use simple rhyming words and innovate on nursery rhymes by changing words/characters and settings.

e.g.:

> HUMPTY DUMPTY WENT TO
> A_____, AT THE_____
> HE SAW A_____.

RECOUNT

Write about events – give sentence starters *(On the weekend, I/ At the Zoo, I)*.

Write a journal pretending to be a character from a story.

Respond to stories or learning – *This week, I learnt...*

Keep a journal of all the things that happened that week or of daily reflections.

NARRATIVES

Re-write and illustrate favourite stories.

Create their own fictional story using a picture or event as a stimulus – Try using images or short clips from **Pobble 365** and **Literacy Shed** found online.

Give narrative starters:
- "The boy and girl screamed and ran out of the house..."
- "He couldn't believe his eyes..."
- "Footsteps slowly creaked down the hallway..."

YEAR 2

WORDS

Explore: contractions, synonyms, antonyms, homophones, homographs, noun groups, proper nouns, pronouns and compound words.

Expand vocabulary by adding new words to Word Bank book **(explained on page 94)**. Revise words regularly.

Play word games such as Hangman, Boggle, Junior Scrabble, Up Words and Scattergories.

Draw an image and label it. Take photographs of still objects *(e.g., a shelf)* and label using digital apps.

Learn Year Two spelling rules **see page 75**.

Explore how prefixes and suffixes can alter the meaning of a word. Change words using in-, ex-, dis-, -ful, -able, -ly, to name a few.

SENTENCES

Explain the difference between a question, command, and statement. Write three questions you would like to ask one of the characters in the story. Write three statements after reading a text. This is explained in more detail on **page 42**.

Focus on grammar and punctuation: capital letters, full stops, exclamation marks, question marks, ellipses, quotation marks, commas to separate list items and within complex sentences **(see appendix pages 227, 228, 234, 235)**.

Make a book of inspirational quotes or interesting words with definitions.

Learn to write simple, compound and complex sentences.

Teach children to respond in full written sentences when answering comprehension questions (they should use parts of the question when answering) *e.g., Why should animals be kept in cages? Animals should be kept in cages because...*

Explore figurative language: Used to enhance our writing. Some examples include:

- **Personification** – giving human qualities to inanimate objects *(e.g., The gate groaned as the old man pushed it open, the wind howled as the tiny girl walked down the street).*
- **Onomatopoeia** – using sound words within the writing *(CRASH! Meow).*
- **Repetition** – used to emphasise ideas or give rhythm to a text *(Wombat Stew, Wombat Stew).*
- **Similes** – compare two or more things using the words *'like'* or *'as'. I am as hungry as a horse, he boiled over like a volcano, as quiet as ...*
- **Alliteration** – repeating the same beginning sound of words *(e.g., tongue twisters).*

PARAGRAPHS

Discuss and identify paragraphs in a text by highlighting similar ideas. Information reports and recounts are great starting texts to explore and connect ideas using paragraphs. **(Note - This is not expected or required until Year Three).**

Write four sentences about trees and four sentences about cats. Jumble them up into one big paragraph and model how to separate into similar ideas.

COMIC STRIPS

Read comics in books and newspapers and encourage children to create their own using a section or a whole familiar text they have read.

DIALOGUE

Write a screenplay of a familiar story.

Write speech bubbles and captions for photos.

Give scenarios such as, *"You are about to start chopping down a tree, but suddenly, it starts talking to you. What would you say back?"*

EXPOSTION/PERSUASIVE

Convince your parents that they should swap rooms with you or that you need a pet tiger.

Explain why we should follow the rules. Why is it important to be honest? Why should dogs be kept on a leash? Should animals be kept in captivity? Should homework be banned? Should weekends be three days long?

Explore multi modal text formats including pamphlets, signs, TV advertisements and written texts **see pages 254-255**.

POEMS

Explore a variety of poetry styles- acrostic, free verse, rhyming, haikus.

Re-write popular poems and create a Poetry Book.

Write a poem about someone/something they love.

LISTS

Write the grocery list, lists of things you cannot live without, a list of items you would take to a deserted island, class rules, a list of what you would buy at the toy shop with unlimited money, ways to fall asleep, ingredients in your favourite recipe.

Write an A-Z list using words from a text, names, different food.

Create silly lists (ingredients for a witch's brew, three gross flavours of ice cream, what to pack for a trip to another universe/outer space).

PROCEDURE

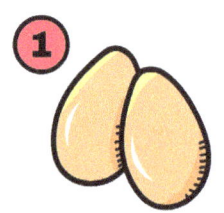 

Write steps for how to brush your teeth, play a game, make a sandwich, build a rocket/train/car/robot out of boxes.

Start a recipe book and fill it with your favourite recipes.

Read and write science experiments.

LETTERS

Write a persuasive letter to the school principal/letter to the council requesting something (swimming school, skatepark etc.).

Write to mum/dad/ distant relative/a pen pal.

Write a letter to an author reviewing or asking questions about their book.

Write letters to respond to characters in texts.

REPORTS and EXPLANATIONS

Report on their favourite animal, country, hero or any topic of interest. Explore how to research information in books and from unreputable websites, summarise and then turn notes into sentences. See note taking page and report template for writing a report on animals in appendix on pages 256-259.

Explain the life cycle of an oak tree, why rain falls, how to care for the world etc.

NARRATIVES

Choose a goodie/baddie/setting/problem/solution and use the template on **page 247** to create a story map.

Use Pobble 365 and Literacy Shed online for fantastic pictures and clips to promote writing.

Innovate on familiar texts by changing character/setting or problem/solution.

Retell narratives using story board on **pages 246-247**.

Use **sentence starters** as a stimulus:

- I could not believe it! One minute it was there and the next it was... gone. Where had my snowman disappeared to?
- I heard a strange noise, so I walked outside to investigate. There, standing before me was...
- As she walked timidly through the school, a tiny person was wiggling around restlessly in her pocket.

RECOUNTS

Write about family events and holidays. See sample in the **appendix on page 241**.

Make up some fictional recounts—
e.g., *The day I woke up with wings... I jumped in the water, only to find... On the day I was in charge of the school...*

Write a historical journal entry, as someone who lived in the past.

Write a simple autobiography: *When I was a toddler...*

GENERIC EARLY YEARS ENGLISH ACTIVITIES

ALL ABOUT CHARACTERS

Tell Me About Them: Discuss characters you like and dislike and explain why. Draw and label your favourite character. Write a list of inner *(personality)* and outer *(appearance)* traits.

Describe Them: Write a descriptive paragraph about a character from your story – find and use adjectives from the text. After writing adjectives to describe a character you have read about, write some antonyms *(opposites)*.

Find Them: Create a Wanted Poster for the baddie in the book. Include headings *'Wanted For'* *'Description/Appearance'* *'Last Seen'* and *'Reward'*.

Talk For Them: Use post-it notes to add speech bubbles to each page. What might the character be saying/thinking/feeling?

Connect With Them: Explore the character's emotions/facial expressions. Discuss a time they have felt this way.

Draw Them: Draw themselves or family members as characters from stories and surround the images with adjectives to describe what each character is like.

Visualise Them: Complete visualisation strategies – write down what the character saw, smelt, heard, felt, tasted.

SUPER SETTINGS

Escape Time: Draw and label a picture of a setting from a book that you would love to escape to. Give two reasons why you would choose this setting. Draw transport needed to get there.

WORD DETECTIVES

Word Families: Write all the words you can think of that end with... in/at/ug etc.

Dead words: Write a list of words that are better than *(synonyms for)* the following overused words = said, went, then, nice, big, get. Make posters using the lists you create.

Rhyme Time: Choose a word and write as many rhyming words as you can think of – use high-frequency words, spelling words or words from a text.

Call out sound words *(onomatopoeia)* for students to identify an object that makes that sound *(e.g., bang, quack, hiss, squeak, cluck, rattle)*.

Grammar hunt: write a list of all the *(adjectives/nouns/verbs/adverbs)* you can find in the book.

Specialised Edition

PUNCTUATION DETECTIVE

Punctuation Hunt: *Can you find two capital letters on this page? Can you find an exclamation mark?*

Fix It Up: Give children unedited sentences/paragraphs with a list of mistakes *(I'm missing 3 capital letters and 2 full stops).*

MAKING CONNECTIONS

Exploring Emotions: *Finish my sentences: I feel happy when/sad when/worried when/scared when/angry when/excited when.* Draw a picture to match the sentence.

ALL ABOUT BOOKS

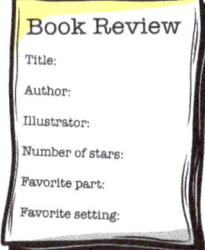

Book Review: Include title, author, illustrator, number of stars, favourite part, favourite setting.

Change It Up: Create a new cover and title for your favourite book.

Explore: Read a variety of texts including magazines, game instructions, newspaper articles, recipes, jokes, poems, etc.

Wish Time: *If someone gave you three wishes, what would you wish for?*

Storyboard: Create story boards after reading simple narratives. *In the beginning, the problem was, the solution was... in the end...* **See the three part storyboard on page 248 and the four part storyboard on page 249.**

Magazine Search: *Cut pictures from magazines:*

- Items characters may be able to use.
- Pictures that start with the sound you are learning.

Hidden Pictures: Read a text without showing illustrations and encourage the children to draw what they imagine the character/setting to look like.

Faves: Draw your favourite part of the story and explain why it's your favourite.

Purpose: Discuss texts read and the author's purpose *(e.g., to entertain, to inform, to give instructions, to convince us that the author is right, etc.).*

Review All: Describe why they chose a certain book and start up a rating system for all books read *(5 stars / A+).*

Teach: *Show what you've learnt* - create a timeline of events after fictional stories or posters of information learnt after non-fiction texts.

Act: Retell and role play familiar stories *(Goldilocks, The Three Little Pigs, etc.).*

Discuss: Compare fiction and non-fiction texts. What is different and similar about them?

Book By Book

These books are not age prescriptive; all of the following texts can be used over the early years to support literacy development. We have however, tried to order them from simple to more complex texts.

The child's reading and writing level will determine the level of support you will need to give them. For example, very early writers will be focusing more on single words and letter formation, whereas competent writers will be focusing on sentence structure and creating the text.

Suggestions for supporting beginning writers:

- Write words/sentences very lightly in books or use dotted words for them to trace over.

The cat sat on the mat.

- Write words/sentences on mini whiteboards or clear plastic sleeves for them to copy into their books.

- Sound out and write each letter/word with them, using an alphabet chart to find the most appropriate sound *(which may not be the correct one every time)*.

- Write sentences clearly in books, leaving gaps for them to have a go at writing focus words.
E.g. The __ sat on the __ .

YOU WILL NEED:

- **2 x exercise books**
1. **Working book**
2. **Word Bank book** *(personal dictionary)* prepared by writing one letter in the top corner of each page in alphabetical order
(e.g. pg 1 Aa, pg 2 Bb, pg 3, Cc).
These words should be spelt correctly to refer to, so please assist with spelling.
- **Writing and colouring materials**
- **Blank paper and cardboard** • **Stapler**

For each text, there will be four nights worth of activities. There are many benefits to reading the same book over and over such as developing an awareness that the text remains constant and building a deeper understanding of the content. Use the activity ideas at your discretion, you may only wish to do two out of the four suggestions.

Specialised Edition

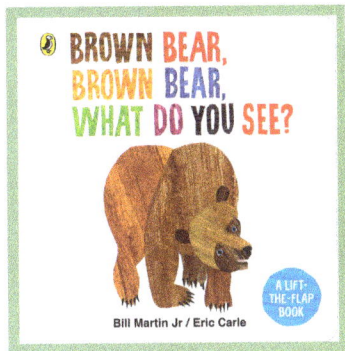

BROWN BEAR, BROWN BEAR, WHAT DO YOU SEE?

BY BILL MARTIN JR AND ERIC CARLE

Always focus on a specific sound and link to text
e.g. **/Bb/** or **/Ss/**.
See explanation on page 48–50

Read 1. Read for enjoyment. Model one-to-one correspondence between written and spoken word by pointing to each word as you read it. Make the **/Bb/** sound in front of a mirror. Ask them what their mouth is doing. Brainstorm and write some words beginning with **/Bb/** in their Word Bank book *(please assist with spelling)*. Or just practise writing the letter b. A little saying may assist your child – *tall back, go back up, big loop.*

Read 2. Ask your child to read along with you or by themselves *(from memory)*. Cut **flashcards** out of cardboard and write words *I, see, a, looking, at, me*. Jumble them up for your child to read. Call out words for children to find and write in their workbook.

Read 3. Ask your child to read the story *(they should be able to do this from memory)*. When finished, ask them to write some sentences using their new words and create their own **animal sentences**

e.g. I see a yellow cow looking at me.

They could draw or have a go at writing the animal name and colour. To encourage writing, have some colour flashcards made up with each colour name and a colour sample.

Read 4. Create a venue-themed book by **folding and stapling blank paper** – *At the beach, I see a...* sentences and pictures. You could create several versions – *At the Zoo, At the park* etc.

Teacher For Early Years

DEAR ZOO

BY ROD CAMPBELL

Always focus on a specific sound and link to text e.g. **/Zz/** or **/Dd/**.

Read 1. Discuss the title **'Dear Zoo'**. Explain that we write *'Dear'* when we are writing a letter. The author's name is written at the bottom of the book. Because there is only one name, this tells us that the author drew the illustrations as well. If this text is unknown to your child, this is a great time to work on **text predictions**. Ask *'What animal do you think will be under here? Why?' 'It says it is heavy.'* Read the text for enjoyment, discuss the animals in the text – *ask your child to think of some other animals that might be at the zoo.* They may want to draw and label a zoo picture.

Read 2. Highlight special sound, **/Zz/** identify other words that start with this sound. Add to Word Bank book. Practise writing **upper and lowercase Zz**. Focus on rhyme */oo/* can you think of some words that rhyme with zoo/dear/sent/me etc (this could be done in the car). Point out *exclamation marks* and *ellipses* and explain their purpose.

Read 3. Discuss an animal they would like to have if the zoo were to send them a pet. They need to be able to describe it and explain their choice. Have a go at writing/finishing the sentence – *I would like a ------ because ------*. Alternatively, create an illustrated list of animals from the story incorporating **adjectives** *(e.g. a jumpy frog)*.

Read 4. Write a letter to the zoo asking for the pet of their choice. Support them to write *Dear Zoo* on the top line, followed by a *comma*, then move down to the next line to begin writing. Remind them to close with a *salutation* stating who the letter is from. See the generic structure of a letter in the appendix on pages 242-243.

Specialised Edition

WOMBAT STEW

BY MARCIA VAUGHN

> Always focus on a specific sound and link to text
> e.g. **/Ww/** or **/Ss/**.

Read 1. Read the text for enjoyment, discuss the animals in the text – see if they can think of more **Australian animals** and predict what they might add to the stew. Choose at least **one animal** and ask your child to describe it using *five describing words* **(adjectives)**.

Read 2. Highlight special sound, **/Ww/** identify other words that start with this sound. Add to word book. Practise writing upper and lowercase **Ww**. Focus on *syllables – how many beats in the word dingo/echidna/kookaburra, etc.* You could create a table with numbers 1-4 at the top and sort the animal names into syllable groups or play orally in the car.

Read 3. Ask comprehension questions *'What ingredient did the echidna put in? What did the dingo want to do with the wombat?'* And inferring questions *'Why do you think the dingo wanted to make a stew?'* Learn about an Australian animal from the story. Draw and label, create a *habitat* using a shoe box and natural materials.

Read 4. Work together to write a procedure for **Wombat Stew**. Use the generic structure of a procedure in the appendix page 244–245. Encourage students to write their own recipes for stew or copy their favourite recipe out of a recipe book.

Teacher For Early Years

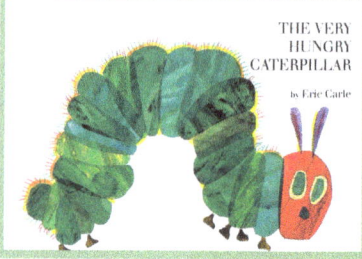

THE VERY HUNGRY CATERPILLAR

BY ERIC CARLE

Always focus on a specific sound and link to text
e.g. **/Vv/** or **/Hh/** or **/Cc/**.

Read 1. Read the text for enjoyment, discuss activities that your child completes on each day of the week.

E.g. On Monday, I have soccer practise.

Read 2. Highlight special sound **/Vv/, /Hh/** or **/Cc/**, go for a *sound walk*, identify other words that start with this sound. Add to word book. Practise writing upper and lowercase letters.

Read 3. Break a page into eight parts and write the names of the seven days of the week *(write Sunday twice)*. Ask students to draw and write what the caterpillar ate on each day.

Sunday	Monday	Tuesday	Wednesday	Thursday	Friday	Saturday	Sunday

Read 4. Fold and staple some blank paper to create a **personalised book** about your family.

The Very Hungry Family. On Monday, daddy ate sixteen sausages, On Tuesday, mummy drank three coffees, etc.

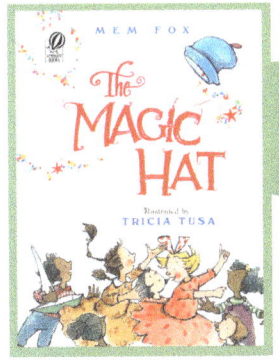

THE MAGIC HAT

BY MEM FOX

Read 1. Read for enjoyment – discuss/explore/list some synonyms to describe **the magic hat** – *stupendous, amazing, wonderful.* Identify *key high-frequency words such as the, this, that, like,* and *over* and play some sight word games using ideas listed on pages 61-63.
Phonics focus - */a/, /m/* or */h/* - practise *letter formation* and add new words to Word Bank book.

Read 2. Create a map showing where the magic hat went – include **labels** and **directions.**

Read 3. Children innovate on the text: *Where will the magic hat go next?*

Read 4. Children can create their own magic hats using *rolled up cardboard* and *decorations.* Write a procedure for making their hat including a list of materials and steps used. See the generic structure of a procedure in the appendix on pages 244-245.

PIG THE PUG

BY AARON BLABEY

Read 1. Read for enjoyment. Ask questions to help make connections *'How would you feel if you were Trevor? Do you think Pig was being fair? Why is it important to share? What games do you like to play with your friends?'* Ask your child to retell the story, using vocabulary from the story.

Read 2. Create lists of rhyming words – They could use these lists to create simple poems:

*There once was a dog, he lived in a log.
His friend was a pig, he wore a pink wig.*

-ig	-ug	-og	-ag	-eg
pig	pug	dog		
wig	dug	log		
fig	mug	bog		

Read 3. Write a description of Pig – *What was he like?* Consider **inner** *(personality)* and **outer** *(appearance)* traits (see page 101 for explanation). Alternatively, use a **Venn Diagram** to compare and contrast the two characters. See template on page 232.

Read 4. Write a letter to Pig explaining why it is important to share.

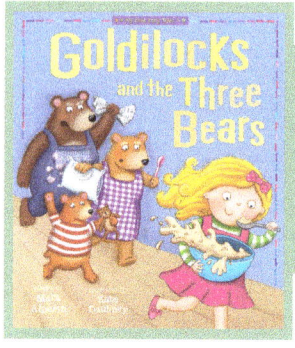

GOLDILOCKS AND THE THREE BEARS

MULTIPLE AUTHORS

Read 1. Read/watch online for enjoyment. **Discuss features of fairy tales** – they start with *'Once upon a time'* and end with the good characters living *'happily ever after.'* They were written a long time ago and have been re-written many times. Discuss syllables in the word **Goldilocks**, *can they think of anymore words with three syllables? (spaghetti, amazing, banana etc).*

Read 2. Create a list of all the items Goldilocks used in the Bear's house.

Read 3. Complete a story board (see appendix page 249) to **break the story into four parts – beginning** (orientation), **problem** (complication), **solution** (resolution), **ending** (conclusion).

Read 4. Pretend to be Goldilocks and write a **sorry letter** to the bears, explaining what she will do to right her wrongs. Use the generic structure of a letter on pages 242-243.

POSSUM MAGIC

BY MEM FOX

Read 1. Read the text for enjoyment. Use the pictures to retell the story. Focus on the **letter p**, practise making the sound and writing the letter. Write some words beginning with /p/ into their Word Bank book. Discuss confusing letters – **b, d, p, q** and explore how they are different. See page 50 for more information.

Read 2. Make a list of all the foods Hush ate to become visible again. For a challenge, write down the names of the cities she visited. Remember to *use a capital letter for proper nouns.*

Read 3. Complete these sentences – *If I was invisible like Hush, I would ... If I was magic like Grandma Poss, I would...*

Read 4. Write a procedure for **making a vegemite sandwich** then follow the instructions to make one. Use the generic structure of a procedure on pages 244-245.

Specialised Edition

DON'T LET THE PIGEON DRIVE THE BUS

BY MO WILLEMS

Read 1. Read for enjoyment, ask some literal comprehension questions:

E.g., What does the Pigeon want to drive?
Why does the Pigeon become angry during the story? **(Easy)**
What does the Pigeon do or say to persuade (convince)
the audience to drive the bus? **(harder)**

And inferred comprehension questions:

Why do you think the Pigeon wants to drive the bus?
Where do you think the bus driver went?

Make connections to the text:

What is something you really want to do but aren't allowed?
Have you ever been on a bus?

Read 2. Write a character description for the pigeon. Focus on inner and outer character traits. **Inner traits** include *behaviours and mannerisms (cheeky, persuasive etc)*, **outer traits** are those *we can observe by looking at him (feathers, beak, two legs etc)*.

Read 3. Draw pictures for the pigeon depicting each of the emotions he went through. Label each picture.

Read 4. Create a **For and Against T chart** and give at least three reasons why the pigeon should/should not drive the bus. Use these points to write an exposition. See examples in appendix pages 250–255.

FOR	AGAINST
He deserves a chance	He doesn't have hands to control the wheel
He might be really good	He won't be able to reach the pedals

EXTENSION FOR YEAR 2

Focus on the word pigeon – read the word slowly, discuss hard and soft 'g.' Explain that sometimes but not always, if 'g' is followed by an 'e', 'i' or 'y' the 'g' will make a soft sound /j/. Brainstorm some other words with a soft 'g' (giraffe, gem, gym, gentle, germ, gypsy, giant, ginger). Write these in Word bank book. Alternatively, look at the contraction 'don't' and explain that before it was contracted to one word, we said 'do not.' Play an online contraction game – search for contraction games online or head to www.learninggamesforkids.com

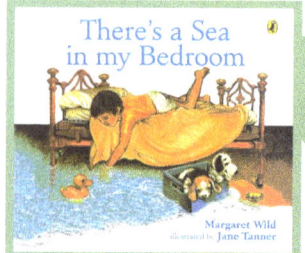

THERE'S A SEA IN MY BEDROOM

BY MARGARET WILD

Read 1. Model reading fluently and expressively as well as changing voice for different characters. Model using **decoding strategies (see page 58)** for the following words - *gobbled, knocked, shaped, curved, waited, listened, wondered, floated*. Discuss new vocabulary. Add words to Word Bank book.

Read 2. Students discuss **'fears'**. *What is fear?* Discuss how David's feelings about the sea changed throughout the book.
Make connections – *'What are you afraid of?' 'What does your body do when you are scared?'* Ask why they think David might have felt that the sea was scary.
Write some noun groups: _____, _____ sea; _____, _____ sea.
(see appendix page 230). Use one of these groups to write a sentence about the sea.

Read 3. Explore the five senses – our senses help us to learn about the world around us. Complete these sentences.
At the beach, I can see...   At the beach, I can taste...
At the beach, I can hear...   At the beach, I can touch...
At the beach, I can smell...

Read 4. Retell the story – This could be done in their exercise book, using the **storyboard sample on appendix page 249** or recording their voice on a device (iPad). Challenge them to use **onomatopoeia *(sound)* words** – *CRASH! Went the waves, splash, ahhhhh.*

KOALA LOU

BY MEM FOX

Read 1. Make connections – *Have you ever been in a race/competition? When have you had to practise/train for something to get better? How do you feel when you lose?* Discuss feelings and emotions, especially jealousy and feeling left out. Discuss and list things some things that they love.

Read 2. Identify what your child knows about koalas. Show them how to do a child-friendly internet search or go to the library and find non-fiction books. **Model how to highlight important information** – *summarising/note taking*. Remind children that they can't directly copy what someone else has written. Start taking some notes.
Use the **note-taking template on appendix page 257.**

Read 3. Read the information found in the previous search – Continue taking notes, reading sentences from the previous search and highlighting/writing down key words on the note-taking template.

Read 4. Model how to turn notes into sentences. **Write an information report using headings** – *Appearance, Diet, Habitat, Special Features/Characteristics* etc. Use the template on **appendix pages 258 and 259** to assist with this. You may also wish to make a *PowerPoint* presentation using *Microsoft* or *KeyNote* using *Apple* products.

Specialised Edition

TAKING A TRIP? LET'S WRITE ABOUT IT!

A DAY AT THE ZOO

BEFORE GOING

- Make predictions of what you might see or what might happen.
- Create a list of animals you hope to see.
- Write down some questions you have about animals.
- Write an invitation for a friend to join you.

AT THE ZOO

- Take photos.
- Read or write interesting facts about animals.
- Draw and label some diagrams of three of your favourite animals.
- Try to get all your questions answered by asking rangers.
- Write a description of your favourite animal.

AFTER THE VISIT

- Use a **Venn diagram** (see appendix page 232) to compare similarities and differences between two animals.
- Write a recount of the day – remember to use time words, write in the past tense, sequential order, include personal feelings (see appendix page 240-241).
- Create an information report on one of the animals (see appendix page 256-259).
- Print photos and label or write captions.

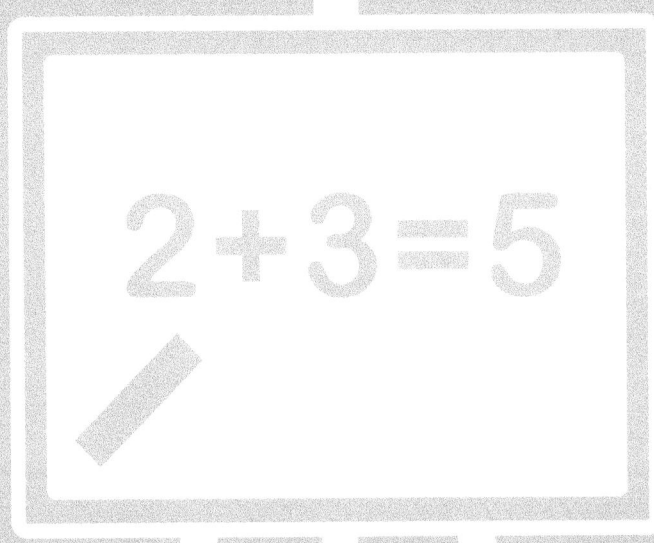
Mathematics
Numbers & Algebra

MATHEMATICS — NUMBERS & ALGEBRA

Mathematics has its own language with a vast array of different terminology that children must master. Please remember that children learn best through repetition so repeat, repeat, repeat.

BEGINNING MATHEMATICAL PROCESSES:

The earliest phases of mathematical understanding.

Children need to be able to master the following skills in the early stages of mathematics:

1. Determining attributes
2. Matching
3. Sorting
4. Comparing
5. Ordering
6. Patterning

Let's explore each of these processes in more detail:

1. DETERMINING ATTRIBUTES
(Starting from around one year old).

Supporting vocabulary development is the most important part of being able to describe attributes or qualities of objects. Children should be encouraged to use all their senses when describing attributes. This will assist them with identifying similarities and differences.

Explore: Encourage this language, in everyday conversations, as much as possible.

SIGHT	TOUCH	SOUND	TASTE	SMELL
colour	hot/cold	loud/soft	sweet/sour	strong/weak
size	roguh/smooth	noisy/quiet	delicious	sweet
shape	heavy/light	high/low	salty	fragrant

2. MATCHING

Matching is an important process that supports children's ability to find likeness or sameness to an object's attributes.
(Starting from around two years old).

Explore: Play lots of matching games:

- Can you make/copy this sound? Clap, play music on instruments or make noises with your mouth (this also supports early listening skills).

- Play games such as Follow the Leader, Concentration (Memory), Simon Says or Snap.

- Point out 'sameness' in the world, "Look, that girl is wearing the same colour dress as you!"

- Can you find two things that are the same colour in this magazine? At the hardware store - can you find the same colour paint sample as mine?

- Can you find the puzzle piece to match this space? (start with inset puzzles).

Specialised Edition

3. SORTING
(Starting from around three years old).

Children need the MATCHING skills of determining similar attributes. They need to be able to decide attributes for separating items into groups. The end goal is that children can **DO** and **DESCRIBE** the sorting they have done.

Explore: Encourage children to sort collections into groups and explain their reasoning.

Suggestions include using **fabrics** *(patterned/striped/spotty).*

Images of people *(glasses/brown hair).*

Buttons/pebbles *(colour, size, texture).*

Plastic animals *(dinosaurs/insects)* etc.

4. COMPARING
(Starting from around four years old).

This is based on the relationship between amounts of an attribute. Once children can match and sort items according to attributes, they should be encouraged to compare them. This is essentially noting similarities and differences between an object's attributes. *(e.g., longer/heavier/sweeter).* We often use the suffix **'er'** when comparing items. E.g., tall/tall**er**; fast/fast**er**.

The language of comparing supports learning in many areas of mathematics.

- Measurement – length, mass, time, temperature, area, capacity.
- Number – more (greater), less quantities, smaller, bigger.
- Texture – rough, smooth, bumpy.

Explore: Take the time to compare **characters/objects/buildings, etc**. Be sure to compare similar objects of different shapes, sizes, colours, etc. *(E.g., That kangaroo is taller than this one, but the smaller one is darker brown. This ball is smaller, but it is bouncier than the bigger ball).*

When comparing numbers, look at the child's age, number of siblings/pets/TV's, shoe size, height, etc.

Comparative Language List

Longer/shorter	Thinner/thicker	Heavier/lighter	Softer/harder
Louder/quieter	Smaller/bigger	Shorter/taller	Slower/faster
Older/younger	Wetter/drier	Hotter/colder	Rougher/smoother	More/less

Use this list to challenge your child to find, draw or compare items.

5. ORDERING
(Starting from around five years old).

Ordering is the process of arranging pictures, objects, or events according to some attribute. Ordering involves three or more items. In addition to using the suffix **'er'** we also use the suffix **'est'**. *E.g., tall, taller, tallest.* The children must be able to make comparisons and detect differences.

Explore:

- Cut 3-5 cardboard squares out of card and draw five different sized shells on them, ask your child to put them in order and explain the order (see above).

- Write 3-5 numbers on post it notes and ask your child to put them in order and explain the order.

- Use toys/number cards/pieces of cut up paper/books, etc. for children to put in order.

6. PATTERNING
(Starting from around five years old).

For children to experience success with patterning, they must be able to use the previous processes of matching, sorting, comparing and ordering objects. When creating patterns in the early years, focus on **repeating** and **growing** patterns. See page 109 for examples.

REPEATING　　　　　　　　　**GROWING**
a b a b a b /　　　　　　　　　a b a b b a b b b
red, blue, red, blue, red, blue

Explore:

- Make patterns using a variety of different materials, including colours, shapes, sizes.

- Create pattern collages using buttons or cut up pieces of paper, use paint and stamps.

- Draw a pattern for them to copy, draw a pattern for them to continue, draw a pattern with missing elements.

- Build towers that are growing in height: one block, two blocks, three blocks tall.

Specialised Edition

PATTERN FORMATIONS

Commonly used patterns that five-year-olds should be exposed to.

AB pattern:
Two parts that repeat

ABC pattern:
Three parts that repeat

AAB pattern

ABB pattern

Growing Pattern

Missing elements

109

NUMBERS

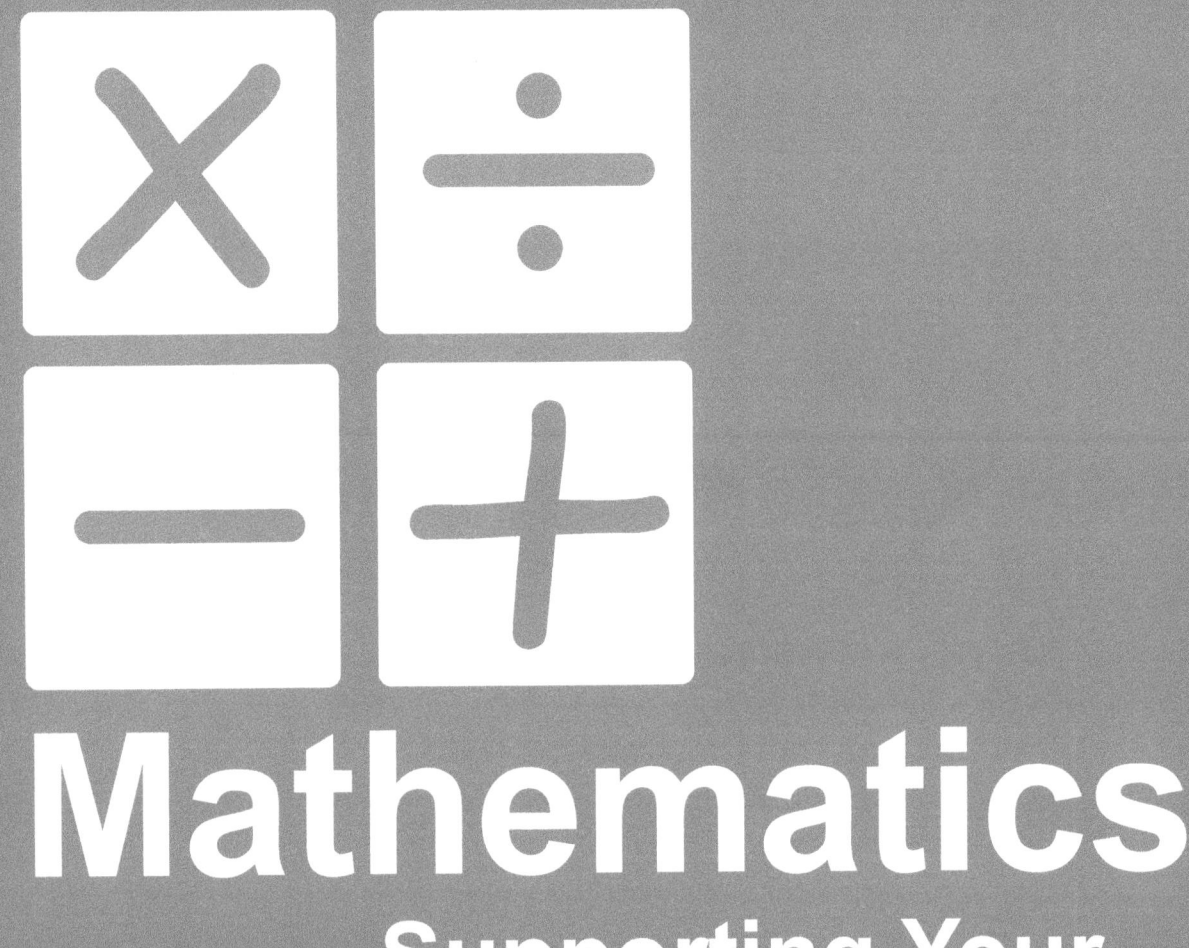

SUPPORTING YOUR EARLY MATHEMATICIAN: 0 - 4 YEARS

Please use these activity ideas to support your young child to build upon their knowledge at their own pace.

✓ Explore the six **Beginning Mathematical Processes** explained on the previous pages, as this will support all areas of mathematical understanding.

✓ **Count orally to three/five/ten forwards and backwards:**

- Count down *(backwards)* to signal the end of an event. *E.g., bath time/car ride.*
- Count in your everyday life, *E.g., count aloud to play hide and seek, count how long it takes to change a nappy, count tomatoes on the vine etc.*
- Count fingers and toes.
- Count aloud – One, mmmmm, three and ask what number was missing - count aloud to five incorrectly, ask the child to help fix the mistake.
- Stress that when we are counting, we are saying **NUMBERS** *(many children confuse letters and numbers).*
- Explore the word **'order'**. Teach children that numbers are counted in order, and that the order doesn't change.

✓ **Sing number rhymes** using bodies and fingers such as:
- **Dr Knickerbocker**
- **1, 2, 3, 4, 5, Once I Caught a Fish Alive**
- **Five Little Ducks**
- **Five Cheeky Monkeys**
- **Five Little Speckled Frogs**
- **Five Fat Sausages**
- **One, Two, Buckle my Shoe**

Check out Super Simple Songs, Bounce Patrol or The Wiggles on YouTube for number rhymes.

Begin to count three/five/ten objects using one to one correspondence:
(say one number name while touching one object)

- Model counting at the shops *e.g., I need five oranges; can you help me get five? Let's count together.*
- Count stairs, bath toys or toys you will take to the park.
- Collect shells, pebbles, buttons etc. and model careful counting.
- Use store-bought puzzles requiring matching a picture with numeral.
- Ask the child to close eyes while an adult taps out a given number of beats on a drum. The child must count in his/her head and say the number.
- Count when cooking or packing lunchboxes – *I need three cups of flour, 5 pieces of apple, 10 sultanas etc.*

 Explore colours, shapes and sizes of objects:

- Blow up balloons in a variety of sizes and colours and use language to compare and sort (see pages 106-108). Can the child sort them into groups *(colours)* or order them *(sizes- smallest to biggest)*?
- Play **Spotto** as you drive around – look for a car to match each colour.
- Complete inset puzzles to support size matching.
- Use nesting toys, shape sorters or containers that fit inside each other to identify and problem solve according to size differences.
- Use story books to identify colours, shapes and sizes in context.
- Explore art media *(paints, crayons, oil pastels, pencils)* to mix colours and draw objects of different shapes and sizes.
- Name and describe lines and shapes in the world around them, including highlighting their attributes – *Can you find the corners on the table? What shape is it? This is a triangle; it has three straight sides and three corners. This circle is round and has one curved line and no corners.*

 Copy and create simple two-part patterns:

- Make concrete patterns using beads, cereal (**Fruit Loops**), paint, colours and stickers.
- Look for patterns in nature *(plants and animals)* and the world *(buildings and clothing)*.
- Read pattern books *E.g.,* Pattern Bugs *or* Pattern Fish *by* **Trudy Harris.**
- Practise movement patterns- copy my clapping pattern, sit, stand, sit, stand/hands in the air, touch toes, hands in the air, touch toes.

- **Recognise numerals to three/five/ten:**
  - Write numerals to three/five/ten all over a piece of paper and ask your child to point to them as you call them out.
  - Learn numeral rhymes to support correct formation **(see appendix page 260–261).**
  - Practise writing numbers: use tracing sheets/whiteboards or blank sheets of paper inside clear plastic sleeves to practice tracing or writing numerals to three, then five, then ten.
  - Practice writing/making numerals in fun ways – shaving foam, sand trays, playdough, cooked spaghetti, painting with water on concrete.
  - Adapt the activity ideas on **Learning High-Frequency/Sight Words on page 61-63** to explore, practise and learn how to write numerals to ten.

- **Order numerals to three/five/ten:**

  - Make your own number lines (or print off the internet) to identify each number's position in order, and use this to support learning numbers to three, five or ten.
  - Write numbers to three, five or ten on flashcards and give cards to the child (depending on ability) to put in **ascending** *(smallest to biggest)* or **descending** *(biggest to smallest)* order.
  - Write all numerals to three, five or ten on flashcards and place in order, leaving out one or two cards. See if children can identify missing number.
  - Write numbers to five or ten on flashcards, pick out three cards and ask the child to put these three numbers in order.
  - Write dotted numerals in order on a piece of paper for the child to trace, learning numeral rhymes will support this **(see appendix page 260-261).**

- **Learn mathematical language used to describe amounts such as 'bigger, smaller, more and less':**

  - Compare characters/buildings/objects in story books using the language of bigger or smaller.
  - Use balance scales and marbles to compare weight using the language of ***more/less.***
  - Use the language of measures to compare everyday objects – **size** *(bigger/smaller)*, **volume** *(more/less which leads to full/empty)*, **weight** *(more or less, which leads to heavy/light)*, **height** *(short/tall)*.

Specialised Edition

SUPPORTING YOUR FOUNDATION AGED MATHEMATICIAN

These are the goals for children to master by the end of Foundation/Prep/Kindy and activities to support this learning. Please check that children have mastered the skills listed earlier for 0 to 4-year-olds.

✅ **Explore numbers in the world around them,** children need to know that numbers are everywhere and are an important part of our world:

- Point out numbers on licence plates, money, road signs, addresses, age of peers, etc.

- Play dice games, card games, board games and games that require a spinner. Some great choices are **Uno, Go Fish, Old Maid, Snap, Concentration, Orchard Board Games, Battleships, Snakes and Ladders, Trouble, Bingo.** See more dice and card games *on pages 186-187*.
- Stress that when we are counting, we are saying **NUMBERS** (many children confuse letters and numbers).
- Play games involving numbers such as hopscotch, What's the Time Mr. Wolf and using numbers as target practice or to keep score in competitions.

✅ **Continue to explore colours, shapes, sizes, and attributes of objects** as this will support all areas of mathematical understanding:

- Collect shells/rocks/leaves/buttons and sort them into groups *(colour, size, texture)*.
- Sort toys according to properties and explain groups. *E.g., sort vehicles according to land/sea/sky. Sort toys into feathers/fur/scales.*
- Read books about matching – *E.g.* **A Pair of Socks by Stuart J Murphy.**
- Read books about sorting – *E.g.* **Sort It Out! By Barbara Mariconda.**

- Complete puzzles with increasing numbers of pieces (10, 20 or 50).
- Explore lines – zig zag, sloping, curved, swirly, dotted, broken *(dashes)*.
- Describe shapes according to geometric properties – *a rectangle is made using four, straight lines, two are long and two are short. It also has four corners.*
- Mix paint colours, complete colour by number activities.

✅ **Sing number rhymes** such as those mentioned in *0-4 years (on page 112)*, as well as:

- **Ten in The Bed**
- **Ten Green Bottles**
- **Ten Fat Sausages**
- **The Ants Go Marching**
- **One Grey Elephant**
- **Alice The Camel**

NUMBER: FOUNDATION

Teacher For Early Years

 Recognise, count, use, and order all numbers to 20:

- Make or buy a set of flashcards. Start with numbers to 5, then 10, then 20. Encourage your child to lay all cards on the ground, face up. See if they can find 1-20 and lay them in order. When that becomes too easy, keep the cards in a pile. Show them where 1 and 20 will lay when the line is complete. Hand them one card at a time and see if they can reflect on the sequence of numbers and where each one would fit into the number line *(e.g., Is 17 going to be closer to 20 or 1?).*
- Use flashcards to 20, to pick a random card and use collage materials to represent that amount. *E.g., pick card (14) and decorate a collaged bug using 14 stickers, 14 sequins, 14 strips of paper, 14 stars, etc.*

- Use flashcards to 20, to pick a random card and complete the corresponding number of actions, *E.g., "You rolled a 14, so jump/bounce the ball 14 times."*
- Play **Guess My Number** (Think of a magic number, then give clues for your child to *guess* your number). Using flashcards to 20, encourage your child to lay them out, then give clues – *E.g., "I'm thinking of a number that is written using two straight lines, I'm thinking of a number that is more than seven but less than nine."*
- Consolidate the word **'order'**, ensure children understand that numbers are counted in a special way called order.
- Complete mazes and dot-to-dot puzzles to 20.
- Hide number cards to 10/20 (and beyond) around the yard and time your child to find them all, and lay them in order.

- Play with numbers: write numbers with chalk on the ground, throw a ball at the number… write on post it notes and stick on the wall, hit numbers with a nerf gun/water pistol.
- Count forwards and backwards to and from 20, from any given number (don't always start counting from one or 20). Use flashcards to 20, ask the student to select a card and start counting forwards or backwards from that number.
- Model how to lock a number in our head and count on or back. Use number lines to 20 to support this learning.
- Complete missing number sequences using numbers to 20 – draw a number line with missing numbers.

- Learn to read number words to 20 - Adapt the activity ideas on Learning High-Frequency/Sight Words on page 61-63 to learn written number words to 20.

> Remember that 'two' has a 'w' in it, because it is in the same family of words as twenty, twelve and twice. Don't forget the w!

- Complete Thinkboards to 10 or 20 to represent numbers (see appendix page 268-269)

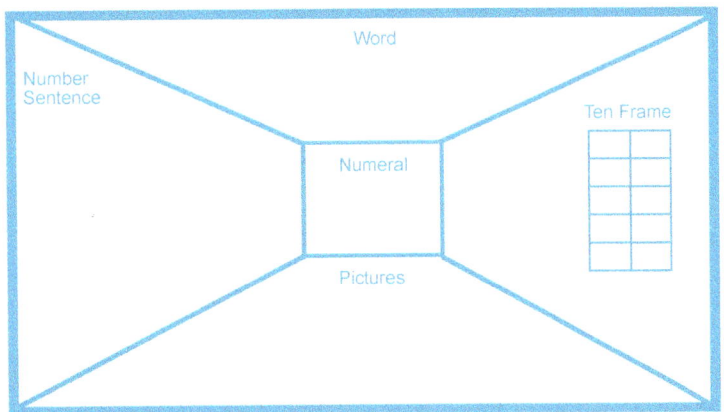

 Estimate – Guess how many? Then model careful counting.

- Randomly scatter five to ten pebbles on the ground. Ask the child to guess the amount and then count carefully by modelling placing them in a line or moving to one side.
- Draw several shapes/dots on a piece of paper, estimate the total, then count carefully by crossing off each as you say each number.
- **Using books:** *E.g. The Bad-Tempered Ladybird* **by Eric Carle**. Flick through the book, discuss, estimate numbers of spots/creatures. Read aloud and, using counters, place a representation of each character on the table. Estimate the number of counters, then count carefully to find the total.
- Hold up a jar with a certain number of objects, estimate the total number and give reasons for estimation, then model careful counting.

 Teach Conservation of number – This is understanding that the number of objects remains the same, even if they are rearranged.
Say *"The last number I count is the total number of items. If I count the same group again, I will get the same number even if I move them around."*

- Place five counters in a line on the table. Ask the child to count. Scatter them around, out of line and ask, *"How many now?"* Repeat with larger numbers.
- Place five counters scattered on the table, ask child to count the total amount. Ask the child to pass you two, say *"Now that there are two in my hand, can you pass me more so that I have five in my hand?"* The child should remember the initial number. Repeat with ten counters, scattered on the table. Ask for five counters and then ten. They should know to grab the whole lot and put them in your hand, as the starting number was ten.

Teacher For Early Years

✓ Learn the language of more/less, before/after, same as:

- Make links to life – *My bowl has **more**, and your bowl has **less**/we have the **same** number of cards. **Before** we go to bed, we will have a bath. **After** you are five, you will be six!*
- Draw two empty lolly bags on paper, ask your child to draw the same number of lollies in each bag.
- Draw two lolly bags, this time draw six lollies in one bag and three in the other. Ask your child, "If you loved lollies, which bag would you want and why?" Model correct answer using the language of more and less.

- Use number lines to 10 and ask questions - *Can you show me the number that comes before 8? Can you show me the number that comes after 2? Can you show me a number that is after 5? Before 5?*
- Use a number line to 20 to find one more/one less/two more/two less than any given number.
- Singing number rhymes (listed on page 112 and 115) will support this language.
- Read number stories exploring more and less – *E.g.,* Ten Seeds **by Ruth Brown**, talk about how there are less and less seeds as the book progresses. Then at the end, there is the same number as at the start of the book.
- Learn ordinal numbers – 1st, 2nd, 3rd etc. exposing them to the word and numeral versions (first and 1st).

- Make towers using construction materials – *which one has **more**? **Less**? **Same**?*
- Draw or display a small bag. Say – *"I have more than 5 counters in this bag, but less than 8. How many counters might be in my bag?"* Change the number of counters. Another example is *"I have more than 10 counters in this bag but less than 20. How many counters might I have?"*

- Draw an empty number line showing zero at one end and 20 at the other end, ask questions about missing numbers such as *"Can you tell me the number that is halfway between these two numbers? Can you tell me another number that is between these numbers? Where would I write 5? Is it closer to 0 or 20? Where would I write 15? Is it closer to 0 or 20? How many numbers are between 15 and 20? Where would number 3 go? How many numbers are less than 3?"*

Specialised Edition

 Represent amounts in any form, to at least 20:

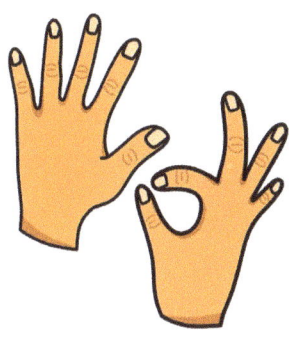

- Use fingers to represent numbers - ask, *"Can you show me 8 fingers? Can you show them in another way?"*
- Hold up your own fingers for children to quickly call out how many fingers you are showing.
- Ask *"If 8 fingers are up, how many are down?"* Model counting the last two fingers to get to ten. Verbalise eight and two makes ten. This will support learning 'Addition to Ten' facts.
- Use adult and child's hands to make teen numbers, adult is the *'tens'* and will hold up ten fingers. Child is the *'ones'* and will hold up the ones to represent the teen number that is called out. *E.g., If the number 17 is called, the* **'ones'** *person must show seven fingers. The adult should consolidate each time* – *"Yes, ten and seven more is seventeen."*
- Use concrete materials to explore counting objects carefully to 20.
- Match pictures, words, numerals to 20.
- Use a variety of thinkboards/number of the day sheets to represent numbers to 20 (see appendix pages 268-269 and 276-277). Encourage children to represent numbers using words, tally marks, pictures, before/after, next three numbers, etc.

 Write numerals to ten and then 20

- Learn numeral rhymes to help write numerals (see appendix page 260-261).
- Use write on, wipe off books, tracing sheets or *iPad apps* to support learning numerals.
- Adapt the activity ideas on Learning High Frequency/Sight Words on page 61-63 to learn numerals and how to spell number words to 20.

 Learn about Zero

- Have two sweets on the table. Share them between you and the child. Explore how there is now none/nothing left. Explain that the number that means 'nothing' is zero.
- Practise writing zero. Note that it is similar to the letter O and an oval shape.

NUMBER: FOUNDATION

Teacher For Early Years

✓ **Subitize: Sight recognition of quantity or the ability to give the number in a collection without counting objects individually** (this is an important part of mathematical development):

- Play board games with dice (*Orchard Games* are great for **3+**).
- Play with dominoes.
- Learn dot (dice) patterns to ten through games and flashcards.
- Play movement games with dice (roll dice, do that many actions).
- Play dice craft games – use a blank template *(e.g., ladybird)*, roll a dice and draw corresponding number of spots on the ladybird. Could use rolled up balls of playdough instead of drawing spots, as this will support fine motor development.
- Show a variety of dot patterns to ten and encourage children to use the language of *"How do you know?"* to demonstrate understanding. *E.g., "I know there are nine dots, because five and five makes ten, but one dot is missing. I know there is nine dots, because three and three and three are nine."*
- Flash **dot cards** using different arrangements of numbers (see some samples below and flashcards in appendix **pages 262-265**) for children to practise instant recognition.

Domino arrangement

Caldwell pattern – rows of three, very easy on the eye

Odd and Even pattern – gets longer and longer

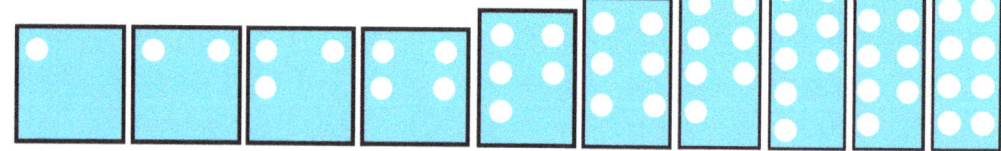

- Show multiple ways to represent the same number. Ask *"How many dots are there? How do you know? How do you see them?"*

- Compare dot cards showing more and less.

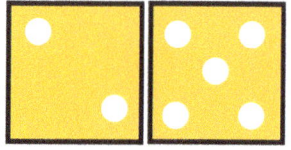   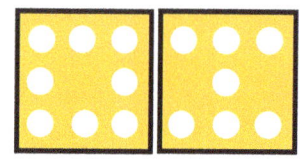

easy comparison   harder comparison

Use Five and Ten Frames – a great way to start teaching addition and subtraction and to learn about part, part, whole. Five and ten frames are <u>equal-sized rectangular boxes in a row</u>, where a box is large enough to hold a counter. A five frame is a 1 x 5 array, and a ten frame is a 2 x 5 array. Fill frames left to right and top to bottom to support subitising *(instant recognition of dot patterns)*. **See the image below for more information and page 267 for a larger version.**

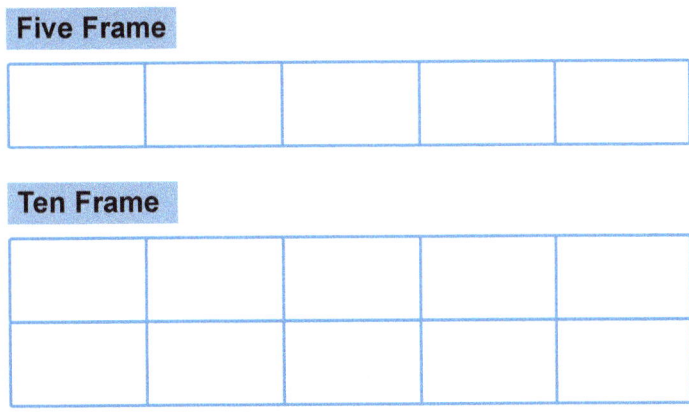

- Use five and ten frames to learn basic number facts that they can verbalise – *E.g., "This five frame has dots in all the boxes except the last box is empty. One less than five is four."* Encourage the child to display three counters in the five frame, identify how many more counters to make five.
- When children are familiar with a five frame, they should move onto a ten frame to support larger calculations. *E.g., "This ten frame, has five dots in the top row and two in the bottom row. Five and two is..."*

- Use this language to link to part, part, whole. *E.g., Using the last example – We can add the part on the top of the ten frame, which was five, with the part on the bottom of the ten frame, which was two, and get the whole amount, which is seven.*
- Use two different coloured counters to fill the frames and make addition sums to five and then ten.

- Flash five or ten frame cards showing a variety of dots (one-ten) and have children share the number they saw. Ask questions like: *"What number was it? How did you know? Is it more or less than 5? How many more do you need to make 10?"* See samples on page 122.
- Read books that explore part, part, whole. *E.g.,* **Ten Black Dots by Donald Crews.**
- Begin to explore basic language associated with addition – and, add, plus, join together, forwards **(see full list on page 152)**.
- Begin to explore basic language associated with subtraction – less, backwards, take away, fewer. See more information in the **Problem Solving section**, pages 152-175.

Five Frames

Ten Frames

10 and 0	
9 and 1	
8 and 2	
7 and 3	

🔥 **Using frames will support addition and subtraction skills and understanding.**

 Start to explore simple addition and subtraction calculations using visual and real-world representations. Make it fun!

- Have a toy tea party, add and subtract toys as they come and go.
- Blow up balloons, play with them, count how many are left at the end. Did any pop?
- Draw pictures such as gardens full of flowers, if some of them dried out how many would be left?
- Have dinner ready on the bench, each family member takes one plate to the table. How many plates are left on the bench?
- Complete sentence strips to support early calculations (_____ and _____ makes _____)
- Use the language of 'and', 'add' and 'plus' when adding, Use the language of 'take away', 'less' and 'subtract' when subtracting.

Please see pages 152–160 for clear explanations of Addition Strategies which have been organised according to level of difficulty – children in Foundation should be exposed to the following:

① Draw a picture
② Word problems
③ Count on
④ Use one ten frame
⑤ Use two ten frames
⑥ Number lines
⑦ Addition to Ten/Rainbow Facts
⑧ Think Big, Count Small
⑨ Doubles facts to 5 (they can do this on their fingers)

Introduce the **addition symbol (+)** ONLY when your child has a solid understanding of addition. Start off by using the word **'and'**
Note: This might not happen until the end of Foundation year or the start of Year 1.

- Complete open-ended addition and subtraction problems.

    E.g., Steph and Amelia were playing a game of soccer. At the end of the game ten goals had been scored altogether. How many goals might they each have scored?

    E.g., I have six counters in this box, some are red, and some are blue. What might this look like? Draw or explain how each colour could be represented.

    E.g. I went to the shop and bought 8 pieces of fruit, some are apples and some are oranges. How many of each type of fruit might I have?

    Using books: Read the book **One Is A Snail, Ten Is A Crab by April Pulley Sayre and Jeff Sayre**. Have lots of pictures of animals with different numbers of legs. Use as a stimulus to add addition and subtraction questions – *E.g., How many legs on a – and a –?*

    Open-ended question – *If I saw 10 legs, how many animals might be there?*

 Use everyday objects to make two- and three-part patterns

– **please see page 109 for samples of patterns**

- Use stickers, shapes and colours to make patterns.
- Use real-world objects (from nature) to make circular artistic patterns.
- Encourage the child to copy the same two- or three-part pattern that you have created.
- Encourage the child to continue a two- or three-part pattern that you have started. Can they explain the repeating part *(rule)*?
- Encourage the child to create their own two- or three-part pattern.
- **Using books:** Read books about patterns *E.g.* **A-B-A-B-A A Book of Pattern Play by Brian P. Cleary.**
- Learn that dance moves can be patterns – watch **Jack Hartmann Pump Up The Pattern** on *YouTube* to support this.
- See sample pattern assessment on page 267.

 Share collections and shapes into equal groups:

- Develop an understanding of the language of 'same' and 'equal'.
- Use real-world problems to share collections into equal groups.
- Break shapes into two equal parts.

Teacher For Early Years

SUPPORTING YOUR YEAR 1 MATHEMATICIAN

These are the goals to master by the end of Year 1. Check that your child has mastered all the skills mentioned previously and continues to build on these.

 Recognise, count, use, and order all numbers to 100:

> Remember that many children find it difficult to count between the decades (e.g., when the tens change from **79 (seven tens) - 80 (eight tens))**. Lots of work using the following activities will support this understanding.

Practise counting to and from 100

- Use posters and hands-on materials such as buttons, rocks or counters.
- Complete mazes and dot-to-dot puzzles to 100.
- **Use a timer:** Time how long it takes them to count to 100? Then challenge them to improve on that time.

Get Fit: Count to 100 using exercise movements

- How many jumps/hops can they do without stopping? How about bouncing a ball?
- View clips on *YouTube* to support counting to 100: *Jack Hartmann* has a fun counting to 100 exercise video available.

Practise counting to and from 100 from any given number

- Tell the child to think of a number between 30 – 40 and start counting forwards or backwards from there.
- Start counting backwards from 84.
- Count forwards from 91, but stop at 98.
- Make real-life problems: Tell the child you have 62 lollies in your jar but need to add 8 more. How many lollies would be in the jar after that? Remind them to start counting from 62 to find the answer.

> **Reinforce the meaning of the words 'before/after' and 'more/less' and 'greater/smaller'**

- Using language: Use this language in your everyday life – *"**Before** we go to bed, we can have some ice-cream," "Your bowl has **more** ice-cream and mine has **less**, you have a **greater** amount and I have a **smaller** amount. **After** ice-cream, we have to go to bed."*
- Learn about more and less/before and after, by asking about people's ages, *"If mummy is 38, how old will she be next? What is one more than 38? How about grandad, who is 87? How old was mum, two birthdays ago?"*
- Using numbers: Find numbers using a hundred grid (see below with options to 99 or 100) and play games to identify one more/one less, two more/two less than any given number to 99. Print out a hundred grid and place it in a clear plastic sleeve, you can use it and a whiteboard marker to play many games (see **100 grid activities and game ideas** on **pages 192-195**). Alternatively, there are many interactive grids available online. Find these by searching *'interactive hundreds grids'*.

0	1	2	3	4	5	6	7	8	9
10	11	12	13	14	15	16	17	18	19
20	21	22	23	24	25	26	27	28	29
30	31	32	33	34	35	36	37	38	39
40	41	42	43	44	45	46	47	48	49
50	51	52	53	54	55	56	57	58	59
60	61	62	63	64	65	66	67	68	69
70	71	72	73	74	75	76	77	78	79
80	81	82	83	84	85	86	87	88	89
90	91	92	93	94	95	96	97	98	99

1	2	3	4	5	6	7	8	9	10
11	12	13	14	15	16	17	18	19	20
21	22	23	24	25	26	27	28	29	30
31	32	33	34	35	36	37	38	39	40
41	42	43	44	45	46	47	48	49	50
51	52	53	54	55	56	57	58	59	60
61	62	63	64	65	66	67	68	69	70
71	72	73	74	75	76	77	78	79	80
81	82	83	84	85	86	87	88	89	90
91	92	93	94	95	96	97	98	99	100

> **Consolidate the word 'order,' ensuring children understand that numbers are counted in a special way called 'order'**

- Make this language a part of your everyday life.
- Link to ordinal numbers (explained on the next page).
- Model counting in the wrong order – 1, 4, 5, 2 and how important it is that we count the numbers in order, so the count is correct.

> **Expand on their understanding of the word 'order' by looking at ordinal numbers to the tenth (10th) place - 1st, 2nd, 3rd, 4th etc.**

- Line up and release cars on a ramp and award them their place at the finish line.
- Watch car races or swimming races on the television.
- Complete running races or other competitions (take it in turns to win and lose, so they get to experience both feelings).
- Line up ten toys or books and award them according to favourites.
- Remember to look at both the number (1st) and word (first) version.

> **Instantly recognise all numbers to 99**

- Make or buy a set of flashcards to assist with instant recognition of numbers to 100 (cut-up cereal boxes make great cards – cheap and strong).
- Hide a selection of number cards to 99 (e.g., numbers 75-85) around the yard or house and time how long it takes for your child to find them and lay them in order.

> **Start using a grid book to practise writing numbers to 20 and beyond. Remind students that each digit/numeral gets its own grid square space**

1	1
not	11

1	2	3	4	5	6	7
8	9	1	0	1	1	
1	2	not		11		

Specialised Edition

Order numbers to at least 100

- Using flashcards to 100, pull out five random cards and ask your child to order them from smallest to biggest or vice versa. Extend, by leaving some blank cards, then working out and writing the numbers before and after each of these numbers.
- Give the child a set of ten cards numbered sequentially *e.g., 60- 70*. Place cards face up, spread on the floor for them to put in order. They will most likely look for numbers in sequence, *e.g., 61, then 62, then 63...* To extend them, place numbers 60-70 in a pile and draw a number line on the ground (or use string). The child must order whatever number comes up in the pile, using their knowledge of each number's position in the number line. *E.g., If they pick up card number 67 first, they have to think about where it would be on a number line showing spaces for numbers 60-70.*

Use number lines to explore and discuss numbers

- Draw a number line and write the first and last number.
- Ask questions, *e.g., Where would I find -----?*
- What number can you see before it? After it?

QUICK GAME

Draw a blank number line on the ground with chalk, about a metre long. Do not write the first and last number as it will change throughout the activity. (Alternatively, use string and pegs and children can pegs cards on the line). Give your child a flashcard saying 20 and ask them to place it where they think it might live on the number line. They may put the card towards the end of the line, thinking the line will be from 1-20. Always ask them to explain the reasoning for placement, *e.g., "Where would 20 go? Why?"*

Do the same with a card showing number 26 asking *"If I gave you this card, where would you put it and why?"* Repeat with more numbers such as 100, 48 – each time, they will most likely need to move previous number cards accordingly and explain their reasoning.

This will support ordering, mathematical language (more/less/before/after), proportions and early fraction discussions (halfway, a quarter of the way), thinking and reasoning and defining the parameters.

Find missing numbers

- Draw a number line in the child's book, starting from any number and leaving out some numbers for them to fill in.

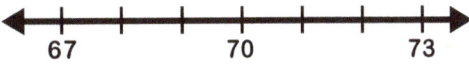

Represent (make/model/write) numbers to at least 100 using a variety of materials:

Learn the words 'digits' and 'numerals'

- Call out two-digit numbers for your child to write. Say *"I'm going to call out a 2-digit number for you to write. This means that the number will have two numerals."*

Explore 'teen' numbers

- Spend a lot of time exploring teen numbers – they are tricky as they are said backwards – children must learn that when we say 18, although we hear the word 'eight' at the start, it is the same as one ten and eight ones. The 8 is indicative of 8 ones, and the ones must be written on the right-hand side of the number. Also, eleven and twelve do not follow the 'teen' pattern like the other numbers.
- Using two ten frames (explored in-depth on **pages 121-122**) will support this learning.

Learn to discuss and describe place value

Each digit in a number has a value, depending on it's placement in the number; the number on the right tells you how many ones, the number on the left tells you how many tens.

TENS	ONES

- Introduce the Tens and Ones Place Value charts **(see page 272)**. These charts/frames help to model two-digit numbers. These will be explored in more detail, using concrete objects/ manipulatives over the next few pages.

Specialised Edition

> **Use bundling (paddlepop or popsicle) sticks to represent two-digit numbers**

- Use bundling (paddle pop or popsicle) sticks, rubber bands and place value charts (see page 272) to model making two-digit numbers and support understanding of place value.

QUICK GAME

Have 100 popsicle sticks on the ground, a few elastic bands and one place value chart displaying tens and ones. Child rolls a six-sided dice, say they roll a six. Place the corresponding number of sticks (6) in the ones column. Roll again. Say they roll another six (so 12 altogether). Remind the child that only 9 sticks/items can live in the ones house, once we get more than 9, we will bundle up 10 sticks using the rubber band and move the bundled group of sticks to the tens house, leaving the leftover/loose ones behind. Keep rolling the dice and making numbers until you get to 99.

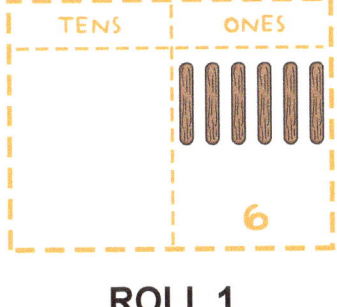
ROLL 1

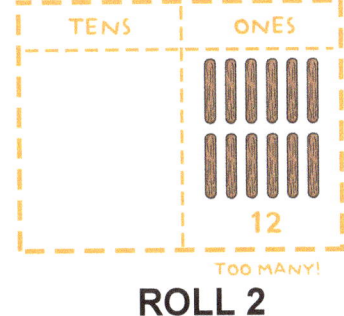
TOO MANY!
ROLL 2

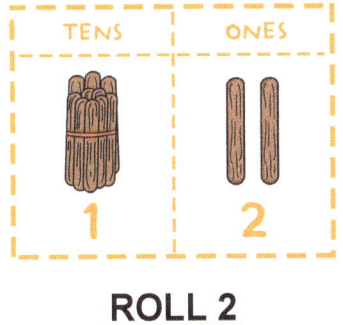
ROLL 2 ADJUSTMENT

Bundling sticks are a fantastic way for children to explore numbers as they help to create a visual of the value or amount in each number. They support the understanding of <u>place value</u> *(the value of each digit in the number)*, <u>partitioning</u> *(breaking the number into tens and ones)*, <u>regrouping/trading</u> *(swapping ten loose ones for one bundle of ten)* and <u>facilitate an early awareness of algorithms</u> *(addition and subtraction)*.

- Another option is to use an object that builds on your child's interests.
  Do they love trains? Have 9 pictures of motors, when they get 10, they can trade up for a carriage; when they get 10 carriages, they can trade up for a train. Explain that a motor has the same value as one, the carriage is worth ten and a train is the same as one hundred or 100 ones/motors.
  You could do the same for unicorns starting with a pony, trading up to a horse and then to a unicorn!

129

NUMBER: YEAR 1

After exploring bundling sticks, introduce MAB/base 10 blocks (most schools will have these – traditionally made from wood but now you can get plastic versions). Children need to know what these are and ideally have a good chance to use them, before moving on to the paper version (see a printable version on page 271). <u>If the child is not using these at school, it may be worthwhile watching some videos on YouTube to explore these blocks.</u>

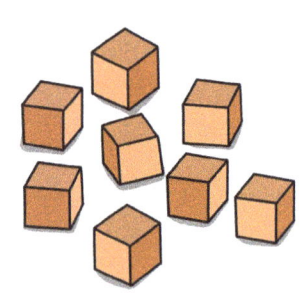

MAB blocks (like bundling sticks) are a fantastic way for children to explore numbers, as they help to create a visual of the value or amount in each number. They support the understanding of place value (the value of each digit in the number), partitioning (breaking the number into tens and ones), regrouping/trading (swapping ten ones for one stick of ten) and facilitate an early awareness of algorithms (addition and subtraction).

- These are available to purchase online; however, they are not cheap. In the appendix, you will find a printable version of MAB's. Photocopy and laminate these and use them to make 2-digit numbers (see **page 271**). Remember, children should have had a chance to use these manipulatives before using the paper version.

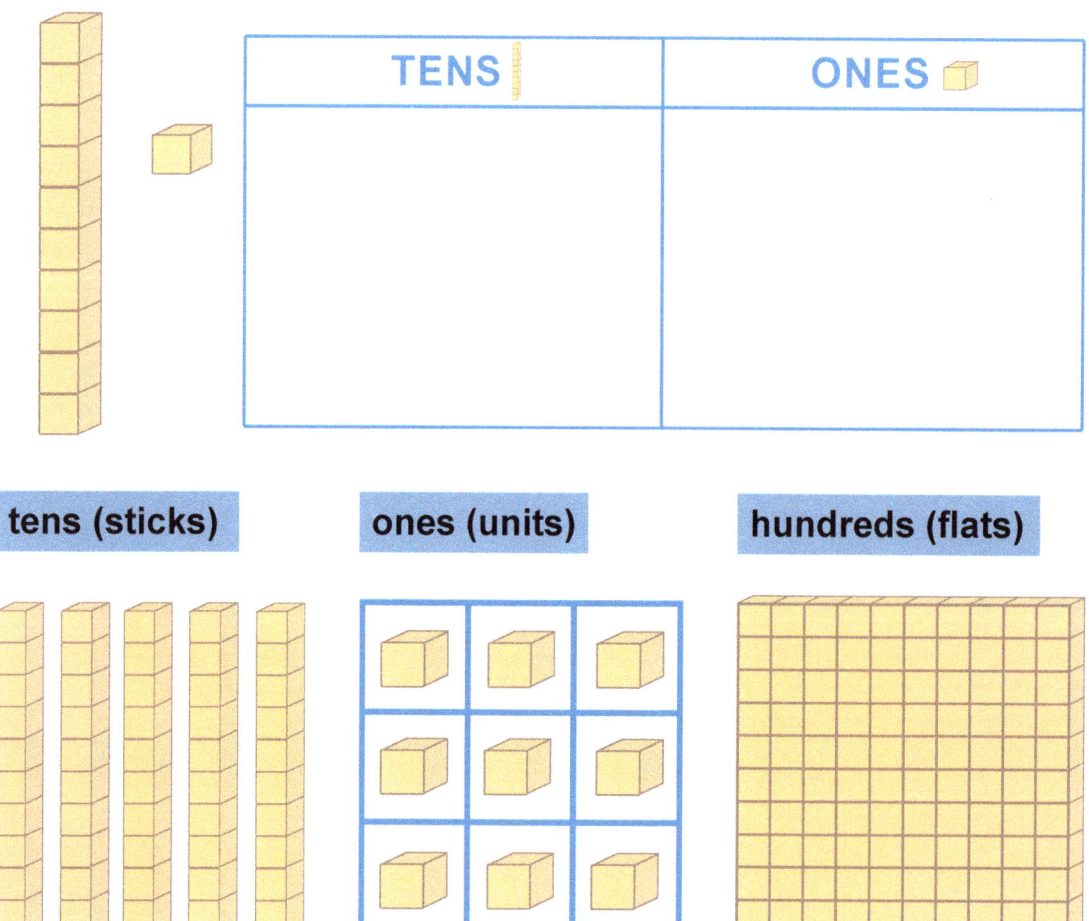

- Use these in the same way as the bundling sticks were used.

Specialised Edition

QUICK GAME

You will need to copy, laminate, and cut a set of printable MAB blocks (see appendix page 271) blocks and give the child **9 ones** and **9 tens**. When children are demonstrating confidence with numbers to 99, you could introduce the hundreds block. Roll a six-sided dice and place the corresponding number of ones in the ones column on the place value chart (page 272). Roll again. Say they roll another six. Remind the child that only 9 ones can live in the ones house. Once we get more than 9, we will swap for a stick of 10 up and move it to the tens house, leaving the loose ones behind. Keep rolling the dice and making numbers until you get to 99.

- Practise partitioning numbers: once children have developed an understanding of place value, they should be encouraged to continue to use manipulatives and practise partitioning numbers (breaking numbers into parts) - **75** is the same as **70 + 5**. The bundling sticks and MAB's will support this learning.

- Hold up flashcards using numbers to 100 or write 2-digit numbers on paper and identify how many tens and how many ones.
  e.g., Look at these numbers – how many tens in: 44? 79? 56? 38? 62?
  Look at these numbers – how many ones in: 23? 54? 19? 89?

Use worksheets and diagrams

- Complete **Think board worksheet** (a partitioned sheet that allows children to show understanding in a variety of ways) (See templates on pages 268-269).
- Complete **Number of the Day worksheet** (a partitioned sheet that allows children to show understanding in a variety of ways) **charts** (see page 276).
- Make a **0-100 picture book** – draw pictures or MAB blocks to match each number.
- Explore similarities and differences between numbers.
  E.g., What is the same and different about the numbers 12 and 21? A **Venn Diagram** (see below) will help to compare and contrast numbers. See blank copy on page 232.

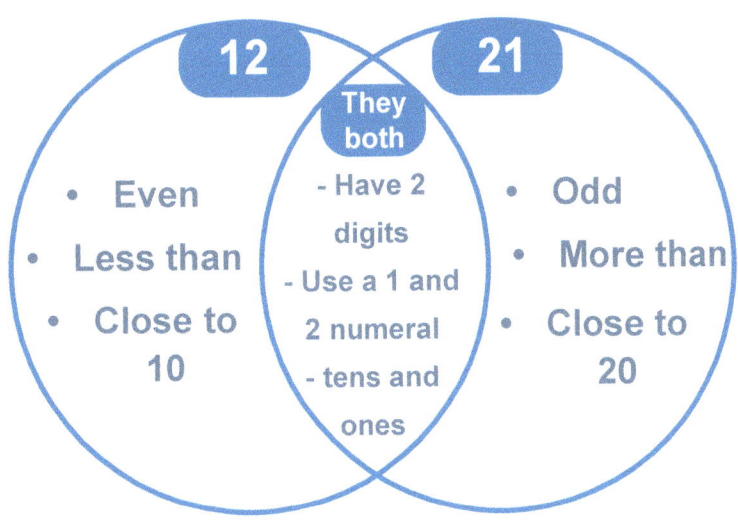

> **Use MAB's, bundling sticks, number lines, hundred grids and place value charts to model and answer questions about numbers**

- Ask questions about features of numbers – *"What features of 23, demonstrate that it lies between 20 and 30?"*
- Take time to distinguish between numbers that sound similar – like 15 and 50 *(stress the **'teen'** and **'ty'** at the end of the word).*
- Pull out random cards from 1-99 (or roll two 10-sided dice - ignoring the tens) to get a 2-digit number. Use bundling sticks or MAB blocks to make the number – *Can you show me how to make 16? What about 74?*

> **Match partitioned 2-digit numbers with whole numbers**

Easy version

Harder version

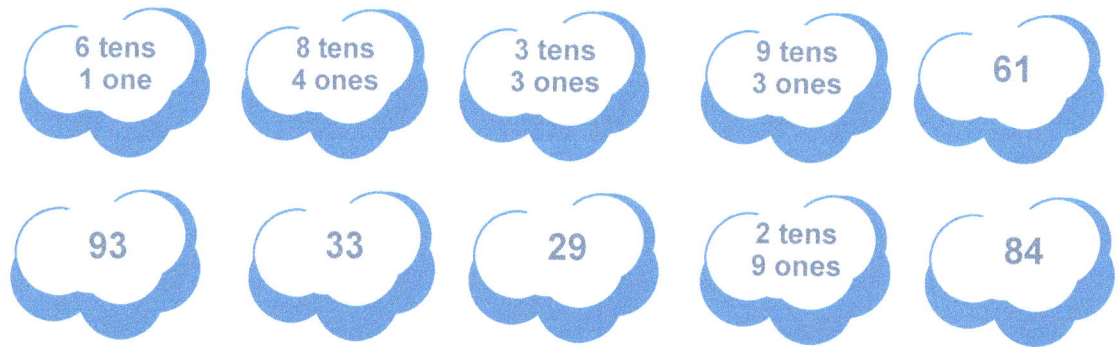

> **Learn to read and write number words to 100**

- Have the child match the number name to the numeral by creating a colour match activity similar to the one above.
- Choose ten numbers between 1-99 and make up two sets of cards that show both numeral and number word. Use these cards to play Memory/Concentration. Turn all cards upside down, take turns to turn over two cards at a time, matching the name to the number. If it is a match, the player keeps both cards, else return them if it is not a match.
- Use whiteboards and race each other to write a number that has been called out, using numerals or words.

Specialised Edition

 Skip count in twos, fives and tens, forwards and backwards to 100:

> **Count real life objects in twos, fives and tens**

- Twos – eyes, feet, hands, pairs of shoes and socks, $2 coins.
- Fives – fingers, toes, sides on a pentagon, $5 notes, use tally marks.
- Tens – total toes or fingers, $10 notes, legs on a **decapod** *(10 footed crustacean)*, **decagons** *(10 sided 2-D shape)*, build towers of ten.

> **Fill the house with counting patterns**

- Draw lily pads on the ground with chalk and count in multiples of two, five or ten, ask your child to jump and count.
- Play hopscotch using multiples of ten.
- Make bunting/hang posters in room or bathroom so they are exposed and practising frequently.

> **Count using familiar mathematical materials**

- Use a number line and a counter to jump along or circle the line to show how we count in twos, fives and tens.
- Use a hundreds grid (paper or interactive) and a counter or marker, jump and circle numbers on the grid to show counting in twos, fives and tens.

- At the time of printing, **ABCya** and **Maths Playground** were both offering free interactive 100s grids.

    https://www.abcya.com/games/interactive_100_number_chart
    https://www.mathplayground.com/interactive_hundreds_chart.html

> **Skip count orally**

- Practise counting orally forwards and backwards using counting patterns (have a laminated hundreds grid in the shower or car to practise anytime).

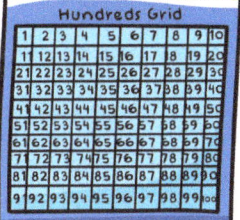

133

NUMBER: YEAR 1

Model how to skip count using large groups of items

- Show a large group of items on the floor (e.g., 72 popsicle sticks) and model careful counting, one item at a time. You may wish to put items in a line after they have been counted. Explain that it took a long time to count, but there could be a faster way. Discuss ways to count quicker, *e.g., putting them into groups and skip counting*. Ask the child to collect items into groups of 10 and then count the total together. Find different ways of grouping the items such as counting in twos and fives.

Find dot to dots online that require skip counting to complete

- Search online (www.education.com has some great examples. You will need to join up with email and search for skip counting dot to dots).

Order flashcards to 100

- Gather all flashcards showing multiples of ten/five/two and ask the child to order cards from smallest to biggest or biggest to smallest.

Continue and complete counting patterns

- Ask the child to continue patterns or complete patterns with missing parts, by helping your child find the pattern rule. Some great questions to ask are:

  Are the numbers getting bigger or smaller?
  Is the pattern counting forwards or backwards?
  Is it jumping in 1's? 2's? 5's? 10's?

  "What is next in this pattern? 57, 47, 37, 27, ---?
  Is the pattern counting forwards or backwards? Is it jumping in 1's? 2's? 5's? 10's? What would the next number be? How do you know?"

  "What is missing in this pattern? 49, ---, 53, 55, 57?
  Is the pattern counting forwards or backwards? Is it jumping in 1's? 2's? 5's? 10's? What would the next number be? How do you know?"

Specialised Edition

Model incorrect skip counting

- Ask for help to correct. — *E.g., 80, 70, 60, 40.* Repeat with counting in twos and fives.

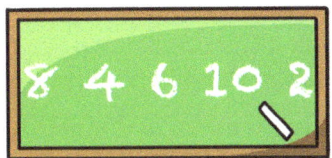

Play 'What Is My Number' using clues related to skip counting

- *E.g., "What is my number? It is a number I would say if I was counting in tens, it is more than six tens but less than eight tens."* See more questions on **pages 192-195**.

Explore multiples

- Start by breaking collections into equal groups *"How many groups of twos are in six?", "How many groups of five are in ten?"* or *"How many groups of ten in seventy?"* Give them concrete material (counters, MAB, bundling sticks, etc.) to work this out. This is the basic skillset needed for future multiplication and division problems.

Learn about tally marks to help with skip counting in fives

- Put 25 objects on the floor. Count in ones, then model grouping objects and counting in fives. Explain how much quicker it was to count in fives, rather than ones. Demonstrate how to make tally marks in groups of five, then complete some activities requiring counting using tally marks.

Skipping

Me	Adult

e.g.,
- Take turns to skip with a rope and record the other person's jumps using tally marks.
- Bounce a ball and record bounces or number of balls caught using tally marks.
- Sit by a 'quietish' road and monitor number of cars using tally marks.

> **Make tally mark flash cards with child (aim for ten matches at a time)**

- Flash them to practise instant recognition or match them with numeral flashcards. To extend, add in number word cards.

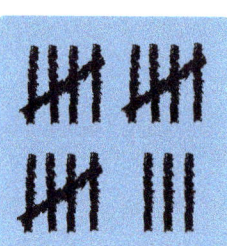

 Explore Addition and Subtraction strategies

> **Please see page 152–165 for clear explanations of Addition Strategies which have been organised according to level of difficulty – children in Year One should be exposed to the following:**

① Draw a picture
② Word problems
③ Count on
④ Use one ten frame
⑤ Use two ten frames
⑥ Number lines
⑦ Addition to Ten/Rainbow Facts
⑧ Think Big, Count Small
⑨ Doubles
⑩ Extending Addition to Ten/Rainbow Facts
⑪ Near Doubles (using small numbers)
⑫ Look for Friendly Pairs
⑬ Use a 100s grid to solve algorithms
⑭ Finding the Difference (using small numbers)
⑮ Extending Doubles Using Multiples of Ten (extension for Year 1)

 Explore odd and even numbers

> **What do even numbers always end in?**

- Use counters, Lego, blocks, magnets and illustrations, to model pairs/partners and odd one out. Use language such as *"Which one is alone? Which one does not have a pair or partner? Which is the odd one out?"*

Specialised Edition

> **As children learn place value of tens and ones (ones on the right, tens on the left), remind them that we look at the ones to decide if a number is odd or even**

- Remind child that if there is a 1, 3, 5, 7 or 9 in the ones place, then the number is odd.

> **Explain reasoning**

- *"Why is 11 an example of an odd number?"* We are aiming for them to be able to say – *"Because it doesn't have a partner/it can't be divided by two or shared into two equal groups/it isn't a number I say when I count in twos."*

> **Use a dice (preferably 10-sided dice)**

- Identify if the number rolled is odd or even. Explain reasoning (see above).

> **Write six numbers on paper: circle all the odd numbers**

- E.g., 33, 42, 10, 6, 99, 85
- Ensure children can explain why they are odd.

> **Play games: Write the words odd and even on cards and draw out of a hat for the following two games:**

- Draw a card each. One player is called **'odd'**, and one player is called **'even'**. Face each other – on the count of 3, each player will hold up a number of fingers from 0-10. Add fingers together. If the answer is odd, the 'odd' player scores 10 points, if it is even, the 'even' player gets 10 points. First to 100 is the winner.
- Draw a card each. One player is called **'odd'**, and one player is called **'even'**. Roll a 10-sided dice. If the number rolled is odd, the 'odd' player scores five points, if it is even, the 'even' player gets five points. Use tally marks to keep track of the score.

> **Using books: <u>One Odd Day</u> or <u>My Even Day</u> by <u>Doris Fisher and Dani Sneed</u> to ignite discussion**

Recognise, describe, and order coins:

Create and compare collections of coins

- Say *"These are all 5c coins, they are worth less than 20c coins. Can you find the coins that are worth the most? Least?"* Order coins according to more or less.

Explore art activities

- Do coin rubbings by placing coins under paper and shading.
- Draw images of animals, people and settings from coins and notes.

Ask child to help you with the groceries

- What brand of canned peaches is the cheapest?
- This item is $2 and this one is $3. How much money will I need to buy both?

Identify and discuss size, shape, colour and imagery on coins

- General discussion throughout the day.

Make small amounts using coins

- *Can you show me how to make 30c? $1.10? etc.*

 Identify halves and quarters of shapes and collections

Ensure children understand the words 'equal parts'

- Use this language in your everyday life: *"I would like a cookie and so would you, but there's only one left. Let's break it into equal parts, equal means 'the same.'"*

Use paper

- Fold square, rectangular and circular paper in half and then half again. Unfold and count the equal parts.

Complete Butterfly symmetry painting

- Fold a piece of paper in half, open it and drop four spoonfuls of different coloured paint on one side. Close paper (into a card), rub paint from the middle line towards the outer side of the paper. Open it up to see a symmetrical butterfly. Identify how each half is the same or equal.

Use 2D shapes

- Draw shapes (square, circle, rectangle, triangle) for children to divide into halves and quarters.

Show unequal parts

- Draw some 2D shapes, draw a line to split shapes in half but very obviously unequal parts. Explain how it isn't equal, so it isn't a half. Repeat with quarters.
- Get a cookie and ask the child to cut it in half. Is it equal? If it isn't, would they be happy to have the smaller part?

Stress that quarters are half and half again

- Say *"If I fold this paper from this side to this side, when I unfold it, I will have two equal parts. These are called halves. If I do it again, I will have four equal parts. These are called quarters."*

Model sharing collections into equal groups using real-world problems

- Share out six lollies and show them by doing it equally and unequally.
- Draw eight circles on paper and model how to share the collection in half and then half again to make quarters.

Teacher For Early Years

✓ **Continue to use Five and Ten Frames** (please see explanation on page 121 and template on page 267).

> **Consolidate use of five frame for those still needing support to understand the number five and how it is made using parts**

- *"This frame shows three dots, I know that instantly because it is two less than five"*

> **Use a ten frame to consolidate addition to ten, this is extremely important and will help develop a number sense within the context of ten, but also later, to 100. The relationship between ten and numbers less than ten, will become apparent via the visual of the frame**

- Use various arrangements of counters on the ten frames to prompt mental images of calculations to ten. *E.g., This ten frame has two dots missing, ten take away two is eight, or two less than ten is eight.*
- Hold up numeral cards to 20 and beyond for children to make numbers on two blank ten frames. Use this learning to support understanding of teen numbers – 18 is the same as 10 and 8.
- Use two different coloured counters to make addition to ten – I have a full ten frame, some counters are red, some are yellow – how many of each could be in my frame?
- Use frames to demonstrate simple addition and subtraction problems.
  e.g., Show me 5 + 4

> **Use multiple ten frames as a visual to support partitioning numbers**

- 54 is the same as 5 tens and 4 ones

> **Use multiple ten frames to prove facts about numbers**

- Which number is larger 13 or 31?

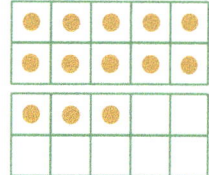 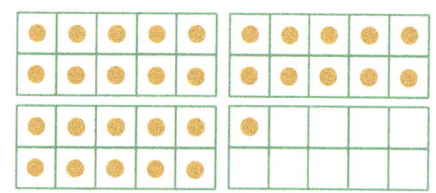

NUMBER: YEAR 1

Specialised Edition

> **Revise previous learning:**
>
> ☐ Check understanding of **zero** (page 119)
>
> ☐ Continue to **estimate** (page 117)
>
> ☐ Check instant recognition of **dot patterns** *(subitisation)* (page 120)

 Copy, continue and create simple patterns using objects (see page 109):

- Use stickers, shapes, craft materials and colours to make patterns.
- Encourage the child to copy the same two- or three-part pattern that you have created.

- Encourage the child to continue a two- or three-part pattern that you have created.
- Ensure that the children are able to explain the repeating part (rule)
  e.g. blue, blue, red, blue, blue, red.

- Check that children understand and can explain the word **'repeat'**.
- Encourage the child to create their own two- or three-part patterns.

- Dance and make musical patterns.
- **Using Books:** A great book to support Year One Mathematical understanding is **Teddy Bear Patterns** by **Barbara Barbieri McGrath** – explores addition, odd/even, sorting, patterns, skip counting.

Teacher For Early Years

SUPPORTING YOUR YEAR 2 MATHEMATICIAN

Please go through all learning from Year One to ensure that they have mastered the skills mentioned previously, even if you are a parent, tutor or teacher of a Year Two student.

 Most **Year Two teachers** will spend at LEAST half of Term One revising two-digit numbers, before introducing three-digit numbers.

 Recognise, count, use, and order all numbers to at least 1000

Count to 1000, forwards and backwards and starting from any given number (e.g., 532)

- Count aloud at every opportunity, the car and shower are great places for counting!
- Roll three dice or pull three cards from a deck of cards (face cards removed) to create a three-digit number, start counting forwards or backwards from that number.
- Count every day on a pre-filled grid.

Reinforce the meaning of the words 'before/after,' 'more/less,' 'greater/smaller' and 'equal/same as'

- Use this language in your everyday life: when discussing the age of people, time words, sizes, etc.
- Hold up two cards (two-digit or three-digit) and ask which number is smaller/bigger/greater/less/larger/fewer.
- See **pages 118 and 125** for activity ideas to reinforce this language.

Consolidate the word 'order'; ensure children understand that numbers are organised and counted in a specific sequence

- Make this language a part of your everyday life: through competitions and races.
- Link to ordinal number by learning ordinal numbers to 20: 1st – 20th, exposing them to both the word and numeral versions. See **page 126** for more ideas.
- Model counting in the wrong order – 101, 104, 105, 102 and explain how important it is that we count the numbers in order, so the count is correct.

Order and compare numbers to 999

- Write a selection of two and three-digit numbers onto cards, put them in order and explain the order – *E.g., I put 204 as the second number because it is less than 467 but more than 91 (91, 204, 467, 599, 700).*

- Write three numbers on whiteboards and ask the child to circle the largest one/smallest one and explain the reasoning for their choice.
- Find the number before and after a range of two and three-digit numbers.

Find numbers on a number line to 999

- Start with a number line to 20 - Draw a number line writing only 0 and 20. Ask the child to help you position number 15. Explain the best way is to start by finding halfway and put 10 on the number line. If they don't know 10 is halfway, this will need to be modelled by counting with a hundreds grid. Ask if they know the number halfway between 10 and 20. If they don't, use the hundreds grid to count all numbers between 10 and 20. Explore that 15 is made using 10 and 5 and that can also help us, as 5 is half of ten. Do the same with a number line from 0-50.
- Remind students that to place numbers on a number line, they have to be very familiar with their place/order in the number sequence.
- Draw a portion of a number line – e.g., 560-580 and locate position of each number.
- Complete number lines with missing numbers.

Revise odd and even numbers

- What do odd numbers always end with? What do even numbers always end with?
- Refer to **pages 136-137** for more ideas.

Play Guess My Number:

- *"I'm thinking of a number between 100-500 (write it down and hide it). I'll give you a clue - It is an odd number. Have a guess. 261? Is that odd? How did you know? My number is more than 261 but less than 300. Have another guess, remember the answer is odd. My number is more than 270, so now we know that it is an odd number, what's the range? It's now between 270-300. Let's write it in our books."* Keep confirming that their guesses are matching the given criteria. *"It could be 281, but my number is less than 280, I'll give you another clue, it has 3 ones..."*

Learn about Friendly numbers

- Any number that ends in 0 is a 'friendly number' because Zero the Hero is easier to work with than other numbers. Put simply, any number with zero in the ones place is considered easier to work with when we are adding or subtracting numbers (i.e., it is easier to add 30 + 1 than 29 + 2). Knowing friendly numbers, will also support 'rounding to the nearest ten.' Any number that we say when we count in tens, is a friendly number – 10, 20, 30, 40 etc.

Teacher For Early Years

✓ **Represent numbers to at least 1000 using a variety of materials:**

Spend plenty of time revising teen numbers

- Remember, teen numbers are challenging for many children as they are said backwards. Children have to learn that when we say 16, although we hear the word 'six' at the start, it is the same as one ten and six ones. Do not move on to three-digit numbers until they have demonstrated a solid understanding of teen and all two-digit numbers.
- Ask students for suggestions of how teen numbers are the same and different, how they can be confusing, what to remember to write them correctly.
- Discuss how easy it is to mix up teen and ty numbers – explore 14/40, 16/60 (teens have 1 team of ten and lots of ones, ty numbers have lots of teams of ten and no ones).

Revise two-digit numbers as having 'tens' and 'ones'

- Play **Listen and Write** – Write the number that has 1 ten and 3 ones, 5 tens and 6 ones, 33 ones, 6 tens and 0 ones. Matching different representations of the same number – 50, 5 tens, 50 ones, fifty.
- See more activity ideas on **pages 124-132**.

Learn place value of three-digit numbers

- Each digit in a number has a value; the number on the right tells you how many ones, the number in the middle tells you how many tens and the number on the left tells you how many hundreds.

Use place value charts, bundling sticks, MAB blocks to practising representing numbers to 999. See pages 126-130 for further explanation.

HUNDREDS	TENS	ONES
▦	│	▫

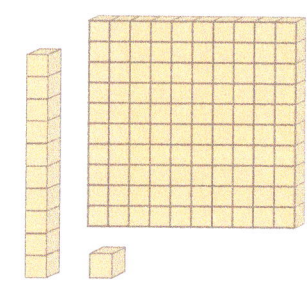

Remind students that 9 is the largest amount we can have in a section or place at any time. When we have more than 9 ones, we must trade up, to two-digits and use two columns on the place value chart. We would have 1 ten and 0 ones. The same thing happens when we have more than 9 tens, we have to trade up to three-digits and make a group of 100.

Specialised Edition

> Represent three-digit numbers using MAB blocks and ask questions to identify place value: How many hundreds? How many tens? How many ones? (Remember to teach children that if there are no tens or ones, we represent this with a zero)

- E.g., 302 has 3 hundreds, 0 tens and 2 ones. Can you represent this number using MAB blocks?

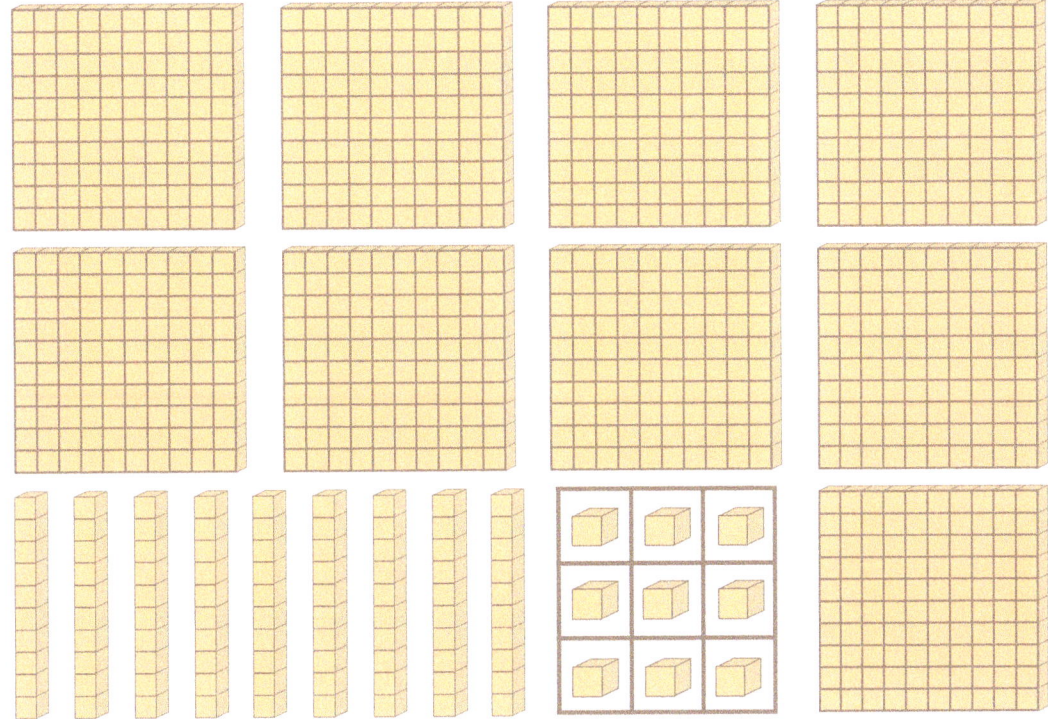

Please see appendix page 271 for some print-friendly MAB/ Base 10 blocks and page 273 for a three-digit place value chart.

Explore numbers

- What can you tell me about the number 180? (it has 3-digits, it is made using 1 hundred, 8 tens and 0 ones, it is even, etc.).
- Describe numbers according to their place value – What number has eight hundreds, three tens and four ones? How many hundreds are in 432?
- Practise partitioning numbers/breaking numbers into their parts according to place value: 743 = 700 + 40 + 3 (This will assist children with adding larger numbers).
- Show a variety of numbers represented using MAB blocks, for children to calculate different amounts.
- Match partitioned 3-digit numbers with their whole number. See sample using two-digit numbers on page 132.

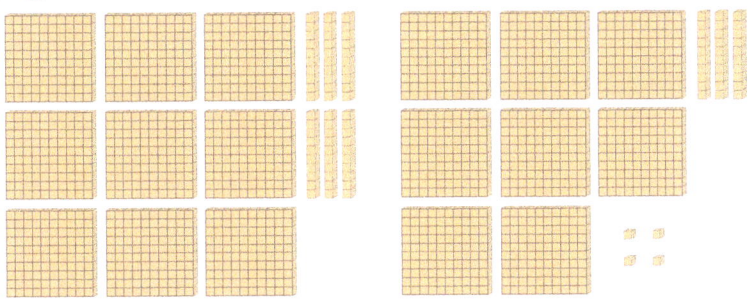

> Use a grid book to practise writing numbers to 1000. Remind students that each digit gets its own grid square, so three-digit numbers would take up three grid spaces

1	1	2
not	112	

Learn to spell number words to 999

- Use the activity suggestions on learning *High-Frequency/Sight Words on page 61-63* to practise reading and writing number words.

Complete worksheets

- **Three-digit Number of the Day charts** (see template on *page 277*).

✓ **Continue counting patterns in twos, fives, tens (and threes) forwards and backwards to 1000, from any starting point. Identify the missing number in a number sequence:**

> Use bundling sticks (page 129) or tally marks (page 135) to reinforce that skip counting is faster than counting items individually

- Drop individual pop sticks on the ground (a number less than 100 e.g., 63) and ask student to estimate how many they think there are. Count in ones to check. Record 63 ones. Ask *"Is there a faster way we could count them?"* (in tens). Help child to make groups of ten. How many sticks do we have? Is it still the same amount?

> Support children to identify counting patterns by finding the rule.

- Write the numbers 1, 3, 5, 7, ___ . Ask child for the next number. If they correctly guess 9, ask for the next number. Ask how they know and encourage the language of skipping one number each time, landing on odd numbers.

> Revise skip counting in twos, fives and tens to 100 before moving on to numbers to 1000

- Count orally and count concrete objects or patterns on grids.
- See *pages 133-135* for more skip counting ideas.

> Find the rule in counting patterns (see page 132 for more questions)

- 100, 95, 90, 85, ____, ____ What is the rule/what is changing each time? Is it getting bigger or smaller?
- 652, 657, 662, ____, ____ What is the rule/what is changing each time?

Identify missing numbers in a sequence such as:

- 220, ____, 240, 250
- 333, 335, ____, 339

Explore growing patterns such as:

- 1, 2, 4, 7, 11, ____
- 1, 3, 6, 10, ____

 Count and order small collections of coins and notes according to their value: Take out your coin jar or buy some play money from the cheap shop:

Practise recognising and ordering coins according to their value

- See activity ideas on **page 138**.

Practicing skip counting in 5's and 10's as often as possible will help your child count money

- Count on grids, using coins or body parts **(see page 133)**.

Play: Can You Make... (start with small amounts)

- 15c? 55c? $3.75? $6.40, etc.
  (after making each amount, challenge them to make it in another way using different coins).

Play: Make It Match (equivalent values)

- Remind children that 100c = $1 and 200c = $2. Expore equivalent values.
  e.g., how many 5c to make $1? How many 20c to make $1?

Model how to write $ and c

- We always write the $ sign before the dollars. We write the c sign after the cents. The decimal place separates the $ and cents. We only write c at the end of the number if there are no $.

Create real-world problems

- I bought a pack of chips using three 50c coins. How much did the chips cost? How do I write that? I want to buy a $4 burger and $3 drink, how much money do I need?

EXTENSION: Finding change from $1 and $2

- I bought a lolly for 40c but paid with a $1 coin, how much change would I get?
- Practise counting larger collections of notes and coins.

Teacher For Early Years

✓ **Identify and use halves, quarters, eighths (and thirds) of shapes and collections:**

Ensure children understand the words 'equal parts'

- Use this language in your everyday life: "I would like a cookie and so would you, but there's only one left. Let's break it into equal parts, equal means 'the same.'"
- Explore that we can split/break a whole into two equal groups called halves. If we split/break it in half again, we will have four equal groups called quarters and if we split/break it in half again, we will have eight equal groups called eighths.
- Show the student a variety of shapes and break them into even and uneven parts. Ask the student to identify whether the parts are equal or unequal and explain why. (This one is bigger than the other one so it has unequal parts).
- See **pages 138-139** for more ideas about exploring fractions.

Read/Watch stories about fractions.

- **Give me Half** by **Stuart J. Murphy** to introduce sharing, halves and whole.
- **My Half Day** by **Doris Fisher** to explore fractions.

Model writing fractions

- We show halves by writing 1/2. This just means that I have split a collection or shape into two equal parts and I have 1 part out of 2 parts.
- 1/4 means 1 part, out of 4 parts.
- Use the fraction chart below, to model splitting the same sized rectangle into equal parts.

1 Whole							
1/2				1/2			
1/3			1/3			1/3	
1/4		1/4		1/4		1/4	
1/8	1/8	1/8	1/8	1/8	1/8	1/8	1/8

Use real-life objects to split into equal parts

- Provide each student with a paper plate. Have them fold it in half and then in half again along the diameter. Have them unfold the paper and then cut along the fold lines to give four quarters. Show students how the four quarters fit together to make a whole circle and two halves (made out of two quarters each) fit together to make a whole circle. Explain that 1/4 is one part of 4.
- Make a pizza and cut it into eighths - You could make a nature pizza with dirt/leaves and flowers or use craft materials or make or buy an edible pizza to explore fractions with.

- Fold strips of paper lengthways in half then fourths (half of a half) and eighths (half of a half of a half).
- Create collages using coloured paper circles that have been cut into fractions (see bird on page 148).
- Can you design a flag that is 3/4 red and 1/4 green?
- How about a flag that is 1/2 red, 1/4 green and 2/8 blue?

Use pre-drawn shapes which have been split in two, three, four or eight equal parts

- Practise shading specified amounts. Draw a rectangle that has been split into 8 sections, ask students to shade a fraction.
- Adult to colour a certain number of parts and child to write the fraction.

Use measuring cups

- Show that two 1/2 cups and four 1/4 cups make a whole cup using water, or explore using recipes and incorporate some cooking.

Compare fractions – draw shapes or use cup measures to check answers

Which is larger?
- 1/2 or 1/8
- 1/4 or 1/8
- 1/2 or 1/8
- 1/4 or 1/8

 Perform simple addition and subtraction problems using a range of strategies, explore the connection between addition and subtraction; represent, solve and write word problems:

- Use the Hundred Grid activity ideas on pages 196-197.
- Identify 1 more/ 1 less, 10 more/10 less, 100 more/100 less using any number to 1000 (this takes time).

> Please see pages 152-175 for clear explanations of Addition Strategies which have been organised according to level of difficulty – children in Year Two should be should be exposed to as many of these strategies as possible.

 Identify multiplication and division problems and represent by repeated addition, groups, arrays and sharing into equal groups:

- See pages 176-183 for clear explanations of Multiplication and Division Strategies which have been organised according to the level of difficulty – children in Year Two should be have been exposed to as many of these strategies as possible.

Mathematics
Problem Solving

ADDITION AND SUBTRACTION STRATEGIES FOR FOUNDATION TO YEAR 2

ORGANISED BY LEVEL OF DIFFICULTY

> Children will ideally understand or will have been exposed to most of these strategies by the end of Year Two.

Please remember:

Every child is <u>different</u> and will learn in <u>different</u> ways and at a <u>different</u> pace. These approaches are to be used as a guide to support children with a variety of strategies they can use, however, not all children will be able to understand or use all of these strategies by the end of Year Two, and that is ok!

It is beneficial for children to be exposed to a range of approaches to solving mathematical problems and explore or identify those that work best for them. They do not need to use these strategies all at once or all of the time, however, they may serve to build up their confidence and basic number skills to help them in the future. Some of these strategies will work well for mental computations, some for written calculations, whilst other methods will be helpful for larger calculations (equations) as they get older.

The strategies explained are recommended for five- to eight-year-olds.
You will notice that all examples only use one or two-digit numbers for Foundation to Year Two as this is all that is required. Bigger numbers will come later, this is a time to focus on the strategy, not the number. Please see **page 122** for a list of strategies to explore with <u>Foundation aged students</u>, **page 136** for <u>Year One</u> and **page 149** for <u>Year Two</u>.

We recommend giving children the time needed to master each strategy, before moving on to the next one.

Please take the time to discuss key language associated with:

Addition **+**	Add, plus, more, altogether, both, another, sum, combine, verbs related to arriving (came, flew in, ran), total, part + part = whole.
Subtraction **-**	Less, away, take away, difference, minus, leave, remain, how many more, subtract, fewer, back, backwards, leftover, not coming, absent, whole – part = part.
Equals **=**	The same as, answer, matches, gives, sum/summation (addition).
Number sentence/ equation/ calculations **2+3=**	A sentence written using numerals and mathematical symbols. **+ - = x ÷**

> Be sure to practise the following strategies using both addition and subtraction examples.

DRAW A PICTURE

Represent addition and subtraction problems using illustrations.

EXPLORE
Draw a picture to match and help solve the problem. Encourage the child to verbalise their thinking when working out the answer, by first considering - is it addition or subtraction and why?

SAY
Can you draw a picture to show this story? What kind of calculation would it be? *(addition or subtraction)*. How do you know? *(E.g., I know this because I heard the words... and ...)*

PROBLEM SOLVING

SAMPLE QUESTIONS:

Kate ate 3 cookies and Mel ate 3 cookies. How many cookies did they eat altogether?

4 people were on the bus and then 5 more got on. How many people were on the bus altogether?

There were 7 birds in a tree but 3 flew away. How many birds were still in the tree?

Murphy the dog got 2 dog treats for being a good boy. He then snuck 6 more. How many treats did he eat altogether?

🔥 Remind children that we can use any easy to draw shape *(i.e., a circle, rather than drawing people or birds)* to represent the parts of the problem and make this strategy faster.

To extend (Year Two): Correct this number sentence (equation) by drawing a picture (use MAB blocks) 80 + 60 = 8060

WORD PROBLEMS

Children need explicit support to connect with the problem and identify the key information that will help them solve the question. Children often find this type of calculation challenging, as they must listen to/read the information given, cypher through it and distinguish what is important and what they can ignore.

E.g., On Monday, at 2 o'clock, I wore a purple dress and caught two fish. On Tuesday at 9 o'clock, I wore a red dress and caught three fish. How many fish did I catch altogether?

EXPLORE
Children need to be taught to listen for and identify the important information within the question and disregard irrelevant information. Lots of visuals (draw a picture, concrete materials, fingers etc.) will support this.

SAY
Today I am going to ask you some word problems. You need to listen very carefully to the information and together, we will decide what is important.

SAMPLE QUESTIONS:

There were 5 red birds in the tree and then 3 more blue birds flew in, how many birds altogether?

On Friday morning, there were 8 flamingos in the water and then on Friday afternoon, 2 more flew in. How many flamingos altogether?

There were 8 apples on the apple tree but then 3 fell off. How many were left on the tree?

11 children were invited to my party but 3 cannot come. How many children will be coming?

To extend (Year Two): Ask children to create their own word problems using only the answer as a stimulus e.g., The answer is 8, make up your own word problem to match the answer (encourage both addition and subtraction).

COUNT ON

Children can lock a number in their brain and count on from there, rather than starting the count from number one each time.

EXPLORE

Use fingers or concrete objects to assist children to visualise the starting number, *e.g., 5 and 2 or 5 + 2* (if the child is ready to use the addition symbol). Fingers are the best concrete object to support this strategy initially – using small numbers in the number sentence.

SAY

When adding two numbers together, it is always easier to put the biggest number in my mind first, and then count on the smaller amount. I can then lock the starting number in my head and count on from there. If I am adding 5 and 2, I can put five fingers up and count on two more numbers from 5. What is the next number after 5?

SAMPLE QUESTIONS:

Peta had 5 pencils in her pencil case, then her mum gave her 2 more. How many pencils does she have now?

Stephanie made a bracelet with 10 beads on it, then she added 5 more. How many beads altogether?

Neve photocopied a book from pages 11 to 14. How many pages did she photocopy? Because these numbers are close together, we can count up to find the answer. Count aloud or model using your fingers: She copied pages 11, 12, 13, 14. How many numbers did I say?

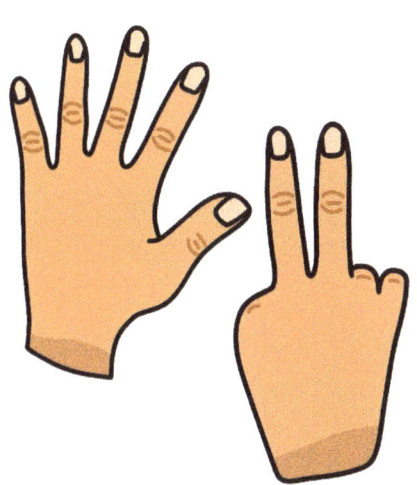

To extend (Year Two): Use larger numbers.

> **Further information:** This is mostly used as an addition strategy, however, it can also be used as a subtraction strategy when finding the difference between two numbers. This will also pose as a 'how many more' question. **Count on strategy** <u>should only be used for subtraction if the numbers stated in the problem are close together</u> *"When I am taking away two numbers that are close together, it is faster for me to start at the smallest number and count on to the biggest number."*

SAMPLE QUESTIONS:

16 - 13 =	97 - 94 =
36 - 34 =	64 - 63 =
57 - 55 =	86 - 83 =

In Year Two, this strategy can also be used when the problem asks you to find the difference but only if the numbers are close together (see above). *E.g., Anna scored 68 points and Lauren scored 72, how many more did Lauren score than Anna?*

(There is more information about the **Finding the Difference strategy** on page 164).

USE ONE FIVE OR TEN FRAME

This is a frame with five or ten equal spaces (see image and explanation on page 121). It is a great visual for developing children's understanding of the parts needed to make number facts to five and ten.

 When exploring addition, we teach the language part + part = whole. In subtraction, we teach whole − part = part.

EXPLORE

Spend time learning about five frames, before moving onto ten frames. You could draw the frame on a piece of paper and use concrete objects such as counters, pebbles, or pasta to create and answer problems. Alternatively, use a laminated copy or slide a frame on a piece of paper into a clear, plastic sleeve and use a whiteboard marker to draw dots.

SAY

(Use a five frame and put 4 counters on). *How many counters? How do you know?* (Encourage children to verbalise that the answer must be four because it is a five frame and one counter is missing, one less than 5 is 4). Repeat with 0, 1, 2, 3, and 5 counters.

Play the More or Less game:

Write on two flashcards – 1 more, 1 less or one more, one less.

Remind students of the terms 'more' and 'less' and link to <u>bigger and smaller</u>. Ask child to select a number between 1 – 5. Put the corresponding number of counters on the five frame.

Put both flashcards in a bag/hat/behind your back and sing the song *"More or less, what will it be? Pull out a card and you will see..."*

Pull out a card, add or remove counter to match the instructions on the card. Ask child to explain why they removed or added a counter and how many counters are now on the frame.

When children are confidently using five frames, introduce ten frames to play the game above and answer word problems and number sentences such as those below.

SAMPLE QUESTIONS:

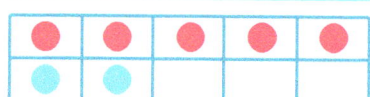

Word problem: I had 5 race cars and I got 2 more for my birthday. How many cars do I have altogether?

Word problem: I had 5 race cars but then 2 of them broke and I had to throw them out. Now how many cars do I have?

Or using number sentences: 6 + 4 = ? 10 − 3 = ?

 Ten frames are also a fantastic resource for learning the **Addition To Ten strategy**, which is explained on page 158.

USE TWO TEN FRAMES

Fantastic visual for adding numbers to 20, as well as learning about 'teen' numbers.

EXPLORE

Use multiple ten frames to solve problems by creating a visual with concrete objects.

SAY

How many frames have I used? How many counters are there? How many are missing? How many are in the top row? How many are in the bottom row? How do you know?

SAMPLE QUESTIONS:

There were 10 birds in a tree and then 6 more came. How many birds are there now?

I had 20 pebbles but then I lost 4. How many do I have left?

Amelia had 13 building blocks and Myla gave her 4 more for her tower. How many does she have altogether?

(Harder) I had 20 party bags, but only 14 people came to my party. How many party bags are left over?

NUMBER LINES

A great strategy to learn each numbers' relative position in the number sequence as well as see the visual of numbers used in the problem, when counting forwards or backwards.

EXPLORE

Give word problems or number sentences to solve, initially using numbers that are close together.

SAY

We are going to use the number line to jump forwards or back to find our answers. Ready? Listen carefully to the number sentence to see which number we should start on and how many numbers we will have to jump. If we are adding, we will be jumping to a bigger number but if we are subtracting, we will be jumping towards zero.

SAMPLE QUESTIONS:

I had 10 crackers but then I ate 5, how many are left? Let's use the number line and jump back from 10, five times.

If I had 13 red marbles and 5 blue marbles, how many marbles do I have altogether? Show me on the number line.

If there were 10 people in our footy team but 3 were away, how many were there to play the game? Show me on the number line.

To extend (Year Two): Draw a line. If 60 is the first and 80 is the last number on this number line, where would 70 go? Use number lines to model addition and subtraction problems.
E.g., 70 – 5 means I jump back five numbers

ADDITION TO TEN/RAINBOW FACTS

Children should be able to instantly recall addition facts where two numbers add together to make ten. These are also sometimes called Rainbow Facts as the image of the rainbow supports us to make connections between numbers.

EXPLORE

Start exploring this strategy using fingers and then moving to ten frames. Introduce the rainbow (see below) as another visual strategy. Some children will learn best by writing these facts out and memorising them.

SAY

I have 10 fingers altogether; I am going to put up 7 of them. If I put 7 up, how many are down? Yes, 7 and 3 are a pair of numbers that make 10 (repeat with all combinations).

SAMPLE QUESTIONS:

When adding two numbers together to make 10, what number pairs up with 0? 1? 2? 3? 4? 5? 6? 7? 8? 9? 10?

(E.g., If x fingers are up, how many are down? If there are x counters on my ten frame, how many more would I need to make 10?)

Using concrete materials

Use 10 bowling pins – roll the ball, how many are up and how many are down? Write the sum.

Prepare 10 tennis balls and a bucket. Throw balls in the bucket and work out calculations – if 4 are out of the bucket, how many are in? If 2 are in, how many are out?

Keep practising this until they can instantly recall pairs of numbers that add together to make ten.

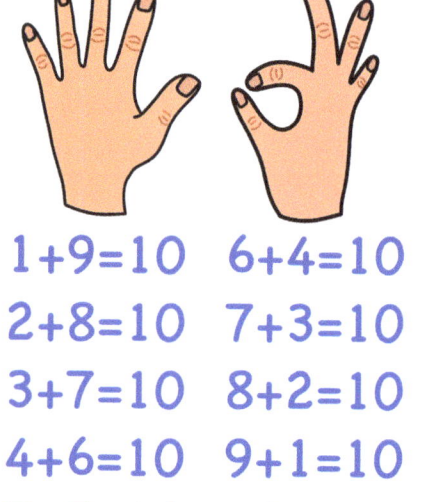

1+9=10   6+4=10
2+8=10   7+3=10
3+7=10   8+2=10
4+6=10   9+1=10
5+5=10   10+0=10

THINK BIG, COUNT SMALL

Remind children that if one part (addend) of the addition problem is bigger than the other, they should use a turnaround (see below) to put the biggest number first and count on the smaller amount.

Turnaround swap the numbers in the sum to put the largest amount first, knowing you will still get the same answer. This works for addition and multiplication (explained on **page 183**).

E.g., 3 + 7 = 10 and 7 + 3 = 10
3 x 7 = 21 and 7 x 3 = 21

EXPLORE

Give a range of addition problems where the second number (addend) is larger than the first. Practise using turnarounds to put the biggest number first.

SAMPLE QUESTIONS:

2 + 7 = We should turn this around to 7 + 2 and then count on

3 + 9 = We should turn this around to 9 + 3 and then count on

2 + 22 = We should turn this around to 22 + 2 and then count on

4 + 45 = We should turn this around to 45 + 4 and then count on

SAY

Today we are going to use the **Count On strategy** (page 155) to add some numbers. We listen to the number sentence, then lock the first number in our brain and count on the second amount. Let's add 1 and 7. I lock 1 in my brain and count on 7 more (model counting). That took a really long time, I wonder if there is a faster way we could do this... Let's try **Think Big, Count Small strategy**. This strategy helps us put the biggest number first and the smaller number second. It tells us to turn the numbers around, so the larger number is always first. So instead of 1 + 7 =, turn this around so that the number sentence is 7 + 1, then we will count on from there. It's called Think Big, Count Small, because we want to think about the biggest number first and count on the smaller amount.

DOUBLES

Children should be able to instantly recall Doubles facts using numbers to ten.

PROBLEM SOLVING

EXPLORE

First, they need to understand the language of *'double'*. Explore *'doubles'* in real-life e.g., double-decker bus, double scoop of ice-cream, doubles in tennis. Practise recalling facts every chance you get (see list below). Write them out, use fingers or listen to doubles facts songs on **YouTube**.

SAY

Today we are exploring doubles facts. What does double mean? Yes, double means two of something.

 Use child's hands to learn Double facts to five and use your hands and child's hands to learn doubles facts to ten.

SAMPLE QUESTIONS:

Learn doubles to 10:

Double 1 is the same as 1 + 1 which is equal to…

Double 2 = 2 + 2 which is equal to…

Double 7 = 7 +7 (and so on) which is equal to…

Please help children to see the pattern when writing doubles, each time the answer gets larger by two.

1+1=2	6+6=12
2+2=4	7+7=14
3+3=6	8+8=16
4+4=8	9+9=18
5+5=10	10+10=20

EXTENDING ADDITION TO TEN/RAINBOW FACTS

Children should be able to instantly recall **Addition to Ten facts** (where two numbers add together to make ten) and use this knowledge to apply to multiples of ten.

 Children need to be confident with **Addition to Ten** and be able to count in tens to at least 100, to understand this strategy.

EXPLORE
Use bundling sticks or MAB blocks to help children visualise the connection between single digits (4 + 6) and multiples of ten (40 + 60).

SAY
I know 3 + 7 makes 10 so I can extend this fact using multiples of 10, 30 + 70 = 100.

SAMPLE QUESTIONS:

1 + 9 = 10, so 1 ten + 9 tens = 10 tens. This is the same as saying 10 (ones) + 90 (ones) = 100

6 + 4 = 10, so 6 tens + 4 tens = 10 tens. 10 tens is the same as 100. We can check by counting in tens, ten times.

8 + 2 = 10, so 8 tens + 2 tens = 10 tens. 10 tens is the same as 100. We can check by counting in tens, ten times.

0+10=10	0+100=100
1+9=10	10+90=100
2+8=10	20+80=100
3+7=10	30+70=100
4+6=10	40+60=100
5+5=10	50+50=100
6+4=10	60+40=100
7+3=10	70+30=100
8+2=10	80+20=100
9+1=10	90+10=100

NEAR DOUBLES

Children use knowledge of **Doubles** (see page 160) and add or subtract the extra parts to help them quickly answer these questions.

 Children need to be confident with instant recall of doubles facts to ten before moving on to this strategy.

EXPLORE
Assist with breaking numbers into easier to calculate parts, to make the problem easier.

SAY
If 8 + 8 = 16, then 8 + 9 = 8 + 8 + 1 more = 17 or if the number sentence is 8 + 7, remember, we know that 8 + 8 = 16, so the answer will be one less than 16, 16 − 1 = 15. This could also be calculated as 7 + 7 + 1 =

SAMPLE QUESTIONS:

7 + 8 =	9 + 10 =
6 + 5 =	8 + 9 =

LOOK FOR FRIENDLY PAIRS

We use this strategy when we are adding three or more addends (parts) and two of the numbers can be added easily.

EXPLORE

Give addition number sentences with three or more parts where at least two of the addends are familiar (e.g. using **Addition to Ten** or **Doubles** facts).

SAMPLE QUESTIONS:

4 + 5 + 6 =	
5 + 3 + 5 + 7 =	
3 + 3 + 4 =	
6 + 3 + 6 =	

SAY

Today we are going to look for friendly pairs when adding number sentences with three or more parts. Let's look at the problem: 7 + 5 + 3. Remember, we can add these three numbers in any order; are there any numbers that stand out as being easier to add, using a strategy that we have learnt? 7 + 5 is not that easy... 5 + 3 is not that easy... Is 7 + 3 easy to add? Yes, we can use the **Addition to Ten strategy**. If we put the 7 and the 3 together, the new sum would be 10 + 5.

Let's look at another number sentence:

$$4 + 1 + 4 = 8 + 1.$$

Repeat script from above but use the language of **Doubles facts** - see page 160 for more information.

USE A 100 GRID TO SOLVE ALGORITHMS

Children will begin to see patterns when completing algorithms on a 99 or 100s grid.

EXPLORE

Use a 100 grid – either paper with a pencil, in a clear plastic sleeve with a whiteboard marker or interactive version. Use the grid to explore one more/one less, ten more/ten less than any number to 100. We want children to start seeing patterns – E.g., when adding 10 - I was on 36, 3 tens and 6 ones, and now I am on 46, 4 tens and 6 ones.

SAY

Today we are going to roll two six-sided dice to find a two-digit number to start on. Then we are going to play a game called the More or Less game.

More or Less game:

Write on four flashcards – 1 more, 1 less, 10 more, 10 less. Put these in a bag or hat.
Remind students of the terms 'more' and 'less' and link to bigger and smaller. Roll two six-sided dice to find a two-digit number to start on – E.g., Roll a 3 and a 6, start on 36 or 63. Circle starting number on hundred grid.
Shake cards around in bag or hat while singing: "More or less, what will it be? Pull out a card and you will see..."
Pull out a card, follow the instruction and circle the matching number.

SAMPLE QUESTIONS:

Ask the same question in a variety of ways –

Ten more than 22 or 22 + 10

One more than 78 or 78 + 1

Ten less than 99 or 99 – 10

One less than 54 or 54 – 1

flashcards

1 more
1 less
10 more
10 less

Please see pages 192-197 for more strategies to utilise the 100 grid.

0	1	2	3	4	5	6	7	8	9
10	11	12	13	14	15	16	17	18	19
20	21	22	23	24	25	26	27	28	29
30	31	32	33	34	35	36	37	38	39
40	41	42	43	44	45	46	47	48	49
50	51	52	53	54	55	56	57	58	59
60	61	62	63	64	65	66	67	68	69
70	71	72	73	74	75	76	77	78	79
80	81	82	83	84	85	86	87	88	89
90	91	92	93	94	95	96	97	98	99

Extend – write the sums for the path taken

(36) + 10 = (46) – 1 = (45) + 10 = (55)

PROBLEM SOLVING

FINDING THE DIFFERENCE

When a problem asks children to 'find the difference' between two numbers (also written as 'how many more?'), they should subtract the smallest number from the biggest number. The answer will tell them the difference between the two numbers.

 When calculating the difference between two numbers and the numbers are close together in sequence, it is easier and faster to just count up to find the difference, rather than subtracting. Please see **Count on strategy** page 155 for further explanation.

EXPLORE

Use number lines to support the visual, remind children of the key words to know they will be subtracting – <u>what is the difference</u> or <u>how many more?</u>

SAY

When a problem asks you to find the difference between two numbers or you hear the words *"How many more?"* or *"How much more?"* we will use subtraction to find the difference. Unless... the numbers are close together, then we will just count up to find the difference.

SAMPLE QUESTIONS:

What is the difference between number 2 and number 5?

Michael scored 10 points and Misa scored 4. How many more did Michael score than Misa?

Claire had $3 and wanted to buy a $5 hat. How much more money does she need?

Macca had 12 cards but needed to collect 30 for the whole set. How many more did she need?

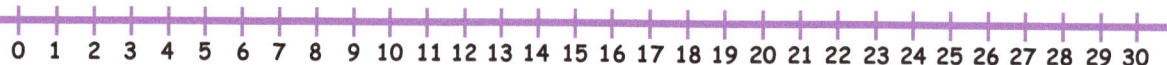

EXTENDING DOUBLES USING MULTIPLES OF TEN

Children should be able to make a link between **Doubles** facts using single digits, and doubles facts using multiples of ten.

EXPLORE

We have learnt that we can extend on our **Addition to Ten facts** using multiples of ten, or numbers that we say when we count in tens (e.g., 3 + 7 = 10, so 30 + 70 = 100). We can do the same with **Doubles facts**. Children will benefit from using bundling sticks and MAB blocks to reinforce this concept.

SAY

Today we are going to revise Doubles facts and apply this strategy to larger numbers. We know that 2 + 2 = 4, so we can use this knowledge to work out 2 tens + 2 tens. How many tens would I have? What about 5 tens + 5 tens?

SAMPLE QUESTIONS:

1 + 1 = 2, so 1 ten + 1 ten = 2 tens. This is the same as 10 + 10 = 20.

6 + 6 = 12, so 6 tens + 6 tens = 12 tens. 12 tens is the same as 120. We can check by counting in tens, twelve times.

9 + 9 = 18, so 9 tens + 9 tens = 18 tens. 18 tens is the same as 180. We can check by counting in tens, eighteen times.

8 + 8 = 16, so 80 (8 tens) + 80 (8 tens) will equal 16 tens or 160.

1+1=2	10+10=20
2+2=4	20+20=40
3+3=6	30+30=60
4+4=8	40+40=80
5+5=10	50+50=100
6+6=12	60+60=120
7+7=14	70+70=140
8+8=16	80+80=160
9+9=18	90+90=180
10+10=20	100+100=200

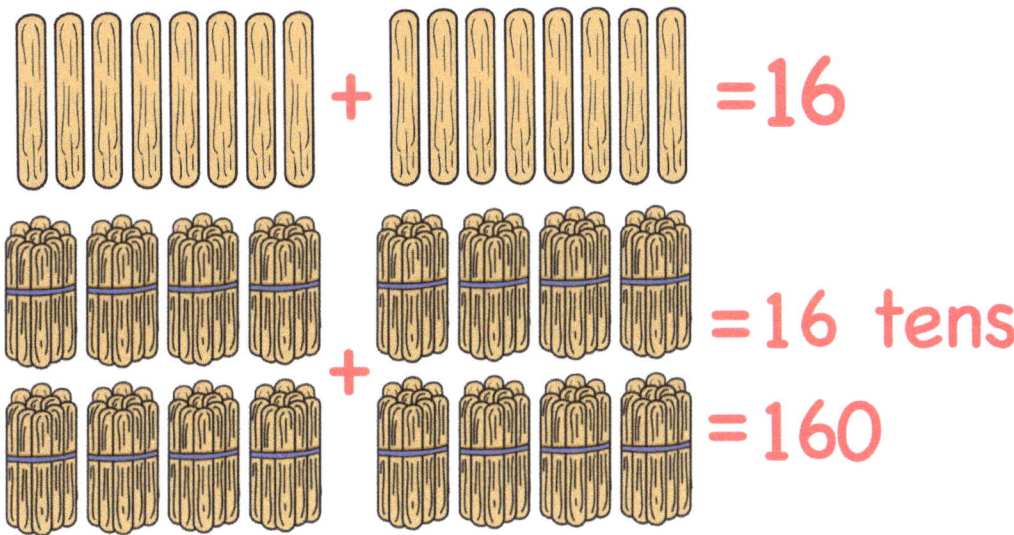

FACT FAMILIES/INVERSE OPERATIONS

Children need to know that there is a connection between addition and subtraction.

EXPLORE

Our Rule is – **I know one number sentence; I know four number sentences**. First, we take one addition problem and re-write it using a **turnaround** (switch the place of the addends). Then, we **backflip** the problem to bring the answer to the front of the number sentence and turn it into a subtraction, using the same three parts.

SAY

Today I'm going to give you some addition or subtraction number sentences with the answer. I want you to turn one number sentence into four number sentences. Remember, it does not matter if the numbers get bigger, if you know the answer and the rule; you can turn one number sentence into four number sentences. (Remember when using subtraction, that the 'whole' amount or biggest number, must be at the start of the number sentence).

E.g., Let's start small

3 + 7 = 10

7 + 3 = 10 (turnaround)
We can now use these three numbers to write a subtraction problem.

10 – 3 = 7 (backflip)

10 – 7 = 3 (backflip)

8 + 9 = 17

9 + 8 = 17 (turnaround)

17 – 8 = 9 (backflip)

17 – 9 = 8 (backflip)

36 + 51 = 87

51 + 36 = 87 (turnaround)

87 – 51 = 36 (backflip)

87 – 36 = 51 (backflip)

SAMPLE QUESTIONS:

Q – If 6 + 4 = 10, what else can you tell me about these numbers?

A – 4 + 6 = 10 (turnaround) and 10 – 6 = 4 (backflip) and 10 – 4 = 6.

Q – If 13 + 9 = 22, what else can you tell me about these three numbers?

Number Bonds also known as Fact Families

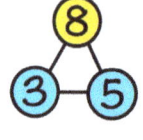
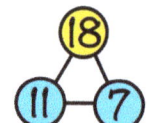

5 + 3 = 8
3 + 5 = 8
8 – 5 = 3
8 – 3 = 5

11 + 7 = 18
7 + 11 = 18
18 – 11 = 7
18 – 7 = 11

This will also assist students with finding the missing part of the number sentence –
E.g., *I had 4 cookies, then my friend gave me some more and I then had 7 altogether. How many cookies did my friend give me?*
Knowing the relationship between addition and subtraction will assist children in finding the missing part 4 + -- = 7. I know I can backflip this number sentence to find the missing part: 7 – 4 = 3.

BRIDGING THROUGH TEN

When adding two numbers and one addend (number or part) is close to ten, we can use the **Bridging through Ten strategy**. Children need to be very confident with **Addition to Ten/Rainbow** facts (see page 158) to be able to complete this strategy. Please note, this strategy is also called **Building to Ten and Making to Ten**.

EXPLORE

Numbers such as 8 and 9 are very close to 10, so when we are adding, it is helpful to make these numbers friendly. We can do this by stealing some parts from the second number. Number lines and tens frames are very useful for supporting learners with this strategy. Children need to know about friendly numbers and **Addition to Ten** to be able to use this strategy.

SAY

10 is a friendly number, it is easy to add numbers to 10. Numbers with a 0 in the ones place are called friendly numbers because 0 is the easiest number to work with. Today, we will be using a strategy called **Bridging Through Ten**, to help make number sentences easier to work out.

For example:

4 + 9 =
Let's start by doing a turnaround to put the largest number first (**Think Big, Count Small strategy on page 139**) so the number sentence will now be **9 + 4 =**
Looking at the first number, how many more to get to 10? **(9 + 1 = 10)**
So, we can break the second number up into two parts – **1 and 3**
9 + 1 + 3 = 10 + 3 = 13

7 + 8 =
Let's start by doing a turnaround, we always put the biggest number first... **8 + 7**
How many more are needed to make 10? **2!**
If the 2 is taken from the 7, how many are left over? **5!**
So, **8 + 7** is the same as **8 + 2 + 5**, so **10 + 5, or 15.**

SAMPLE QUESTIONS:

Complete number sentences, where one addend is close to ten:

E.g., Remember to make the first number friendly (a number that ends in zero), by breaking the second number into parts and stealing from the second number.
E.g., 9 + 5 = is the same as 9 + 1 + 4, is the same as 10 + 4

Try these:

9 + 6 =   8 + 3 =   9 + 7 =

BRIDGING THROUGH TEN USING MULTIPLES OF TEN

Bridging through Ten strategy works using multiples of 10 (numbers we say when we count in tens such as 10, 20, 30, 40, etc.) too. Please note, this strategy is also called **Building to Ten and Making to Ten**.

EXPLORE

Complete some number sentences with numbers that are close to multiples of 10 (e.g., 29 + 6, 68 + 9). Remember to break the second number into parts, to give to the first number. Then add the remaining part. See the visual below for further explanation.

SAY

Today we are going to use the **Bridging Through Ten strategy**, using larger numbers. Let's look at the number sentence:

$$29 + 6 =$$

29 is very close to a friendly number. Remember, friendly numbers are numbers with zero in the ones place, or numbers we say when we count in tens. Tell me to stop when you hear me say a friendly number that is close to 29. 10, 20, 30... (If they can't recognise the closest friendly number, you will need to use a number line to 40 or a hundred grid to support this). Now we need to work out the difference between 29 and 30... 1! So we will steal 1 from the second number, to make the first number friendly. 29 + 1 + 5 will be our new sum, so 30 + 5 is our final sum. See the visual below for further explanation.

$$68 + 2 + 7$$
$$68 + 9$$
$$70 + 7 = 77$$

$$29 + 1 + 5$$
$$29 + 6$$
$$30 + 5 = 35$$

SAMPLE QUESTIONS:

19 + 4 =

39 + 5 =

88 + 7 =

69 + 7 =

79 + 8 =

PARTITIONING

Children need to know that numbers can be broken into parts according to place value. This is called their *'expanded form'*.

EXPLORE

Practise making two-digit numbers on Place Value Charts (page 272) using bundling sticks and MAB blocks (explained in detail in **Supporting Your Year One and Two Learners** pages 128-132 and 144-146). Use the visual to explain that 28 is the same as 20 + 8 or 2 tens and 8 ones.

SAY

Today, we are going to learn how to break numbers into parts; this is called partitioning. When I say the word *'partitioning'*, you can hear me say the word *'part'*. We are going to be breaking numbers into parts to make calculations easier.

SAMPLE QUESTIONS:

Practise partitioning two digit, then three-digit numbers into different layouts.

19 is the same as 1 ten and 9 ones or 10 + 9

85 is the same as 8 tens and 5 ones or 80 + 5

389 is the same as 3 hundreds, 8 tens and 9 ones or 300 + 80 + 9

When children are confident, they can use this strategy to explore doubling tens and ones by partitioning numbers: Double 13 is the same as double 10 and double 3 so

$$13 + 13 = 10 + 3 + 10 + 3 = 20 + 6.$$

SAMPLE QUESTIONS:

Work out doubles of the following numbers by doubling the tens and ones separately:

Double 22   Double 41   Double 32
Double 14   Double 43   Double 24

If you really want to challenge children, once they understand standard partitioning, you can then introduce **non-standard partitioning**.

32 is the same as 2 tens + 12 ones, 20 + 12

425 is the same as 3 hundreds + 12 tens + 5 ones or 3 hundreds and 125 ones

SPLIT STRATEGY

In this strategy, we partition (*break into parts*) both numbers. This strategy is mostly used when no regrouping is required.

EXPLORE

Model addition and subtraction by partitioning **BOTH NUMBERS** – explain that this is called **SPLIT** strategy.

SAMPLE QUESTIONS:

52 + 26 =	
24 + 43 =	

61 + 14 =	
26 + 33 =	

SAY

Today we are learning to use the **split strategy**. We will break both numbers into parts, to make the equation easier. Let's look at the number sentence:

36 + 43 = ____

I can split or partition these numbers into tens and ones and then add them together. I can add **30** and **40** to get **70**.
I can add **6** and **3** to get **9**.
70 and **9** make **79**.
So, I know **36 + 43** makes **79**.

Let's look at another number sentence:

75 + 23 = ____

I can split these numbers into tens and ones and then add them together.
I can add **70** and **20** to get **90**. I can add **5** and **3** to get **8**.
90 and **8** makes **98**.
So, I know **75 + 23** makes **98**

$$75 + 23$$
$$70 \quad 5 \quad 20 \quad 3$$
$$70 + 20 = 90$$
$$5 + 3 = 8$$
$$90 + 8 = 98$$

And with subtraction:

$$67 - 31$$
$$60 + 7 - 30 + 1$$
$$60 - 30 \quad 7 - 1$$
$$30 \; + \; 6$$
$$36$$

JUMP STRATEGY

In this strategy, we partition (break into parts) the second number and perform jumps on a number line. This strategy is mostly used **when regrouping is required.**

EXPLORE

Model addition and subtraction by partitioning the **SECOND NUMBER** and jumping on a number line – Remember to explain that this is called the **Jump strategy**. One of the addends in the sum is partitioned (broken up into its expanded form) and added or subtracted in parts. Children must be able to partition numbers and use a number line to experience success with this strategy.

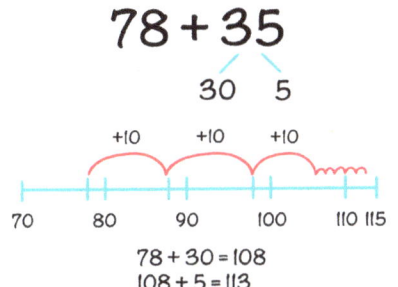

78 + 30 = 108
108 + 5 = 113

SAY

Today we are learning to use the **Jump strategy**. We will break the second number into parts, to make the equation easier. We will use the number line to help us (model using a number line). Let's look at the number sentence:

57 + 38 = ___

We can partition the **38** into **30 + 8**. First, we will add the tens, then we will add the ones.
57 + 30 = 87 (but we still need to add the **8** ones from **38**)
87 + 8 = 95 (model using a number line)

39 + 43 = ___

We can partition the **43** into **40 + 3**. First, we will add the tens, then we will add the ones.
39 + 40 = 79 (but we still need to add the **3** ones)
79 + 3 = 82

SAMPLE QUESTIONS:

| 22 + 23 = | 22 + 20 + 3 | 45 + 47 = | |
| 37 + 37 = | 37 + 30 + 7 | 69 + 15 = | |

ROUNDING UP OR DOWN

Rounding two-digit numbers to the nearest ten, to assist with mental computations.

EXPLORE

Count in tens up to 200. Remind students that 0 is a friendly number and all the numbers that have zero in the ones place are friendly because 0 is the easiest number to work with. Explain that all numbers five and above round to the higher tens and numbers below five, round down.
First children need to be explicitly taught how to round to the nearest 10, this should be done using number lines such as the ones below:

Round the numbers below to the nearest 10:

42 = 40   58 = 60

40 41 42 43 44 45 46 47 48 49 50   50 51 52 53 54 55 56 57 58 59 60

SAY

Today we will use a number line to identify the closest friendly number to any two-digit number. Then we will use this to help solve addition and subtraction problems.

19 + 11 is about…	20 + 10
48 + 21 is about…	50 + 20
37 - 21 is about…	40 - 20
52 - 28 is about…	50 – 30

SAMPLE QUESTIONS:

| 29 + 32 = | | 99 – 49 = | |
| 31 + 59 = | | 68 – 39 = | |

COMPENSATION STRATEGY

Knowing friendly numbers (numbers that have zero ones or numbers that are multiples of 10, such as 20, 30, 40, 50) can help us with another strategy called **Compensation strategy**. Using the **Compensation strategy**, you swap a compatible number, for a number that you can more easily mentally compute.

EXPLORE

Use a hundred grid, MAB blocks or number lines to model adding or subtracting 10 (friendly number) and then compensating by taking away or adding the extra part. Repeat, repeat, repeat as this concept is challenging.

SAY

Today we are going to be using **Compensation strategy**. Knowing friendly numbers will help us, let's count in tens to 100 because all the numbers we say are friendly numbers. Remember, friendly numbers are easier to add than other numbers, it is much easier for the brain to add 10 more, than 9 more.

Lets look at the sum: 25 + 9 = ___ In my brain, I am going to do 25 + 10, which I know will be 35. But remember, I added too many – I was only supposed to add 9. I added 10 because that is easier for my brain to work out. 10 is one more than 9. So, because I added too many (10 instead of 9) I will need to take one away.

SAMPLE QUESTIONS:

Change the 9 to 10 and complete the problem, then compensate by correcting the adjustment to match the original equation.

| 37 + 9 = | 55 + 9 = | 56 – 9 = |
| 72 + 9 = | 33 – 9 = | 91 – 9 = |

When you see that children have grasped this concept, try using trickier calculations:
25 + 49

SAY

I know that 49 is very close to 50. Multiples of 10, or numbers that I say when I count in tens, are much easier to add. First, I am going to use **Think Big, Count Small strategy** (see page 159) to turn this number sentence around and make it 49 + 25. Then I am going to adjust it to 50 + 25 to make it easier. Then I will compensate by taking one, as I was supposed to add 49 + 25, not 50 + 25.

Model doing the same using jumps on a number line or on a hundred grid.

SAY

The sum is 25 + 49 but using **Think Big, Count Small** strategy, we know to turn the number sentence around and start with the larger number. 49 is not easy to work with, so we make it 50. We jump on the number line to add the 25, we know that 25 has two tens and five ones. (Model making the jumps on the number line). Then we have to minus (take away) the extra one that we added earlier. Remember, we only wanted to add 49 but we added 50, so now we need to take 1 away.

SAMPLE QUESTIONS:

Model adding and subtracting two-digit numbers –

| 54 + 29 = | 29 + 35 = |
| 77 + 19 = | 47 + 19 = |

$$54 + 29$$
$$\downarrow +1$$
$$54 + 30 = 84$$
$$\downarrow -1$$
$$84 - 1 = 83$$

VERTICAL ADDITION AND SUBTRACTION (NO REGROUPING)

When completing vertical addition and subtraction, always calculate the ones first. Please introduce new vocabulary – vertical, horizontal, rows, columns.

EXPLORE

Write some vertical addition sums in grid book– model how to line up tens and ones under each other. Remember, we only write one digit, per grid space, even if it is a two-digit number. Write this rule together – ALWAYS ADD AND SUBTRACT THE ONES COLUMN FIRST.

SAY

Today we are going to write equations in our grid book. We need to be careful how we write the numbers as we need to line up the tens and ones in each number. Let's write the rule at the top of our page first – Always add and subtract the ones column first.

We will write our two digits numbers, one on top of the other, then we will write the symbol (addition or subtraction) on the left side of the bottom number. (It would be helpful to draw a chart above the tens and ones and label each column when they are starting out – see below in blue). Remember, we always add or subtract the ones first.

SAMPLE QUESTIONS:

```
  42      26      64
+ 35    + 32    + 11
____    ____    ____
```

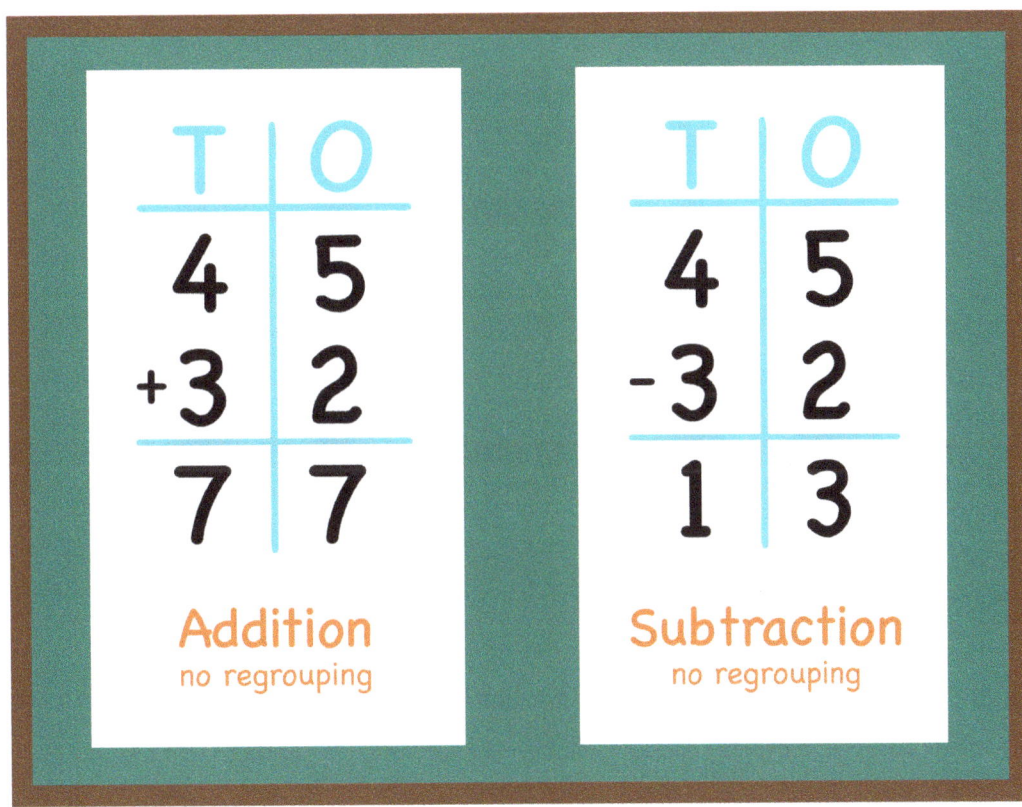

Addition
no regrouping

Subtraction
no regrouping

VERTICAL ADDITION AND SUBTRACTION (WITH TRADING/REGROUPING)

When completing vertical addition and subtraction, always calculate the ones first. Children need to be able to swap 10 ones for 1 stick/bundle of ten using MAB blocks or bundling sticks, as this is the beginning of regrouping/trading. More information about MAB blocks and bundling sticks can be found in **Supporting Your Year One and Two Learners** on pages 128-132 and 144-146.

EXPLORE

Write some vertical addition equations in grid books. Model how to line up tens and ones using grid spaces. Remember one digit, per grid space. Write rule together – ALWAYS ADD THE ONES column FIRST.

SAMPLE QUESTIONS:

```
  49      28      37
+ 15    + 64    + 15
____    ____    ____
```

SAY

Today we are going to write equations in our grid book. We need to be careful how we write the numbers as we need to line up the tens and ones in each number. Let's write the rule at the top of our page first – Always add and subtract the ones column first.

Let's start with the sum 59 + 26 = ___

We will write these two numbers, one on top of the other, then we will write the symbol (addition or subtraction) on the left side of the bottom number. (It would be helpful to draw a chart above the tens and ones and label each column when they are starting out – see below in blue). Remember, we always add the ones first.

Today when we add the ones, our answer will be more than 9. We will need to work out how many tens and ones in the answer, then trade the ten to the tens column and only write the leftover ones in the ones column (see sample below).

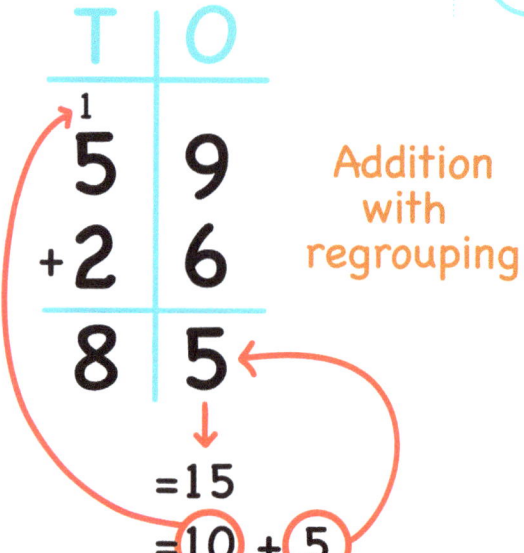

Addition with regrouping

Model this equation and explain:
I added 9 ones and 6 ones and the answer was 15. I know that 15 is made using 1 ten and 5 ones, so I need to move the 1 ten to the tens column and only leave the 5 ones under the ones column. Then I add the tens: 5 + 2 + 1.

When subtracting, sometimes the ones digit in the bottom number will be larger than the ones digit in the top number. If this happens, you will need to borrow ten from the top number to give to the ones of the top number.

> **EXPLORE**
>
> Write some vertical subtraction equations in grid books. Model how to line up tens and ones using grid spaces. Remember one digit, per grid space. Reiterate the rule – ALWAYS SUBTRACT THE ONES column FIRST.

```
  T | O
  2 | 1
  3̸ | 3
- 1 | 7
─────
  1 | 6
```

Can't subtract 7 from 3, so we have to borrow from the tens column. 3 tens will become 2 tens and 3 ones will become 13 ones.

Subtraction with regrouping

 Please emphasize that we always subtract the bottom number from the top number. Many children will reverse the calculation if the bottom number is larger.

Please remember, not all children will be able to use all of these strategies by the end of Year Two, and that is OK. Exposing them to these strategies will only benefit them in the future.

What we want is to create skilled mathematical thinkers who feel confident to solve problems both mentally and in written form, hence the need to arm them with a multitude of strategies.

Many people (both children AND adults) believe they aren't "good" at maths and develop a keen dislike from an early age. We want to avoid that by helping them find ways that work for their brain so they can become confident mathematicians, ready to take on any math problem!

MULTIPLICATION AND DIVISION STRATEGIES

These strategies should be used with Year Two students.

Remember to listen for key words:

Multiplication	Groups of, teams of, bunches of, rows of, bags of, multiply, times, lots of, array, altogether
Division	Shared between, shared equally, halved, divided, split, goes into, equal groups

EARLY SUPPORT:

✓ Remind your child that we use multiplication when we have groups with an equal amount in each group.

✓ Practise skip counting to 100 and beyond in twos, fives and tens (extension - 3's).

✓ Help your child to represent multiplication in a variety of ways *(see this section for a variety of representations)*.

REPEATED ADDITION

We use repeated addition as an introduction to multiplication, as children should already be very familiar with addition.

EXPLORE

Using repeated addition means adding the same number repeatedly, or over and over. We use it when there is the same amount in each group.

SAY

There were 3 trees with 7 birds in each, how many birds altogether? Because it is not easy to skip count in 7's, we could use repeated addition to solve this

7 + 7 + 7 =

SAMPLE QUESTIONS:

I am having a party with 4 friends and I want to give each of them a party bag with 5 lollies. How many lollies do I need to buy?

I have 3 bunches of flowers. Each bunch had 4 flowers. How many flowers were there altogether?

My 5 friends are each holding a bunch of 5 balloons. How many balloons altogether?

Explain that there is a faster way to work out the problems we just looked at and that is by using multiplication. Introduce multiplication (**x**) symbol and explain it – we normally introduce it as meaning 'groups of.'
e.g., 1 x 5 is the same as 1 group of 5

Let's go through our **5 times tables** – use concrete objects to model (fingers, tally marks, pictures, etc.).

1 group of 5 = This just means that I have one group and it has five items in it.

2 groups of 5 = I can count by ones, or I can skip count in 5s, two times. Skip counting is a much faster way to count equal groups.

3 groups of 5 = I can count by ones to get to fifteen, or I can skip count in 5s, three times. Skip counting is a much faster way to count equal groups.

4 groups of 5 = I can count by ones to get to twenty, or I can skip count in 5s, four times. Skip counting is a much faster way to count equal groups.

CONTINUE TO TEN GROUPS OF FIVE: Start replacing the words 'groups of' with the multiplication symbol as they grow in confidence.

REVISE 3 x 5 balloons – we could write this is using repeated addition: 5 + 5 + 5 = 15 but it is much faster to write 3 x 5 because we have 3 groups of balloons with 5 in each.

DRAWING OR MAKING EQUAL GROUPS

All groups must be equal (the same number of items as all the other groups). This pictorial representation is great for visual learners and works for multiplication or division.

EXPLORE

Show a picture of 3 groups of 5

SAY

Look at the picture, there are three groups of stars, with five stars in each. Let's use repeated addition to find the total number of stars.

5 + 5 + 5 = 15.

(Model circling groups and skip counting), 5, 10, 15.

3 groups of 5 is 15. We can write this sum quickly using the multiplication symbol.

3 x 5 = 15

SAMPLE QUESTIONS:

There were 5 cars with 4 wheels on each that needed to be changed. How many wheels does the mechanic have to change altogether? We can represent this by drawing the five cars with four wheels, which will take a long time! Or we could just draw something easier, like five circles (to represent the five cars) and four dots in each (to represent the four wheels)

I have 6 lily pads and there are 2 frogs on each. How many frogs altogether? Revise repeated addition: 2 and 2 and 2 and 2 and 2 and 2 makes 12. Use repeated addition to solve the problem e.g., 2+2+2+2+2+2=12.

Make Links: Let's draw what this sum would look like. We can use circles to represent (show) the lily pads and dots to represent the frogs. Let's count the dots, did we get the same answer as when using repeated addition? Use the frogs and lily pads in the appendix (pages 274 and 275) to make equal groups.

 Remind children that we can use any easy to draw shape *(i.e., a circle, rather than drawing people or birds)* to represent the parts of the problem and make this strategy faster.

Millie the dog loves to eat bones. Every day, she eats 3 bones. How many bones would she eat in 4 days? Can you draw a picture to match this word problem?

Amanda has 4 buckets for her toys. Each bucket has 4 toys in it. How many toys does she have altogether? Can you represent (show) this problem using objects?

Extend – can children match the number sentence with the visual?

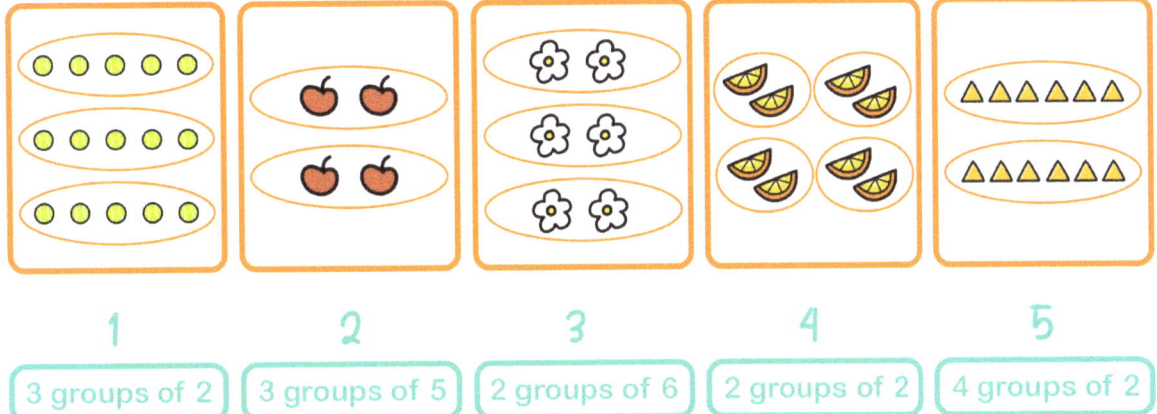

| 1 | 2 | 3 | 4 | 5 |

3 groups of 2 | 3 groups of 5 | 2 groups of 6 | 2 groups of 2 | 4 groups of 2

When using **division**, children are encouraged to group items into equal sets and solve simple problems using these representations. We can use concrete objects (best choice) or draw representations. Remember, children must be exposed to the words *'equally'* and *'evenly'* to be able to start using division.

SAMPLE QUESTIONS:

I had 6 blueberries to share equally between 3 children. How many blueberries would each child get?
Hands on: Use 6 blueberries and 3 dolls. Alternatively, draw stick people and share out some pebbles.

I had 12 lollies to share amongst my 4 friends. How many lollies would each friend get?
Hands on: Use 12 lollies and 4 lolly bags and model sharing them out evenly.

14 children need to be divided (shared) equally into 2 teams. How many children will be in each team?
Hands on: Get two hoops and use dolls or toys placed in each group until you have used 14. Or draw representation on a white board.

16 frogs were sitting on 4 lily pads. How many frogs on each lily pad?
Hands on: Use photocopied and laminated frogs from pages 274-275.

ARRAYS

Another pictorial representation, images or shapes arranged in rows or columns.

Please note: Children need to be explicitly taught new vocabulary **'rows'** and **'columns'**.

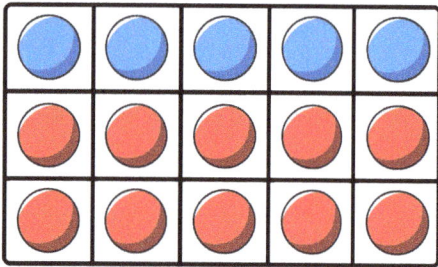

The rows run from left to right.
This array has three rows.

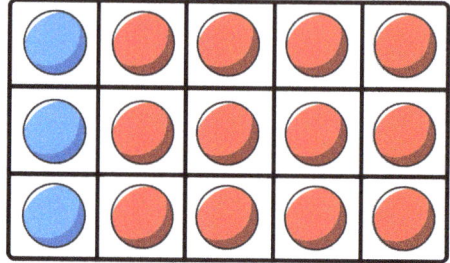

The columns run from top to bottom.
This array has five columns.

EXPLORE

Arrays can not only be used to assist children with a visual image to support understanding, but they also assist in demonstrating the relationship between multiplication and division (explored further on page 183).

SAY

Today I am going to teach you a new word – **ARRAY**. An array is a way of lining up objects so that they are easier to multiply. It is made up of rows going side to side (horizontal) and columns going up and down (vertical).

Show a 3 x 5 array

 Each row and each column must have the same number of objects in them.

Ask "What can you see? How many rows? How many in each row? How many columns? How many does that make altogether?"
Explain that there are 3 rows. Count how many stars are in each row, 5.
Write down 3 rows of 5, which means there are 15 stars altogether the number sentence is **3 x 5 = 15**
Model sum using multiplication symbol. Write **3 x 5 = 15**

Investigate multiple arrays and ask questions to encourage children to verbalise their thinking: "What can you see? How many rows? How many in each row? How many columns? How many does that make altogether?"

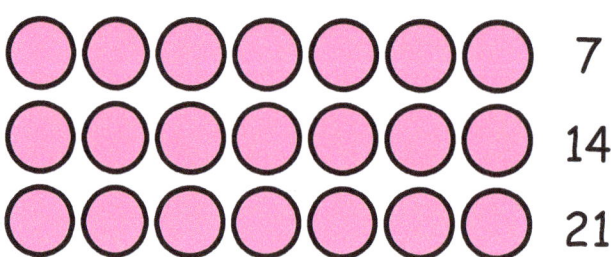

Model how to draw the following arrays using word problems.

> Remember, word problems are challenging as children must carefully listen/read the information given and identify what is pertinent to the question. It might be helpful to first draw a picture of the problem, before representing it in an array.

SAMPLE QUESTIONS:

(Q) There are 4 cars parked in the car park. How many wheels in the car park? **(A)**

(Q) There were 5 cages and each cage had 2 birds in it. How many birds altogether? **(A)**

(Q) I had 6 bowls and each bowl has 3 apples in it. How many apples were there altogether? **(A)**

Extend

Can you draw an array that has three rows, with three circles in each row?

Can you draw an array that has six columns and five circles in each row?

I put 12 circles into an array. What might my array look like? Draw a few options.

I put 20 stars into an array. What might my array look like? Draw a few options.

> Use muffin trays (3 x 4), egg cartons (2 x 6) and egg trays (5 x 5) as a ready-made array holder to match the corresponding algorithm.

NUMBER LINES

Use number lines as a visual aide when skip counting to solve multiplication and division problems.

EXPLORE

When you see a multiplication equation and it is linked to a number line, it is beneficial to think of the multiplication symbol (**x**) as meaning 'jumps of.'
e.g., 3 x 5 = 3 jumps of 5

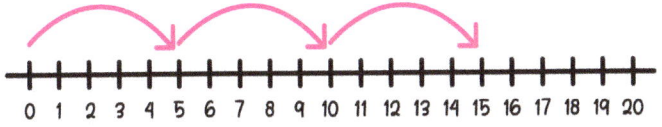

SAY

When we see the multiplication symbol (x) we often think of it as meaning 'groups of' but today, I want you to think of it as meaning 'jumps of' because we are going to be jumping on the number line.

SAMPLE QUESTIONS:

Can you use this number line to show 4 jumps of 3? What number did you land on? (4x3)

Can you use this number line to 20, to show four jumps of five numbers? What number did you land on? What do you think the sum was? (4 x 5)

Using this number line to 30, can you show three jumps of seven? What number did you land on? Can you write the number sentence? (7 x 3)

NUMBER SENTENCES

Practise writing and working out equations.

EXPLORE

Children should have had multiple and extended periods of time exploring all of the previously mentioned strategies. They must have that visual representation to refer to, before they start memorising multiplication facts (times tables).

SAY

Today, we are going to practise number sentences/equations using the multiplication symbol.

SAMPLE QUESTIONS:

Please note: Children do NOT need to have times tables memorised by the end of Year Two.

Write out times tables – 2 x's tables, 5 x's tables, 10 x's tables before moving on to other numbers

Listen to multiplication CD's or songs on YouTube

Roll a dice twice or pull out two playing cards from a deck (take out face cards and Aces). Write down the two numbers shown e.g., 6 and 3. Turn it into a multiplication problem: 6 x 3 or 3 x 6 =

Show images of equal groups for children to write a matching multiplication sentence.

a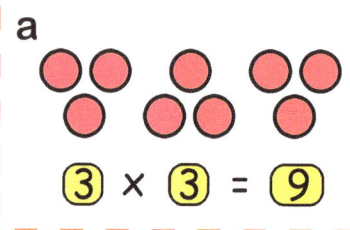

b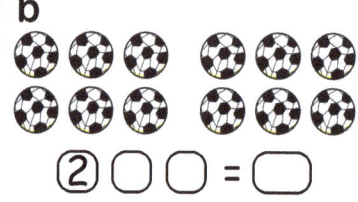

c

d

e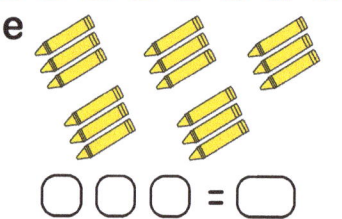

f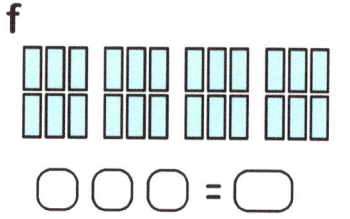

FACT FAMILIES/INVERSE OPERATIONS

Just like addition and subtraction are related, so too are multiplication and division.

EXPLORE

Remember the rule- If I know one, I know four (page 166). So, if I know one number sentence, I can use those same numbers to make four sentences. Begin by reminding students about turnarounds with addition. We know that when we are adding two numbers together, it does not matter which number we add first – we will still get the same amount.

 Don't introduce the division symbol (÷) until children have demonstrated a thorough understanding of how to share into equal groups.

Say: I know 1 sentence, I know 4 strategy

Let's turn this one sentence into four sums sentence.
3 x 5 = 15
5 x 3 = 15 (turnaround)
15 shared between 5 = 3 (backflip)
15 shared between 3 = 5 (backflip)

3 x 5 = 15   5 x 3 = 15

Let's turn this one sum into four sums
2 x 5 = 10
5 x 2 = 10 (turnaround)
10 shared between (divided by) 5 = 2 (backflip)
10 shared between (divided by) 2 = 5 (backflip)

5 x 2 = 10   2 x 5 = 10

SAY

The first picture shows 3 + 10 and the second picture has been turned around to show 10 + 3. It does not matter if I say 3 + 10 or 10 + 3, I will still get the answer 13.

3 + 10 =   10 + 3 =

The same rule applies for **multiplication** – When we are multiplying two numbers together, it does not matter which number we say first – we will still get the same amount.

3 x 4 =   4 x 3 =

Practise using arrays and concrete objects to model making multiplication sums and demonstrate the relationship between multiplication and division by then dividing the total amount back into one of the parts.

3 x 4 = 12   4 x 3 = 12
            4   3
            8   6
            12   9
                              12

SAMPLE QUESTIONS:

Use the numbers in each of these sentences to write four sentences:

| 3 x 4 = |
| 2 x 6 = |
| 3 x 10 = |

Verbalise:
Q – If 4 x 5 = 20, what else do you know?
A – I know that 5 x 4 = 20 and 20 shared between 4 will give me 5, and 20 shared between 5 will give me 4.
Repeat using many examples.

By the end of Year 2, children should be able to show understanding of multiplication problems in a variety of ways including repeated addition, arrays, algorithms and pictorial representations.

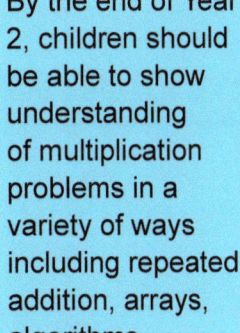

Repeated addition 6+6+6=18
Multiplication 3x6=18
Equal Groups
Arrays

PROBLEM SOLVING

Mathematics
Exploring Numbers with Dice, Cards, and Grids

FOUNDATION

Dice Games
Using six and ten-sided dice

Algorithms:

Roll two six-sided dice and add the two numbers together.

Roll two six-sided dice and subtract the smaller number from the larger number.

Subitising and Number Awareness:

Roll a six-sided or ten-sided dice and instantly call out the number of dots (subitisation explained on **page 120**). Use a timer: How many numbers can they roll and read in 20 seconds? Can they beat that time?

Break a page up into six parts, write 1-6 in each box. Roll a six-sided dice, 20 times and put a mark (or tally marks if you have introduced them) in the corresponding box each time you roll that number. Repeat with a ten-sided dice when they are confident with dot patterns to six. Extend: graph results.

Roll a six-sided dice and start counting forwards or backwards from that number.

Roll a ten-sided dice and start counting forwards or backwards from that number.

Roll a combination of six and ten-sided dice at the same time to make and write a teen number. Represent it using tally marks, tens frames, bundling sticks or on a think board (see **page 269**).

Play against each other – take turns to roll five, six-sided dice, get a point for rolling three of a kind. First to ten points is the winner.

Draw or print rows of dots on a page, the amount of dots is up to you. Next, roll a dice and circle the same number of dots, writing the matching numeral in the shape that you made. Alternatively, use graph paper and colour grid spaces (see **page 190**).

Roll a dice and create a tower using the corresponding number of blocks/Lego. Keep rolling and adding blocks and counting the total number of blocks. See if they can get to 30 or beyond.

Specialised Edition

Using A Deck of Cards
(Remove face cards)

Recognition of numeral or dot pattern (subitisation):

Pull out a card, what number is it? Repeat with multiple cards.

Pull out a few random cards, practise drawing dot patterns using the same representation shown on cards.

Comparing:

Using one set of cards showing Ace (acting as 1) to 10:
Find a card that has a number that is one more than five? One less than ten? Two more than two?

Split deck into two piles, flip over the top two cards, point to the biggest number

Pull out a random card (say 7), Ask how many numbers in the pile are more than 7? Pull out a 4 – How many numbers in the pile are less than 4?

Ordering:

Pull out three to five random cards using one set of cards Ace-10 (Ace acting as 1), ask child to order them and explain the order.

Use a deck of cards to find and order numbers to 10. Draw a number line in chalk on the ground, long enough for ten cards to fit. Leave remaining cards in a pile, turn over the top card and locate the number on the number line. Invite the child to predict whether the next card will be more or less than the previous card. They then turn over the next card to check their prediction. Complete until all 40 cards have been used, by stacking on top of the cards already on the line.

Pull out five cards each and race the child to put them in order from biggest to smallest or smallest to biggest.

MATHS EXTRAS

YEAR 1

Dice Games
Using six and ten-sided dice

Recognition and counting:

Roll two six-sided dice to create a two-digit number, count forwards or backwards from that number to another given number.
E.g., Roll a six and a one, make a two-digit number (16 or 61) and then count on or back from that number.

Roll two six-sided dice, if children get doubles, they get five points, unless they get double six (the magic number), then they get 20 points. First to 100 points is the winner. Use tally marks to keep score, this will support skip counting. You can make many variations on this game, for example double one might be a poison number, lose 10 points or you could make double three the magic number.

Algorithms:

Steal a Ten: Two player game – Both players start with a tower of 10 unifex/Lego/Duplo (ideally all the same colour). Player one rolls a six-sided dice and steals the corresponding number of blocks from their opponent. Player two then rolls a six-sided dice and steals the corresponding number of blocks from the first player. Player one then rolls again, and steals blocks from opponent. The winner is the player who ends up with all 20 blocks.

Children roll two six-sided or ten-sided dice and see how quickly they can add the two numbers together.

Can you roll a ten, using two six-sided dice? What about seven? How many possible combinations are there?

Using A Deck of Cards
(Remove face cards)

Place Value:

Pull out one set of cards, showing Ace (acting as 1) to 10. Using these cards, ask a variety of questions such as:

- Can you make a number between 50 to 65?
- Can you make a number that is smaller than 80 but bigger than 30?
- Can you make an even number?
- Can you make a 2-digit number that has 8 tens and 2 ones? 5 tens and 4 ones?

Algorithms:

Pull out two cards: *How quickly can you add the digits?* (When adding two digits, it is beneficial for students to lock the biggest number in their head and count on the smaller amount - see **page 159** for more information).

Using one set of cards showing 1 (use Ace) to 10, pull out a random card and ask how many more to get to ten?

Comparing:

Turn over two cards, point to the largest number. Make into a game, player one turns one card, player two turns one card, compare who has the largest number. The player with the largest number gets a point. First to ten points is the winner.

Turn over two cards, the first card is representing the ones digit, the second card is representing the tens. *What number did you make? Let's write it. Now I will do the same, and then write it. We will compare numbers, whoever has the highest number will get five points. We will repeat this game 10 times and use tally marks to keep score.*

Using one set of cards showing Ace (acting as 1) to 10, pull out four cards. Ask the child to make the biggest and smallest two-digit number that they can make. Ask the child to pull out two more cards. Can they make a number to fit in between the other two numbers?

MATHS EXTRAS

YEAR 2

Dice Games
Using six and ten-sided dice

Number:

Roll three six-sided dice: *"What is the largest three-digit number you can make? How do you know? What is the smallest? How do you know?"* Make it into a game, take turns to see who can make the largest number for each round. Keep the score using tally marks.

Skip-counting:

Roll two six-sided dice to create a two-digit number. Use a hundred grid, mark that two-digit number as the starting number. Now roll one dice and skip count using that amount. Use the grid to mark the number said each time they count.

Algorithms:

Roll two six-sided dice: can you add the two numbers? Can you multiply them? Make this harder by using one or two ten-sided dice to replace the six-sided dice. Use activities on **pages 176-183** to support multiplication exploration.

Use two blank pages in a grid book, draw an equal-sized border on each page. Player 1 rolls two six-sided dice: use the two numbers presented and make a 2D shape with that area. E.g., roll a 2 and a 4, draw a 2 x 4 rectangle. Player 2 rolls two six-sided dice: use the two numbers presented and make a 2D shape with that area.
E.g., roll a 6 and a 5 and colour 6 x 5 grid spaces. Keep rolling and colouring in grid spaces until one player has filled the page (or as much as possible).

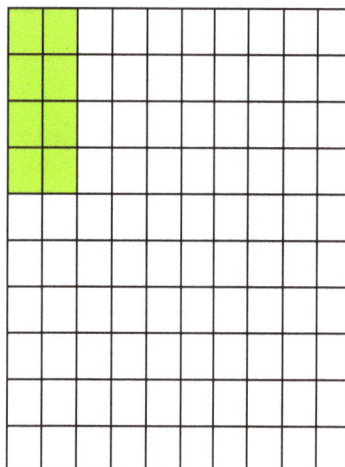 

Using A Deck of Cards
(Remove face cards)

Number:

Using one set of cards from Ace (acting as one) to nine, pull out two or three cards. Make two or three-digit numbers and represent (make) using MAB blocks (see **page 271**).

Comparing:

Using one set of cards from Ace (acting as one) to nine, pull out three cards and ask three-digit number questions - *What possible combinations of numbers can you make using the three cards you pulled out? What is the biggest/smallest number you can make? How do you know?*

Algorithms:

Pull out two cards, use numbers to write a word problem (see **page 155**).

Pull out two cards: *What is the difference between the two numbers?* Remind students that the easiest way to find the difference is to count up if the numbers are close together (from the smallest number to the largest) or subtract the smaller amount from the bigger amount if they are not close together. See **page 164**.

Pull out two cards: Can you multiply them?

Make to Ten game - Remove face cards and tens for this game. Shuffle the cards and lay out twelve cards face down, in a 4 by 3 grid on the table. Leave the leftover cards in a pile. Player one chooses two cards from the grid then adds the cards together. If the sum of the two cards is 10, player one gets to keep the cards and replaces the empty spaces with two new cards from the pile. Keep playing until all combinations have been collected.

Pull out four cards and make two, two-digit numbers. Add or subtract numbers using one of the problem-solving strategies explained on **pages 159-165**.

ACTIVITIES USING THE HUNDREDS GRID

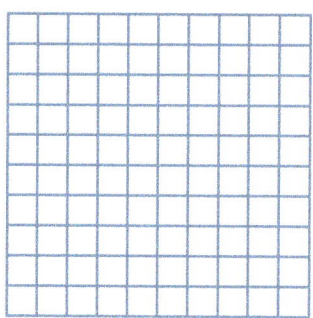

Print out a hundreds grid and place it in a clear plastic sleeve. Use a whiteboard marker to play games. Alternatively, there are many online interactive hundred grids available online (see interactive 100s grid game). **Maths Playground** on tablet or **Splat Square** on computer work well.

YEAR 1

Use a blank hundred grid and ask students to fill in numbers 0-99 or 1-100 (see **page 125**).

> Use grids to count and warm up for the lesson – counting on the hundreds grid daily will support children to learn place or order of the number sequence:

Sit with hundreds grid in front of them, point to numbers as they count forwards and backwards from any starting place in ones. Ask "What's the pattern when we count forwards/backwards in ones (ones change, tens stay the same until there are nine ones). Discuss patterns on the 100s grid and when it becomes tricky (going to next team of ten). Extension kids may close their eyes while counting.

Revise when we count in ones, we are finding 1 more, when we count backwards in ones, it is 1 less. Start from any number, *e.g., 32, 1 more: 33, 1 less: 31.*

Use a recording device on tablet or phone to record counting sequences – *e.g., Can you count to 80?*

Specialised Edition

> Use grids to ask a variety of closed questions (only one answer) about place value. Call out different clues for children to find numbers and explain reasoning "I know this is correct because…"

- Point to a number that has 4 tens and 3 ones, how do you know?

- What about 8 tens and 4 ones? 6 tens and 3 ones?

- Point to the smallest and largest number on the grid.

- Cover a number, ask the student what number is covered and how they know? (They should be using the language of more than, less than).

- Circle five numbers between 50 and 55.

- Circle all the even numbers between 20 and 30.

- Circle the number that is ten more than 56.

- Circle the number that is one less than 98.

- What is two more and two less than 73, two less than 100.

- Play the **More or Less** game

Give the child a hundred grid and whiteboard pen (or use interactive version), call out different closed questions (listed above).
After asking a few closed questions, stop on a 2-digit number and tell the child that you are going to play the More or Less game.
Create four flashcards saying 1 more, 1 less, 10 more, 10 less on them. Hide the cards in a bag or hat to use as a lucky dip.
Sing: *More or less, what will it be? Pull out a card and you will see!*
Model changing the number on the grid to match the instruction on the card.
Repeat several times.
Extend: Predict if they think the number will be bigger or smaller. Describe the part of our number that changed (*was it the ones or the tens?*).
Ask the student to explain what more and less mean.

- Locate numbers to 100 on a hundred grid – *E.g. If I was looking for the number 25, would I be looking in the upper half or the lower half of the hundreds grid?*

Photocopy a few hundred grids onto different pieces of coloured card, then cut up the hundred grids to make into puzzles. Ask questions about their sorting – "How do you know that piece is in the right place? What patterns can you see?" Any children who are finding this challenging, should be given a complete 100's grid use as a base and match numbers.

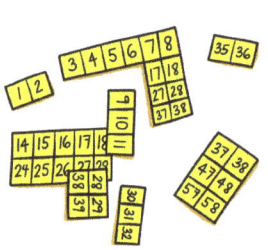

1	2	3	4	5	6	7	8	9	10
11	12	13	14	15	16	17	18	19	20
21	22	23	24	25	26	27	28	29	30
31	32	33	34	35	36	37	38	39	40
41	42	43	44	45	46	47	48	49	50
51	52	53	54	55	56	57	58	59	60
61	62	63	64	65	66	67	68	69	70
71	72	73	74	75	76	77	78	79	80
81	82	83	84	85	86	87	88	89	90
91	92	93	94	95	96	97	98	99	100

Partly fill in a hundreds grid and ask child to complete the missing parts.

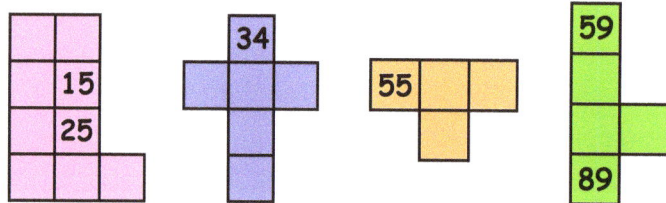

Complete number grid part puzzles such as those below.

Ask open-ended questions using the hundreds grid (there will be multiple answers):

A two-digit number has a 4 in the ones place, what could the number be?

Circle a number with 9 tens.

Find a number between 79 – 84.

Point to a 2-digit number. (How do you know it is a two-digit number?).

- Circle five numbers larger than 50.

- Circle five numbers that are less than 50.

- Find an even number between 10 and 50.

- Circle an odd number between 40 and 47.

> Point to random numbers on the grid and encourage child to partition (break numbers into parts) according to place value:

- 75 is the same as 70 + 5.

- 12 is the same as 1 ten and 2 ones.

> Practise skip counting in 2's, 5's and 10's to any given number:

- Colour in or circle numbers on the grid.

- Look for patterns. When I circle all the numbers said when I count in tens, what do you notice? What about fives and twos?

> Ask number sentence and word problems using the 100's grid:

- One more than... two less than... 10 more than...

- I am thinking of a number that is one more than 54, 2 less than 20, 10 more than 26...

YEAR 2 — Use numbers to 1000

Use a blank hundreds grid and ask students to fill in a series of one hundred three-digit numbers (e.g., 800-900).

> Use grids with 100 numbers to 1000 (e.g., 500-600) to ask questions. The following questions could be given if you were focusing on a 500-600 grid:

- Use the grid to practise counting on or back from any number, *e.g., can you count to 600, starting from 560?*

- Use a grid and a recording device on a tablet or phone to record counting sequences.

> Use grid with 100 numbers to ask a variety of closed questions (only one answer) such as:

Using a 500-600 grid

- I am thinking of a number between 500-600 that has two 9's in it. What number could that be?

- I am thinking of an odd number between 551 and 557, the sum of my digits is 13 (553).

- How many numbers can you find that are between 562 and 568?

- What features of 523, demonstrate that it lies between 520 and 530?

- Point to a number that has 5 hundreds 4 tens and 3 ones.

- How many numerals/digits are in the number 521?

- One more than... two less than... 10 more than...

- Play the **More or Less game** (see **page 193**).

Complete missing puzzle pieces like the one below – Draw your own into grid books. This is very challenging and takes time. It may be beneficial to have a hard copy of a complete grid in front of child to support this learning:

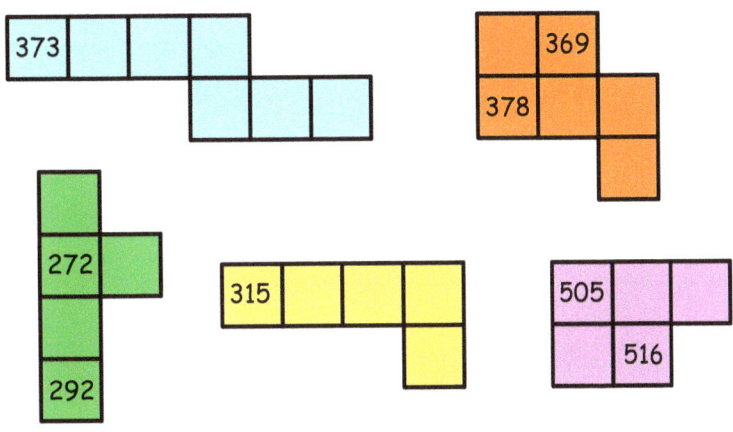

Ask open-ended questions (there will be multiple answers):

- A three-digit number has a 2 in the ones place, what could the number be?

- Circle a number with 8 tens.

- Circle a number that has 5 hundreds and 4 tens (any number of ones).

- Find an odd/even number between – and –.

- Circle a number that would be found in the bottom half of the grid.
(see more ideas on **pages 194-195**).

Point to random numbers on the grid and encourage child to partition (break numbers into parts) according to place value:

- 754 is the same as 700 + 50 + 4.

- 502 is the same as 5 hundreds + 0 tens + 2 ones.

Practise skip counting in 2's, 5's and 10's from any given number to any given number. Circle numbers, ask the child to find the pattern rule – is it getting bigger or smaller? Is it counting in ones? Twos? Fives? Tens?

- Circle 512, then 522, 532, 542. What would be the next three numbers you circle?

EXTRA IMPORTANT MATHEMATICAL LEARNING IN F – 2

- Learn days of the week, months and seasons of the year.

- Learn the number of days in each month.

  - Learn the rhyme: 30 days has September, April, June and November. All the rest have 31, except for February, which has 28 clear and 29 each leap year.

  - **Knuckle mnemonic**

    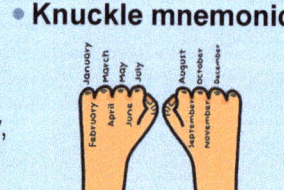

  Make a pattern using knuckles: Starting on the left pinky knuckle, count knuckles as 31 days, depressions between knuckles as 30 (or 28/29) days.

- Use a calendar to identify the date and link months to seasons.

- Tell the time to the hour (Foundation) and half hour (Year 1), quarter past and quarter to (Year 2) using digital and analogue clocks. Extend to five-minute intervals when they master the others.

- Use the language of time, e.g., tomorrow, yesterday, later, before, after, morning, afternoon, evening.

- Learn left, right, horizontal, vertical, clockwise and anti-clockwise.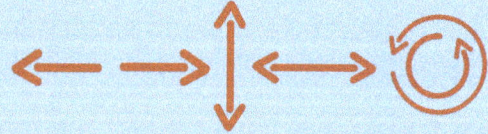

- Read and answer questions about simple maps from zoos and theme parks.

- Learn about alpha-numeric grids (Battleships game is a great intro for this).

- Explore North, South, East and West on a map of a country (Year Two).

  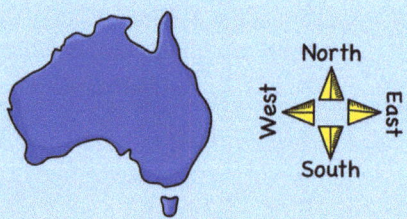

- Use toys or go to the park/playground and give instructions using positional language, e.g., behind, in front, above, below, next to, between, forwards, backwards, on, under, over, near, far, close.

Specialised Edition

- [ ] Use stop watches to time simple events such as competing in running or novelty races, balancing on one leg, handstand, throwing and catching a ball without dropping.

- [ ] Measure objects with non-standard measuring tools (hands/feet/pebbles/popsicle sticks). Note: standard measures (ruler/tape measure) are used in Year Three.

- [ ] Order objects by length, volume, weight or height. Use the Comparative Language List on **page 107** to support this.

- [ ] Compare weight of objects using balance scales.

- [ ] Explore symmetry using paint and mirrors.

- [ ] Describe outcomes for everyday events (likely/unlikely, certain/impossible/equal chance). Answer questions starting with *"What is the chance...?"*

- [ ] Explore halves, quarters, thirds and eighths using real-life objects (pizza, sandwiches, cup measures, paper folding, etc.).

- [ ] Model collating and recording data in tables and graphs:
  - Use tally marks to record how many hops/jumps/throw a ball against a wall and catch it, before recording on a graph.
  - Observe a semi-busy road and record colours of cars or types of vehicle before recording on a graph.
  - Sort and count toys/blocks into groups and graph the results.

- [ ] Answer questions using pre-recorded tables and graphs (Which answer had the most/least? How many more/less?)

- [ ] For Year Two, rotate shapes and objects using full, half and quarter turns both clockwise and anticlockwise.

MATHS EXTRAS

199

SHAPE:

- Get crafty:
  - Using only 2D shapes, draw a robot/house/monster. Describe the shapes you have used.
  - Shape stamping or tracing.

- Play **"Guess My Shape"** by giving clues – E.g., I have three straight sides, I have four straight sides; two are long and two are short (Square, rectangle, triangle, rhombus, diamond, circle, oval, pentagon, hexagon, octagon).

- Draw some 2D shapes for students to label, or call out shapes for students to draw.

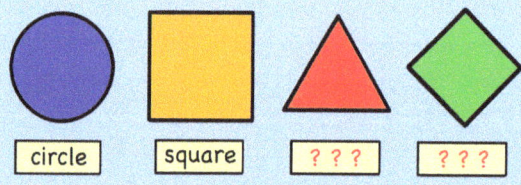

- Learn about curvy and straight lines. Ask students to draw some shapes with curved/straight sides.

- How many sides/corners on a _____? Sort shapes according to number of sides, corners and lines used (straight or curved).

- Be able to explain the difference between a 2D and 3D shape.

Specialised Edition

☐ Identify similarities and differences between shapes. What is similar and different between a ____? (e.g., rectangle and triangle).

☐ Recognise and name 3D shapes (pyramid, cone, cube, cylinder, sphere, prism).

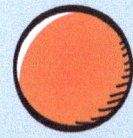
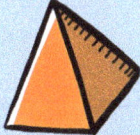   

☐ Find everyday shapes around the house. Go on a shape hunt and find shapes in our world.

☐ Describe 3D shapes (straight/curved sides and number of faces, edges, corners/vertices).

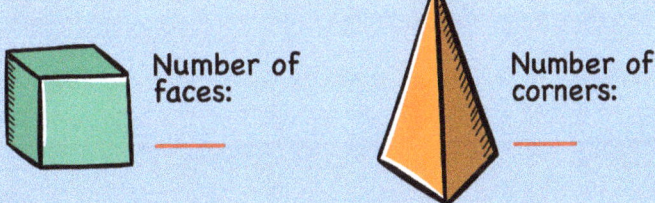

☐ Make 3D shapes using nets (these are available online) or pull boxes apart to see the net.

☐ Identify similarities and differences between a range of 3D shapes. Which ones can roll? Stack?

201

MATHS EXTRAS

Mathematics
Assessment

FOUNDATION ASSESSMENT OVERVIEW

I can...	Date	Date	Date
Count forwards and backwards to 20 from any starting number.			
Count beyond 20.			
Show an understanding of number zero.			
Use ordinal numbers to at least 3rd place.			
Recognise numerals to at least 20.			
Count quantities to at least 20, using one-to-one correspondence (I say one number, I touch one object).			
Demonstrate an understanding that the last number said is the total number of items.			
Make links between number names and numerals initially to 10 and then beyond.			
Order numerals to at least 20.			
Subitise collections up to 10 using a range of images (dice patterns, five and ten frames, random representations).			
Use mathematical language to compare collections such as more than, less than, same as.			
Identify halves of shapes and collections.			
Use a 10 frame to make different amounts and to answer calculations.			
Add small amounts.			
Count on to solve simple addition problems.			
Count back to solve simple subtraction problems.			
Subtract small amounts.			
Compare groups of objects to identify more and less.			
Copy, continue and create two and three-part patterns using colours, objects, movement and sound.			
Sort objects into groups and explain sorting.			
Share items into equal groups.			

Please note: The following assessment piece is a sample only and does not cover everything that needs to be explored and assessed. Use this to identify areas to focus on during learning sessions.

Specialised Edition

FOUNDATION BEGINNING OF YEAR:

One on One Assessment Sample: Number & Algebra

1. Count until I tell you to stop. Accurately counts to _____ . If the child accurately counts beyond 10: Can they count to 10 starting from 4 ____ and 6 ____.

2. Count backwards from 10_____ 20_____.

3. Names these numerals (use flashcards to 10)

1	2	3	4	5	6	7	8	9	10

4. If accurate, can you put those number cards in order from 1-10
(give the pile to the child and see if they can put them in order – check they are ordered left – right)
_____

5. How many counters do I have here? 10 _____

6. Can you put 5 counters in my hand? _____ Now 10? _____
(Did child grab them all, knowing that 10 was the starting number? Did they count on from 5?)

7. Can you make these bags have the same number of lollies in them?

8. What can you tell me about the lolly bags below?
_____
_____

Which one would you like/prefer to have _____
Why? _____

ASSESSMENT

205

Teacher For Early Years

FOUNDATION END OF YEAR:

One on One Assessment Sample: Number & Algebra

1. Counts to: _____ If accurate to or beyond 20, counts from any given number to 20- Starting from 15 ___ and from 6 ___ and from 11____

2. Counts backwards from 20 ___ 10 ___

3. What is one more than 5 _____ 14 _____ 17 _____

4. What is one less than 3 _____ 9 _____ 19 _____

5. Recognise/name these numerals

1	2	3	4	5	6	7	8	9	10

6. If accurate, can recognise/name these numerals

11	12	13	14	15	16	17	18	19	20

7. Shows one to one correspondence (points to one item whilst saying one number name) when counting objects to 5 ___ 9 ___ 14 ___ 20 ___

8. Add these numbers to the number line: 8, 3, 4. How did you know where to put them?

9. Using the number line below, where would number 10 go? Where would 11 go? What about 19? How do you know? _____

10. Can you draw a picture to help answer this question? Can you work it out on a ten frame?

There were 3 birds in the tree eating apples and there were 5 birds on the ground eating grass. How many birds all together? _____

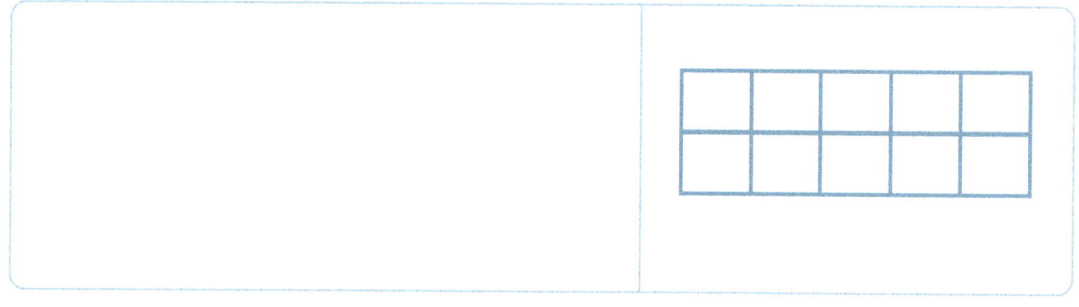

Specialised Edition

YEAR 1 ASSESSMENT OVERVIEW

I can...	Date	Date	Date
Count to and from 100, from any starting number.			
Count beyond 100.			
Demonstrate a solid understanding of number zero.			
Use ordinal numbers to at least 10th place.			
Show an understanding of mathematical language, e.g., order, equal, before, after, more, less, add, subtract.			
Locate numbers on a number line.			
Identify odd and even numbers.			
Order and compare numbers to at least 99.			
Read and write number words to 100.			
Partition numbers using place value (tens and ones).			
Group collections of objects into sets to facilitate efficient counting.			
Investigate and describe number patterns.			
Copy, continue and create simple patterns using objects.			
Identify the missing part in number sequences.			
Skip count in 2s, 5s and 10s, starting the count from zero.			
Represent and solve simple addition and subtraction problems using a range of strategies.			
Identify representations of one half by splitting objects or shapes into two equal parts.			
Identify representations of one half by sharing a collection into two equal groups.			
Recognise and describe (Australian) coins.			
Order coins according to their value.			

Please note: The following assessment piece is a sample only and does not cover everything that needs to be explored and assessed. Use this to identify areas to focus on during learning sessions.

YEAR 1 BEGINNING OF YEAR:

One on One Assessment Sample: Number & Algebra

1. Counts to: _____ If accurate to or beyond 100, counts from any given number to 100- Starting from 18 ___ and from 62 ___ and from 41____

2. Counts backwards from 100 / 20

3. What is one more than 11 _____ 54 _____ 79 _____

4. What is one less than 13 _____ 92 _____ 25 _____

5. Recognise/name these numerals (flashcards out of order)

11	12	13	14	15	16	17	18	19	20

6. If accurate, can recognise/name these numerals (you will need to make up flashcards)

83	36	73	51	47	28	94	100	66	96

7. Shows one to one correspondence (points to one item whilst saying one number name) when counting objects to 15 ___ 29 ___ 54 ____

8. Place these number cards in order 17, 10, 71, 19 How did you know where to put each number? _____

9. Add these numbers to the number line: 68, 63, 71. How did you know where to put them?

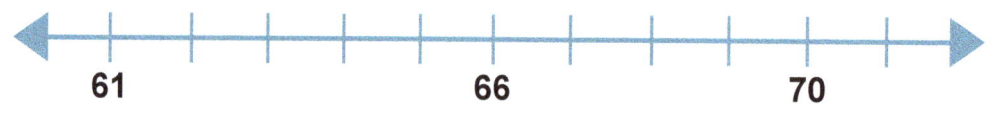

10. Can you skip count to 100 in 5's _____ 10's _____ 2's _____

11. Can you teach me how to work out this word problem? Is it addition or subtraction? How do you know?

> Thirteen cows were in the field and then three of them were moved to another paddock. How many cows are left?

Specialised Edition

YEAR 1 END OF YEAR:

One on One Assessment Sample: Number

1. Counts to: _____ If accurate to or beyond 100, counts from any given number to 100
Starting from 78 ___ and from 12 ___ and from 45____

2. Can you skip count to 100 in 2's _____ 5's _____ 10's _____

3. Can you skip count backwards from 100 in 10's _____ 5's _____

4. Complete the missing parts of the counting patterns

35	34	33			30		28		
4	14	24		44		64		84	
22	24		28	30		34		38	
100	95	90			75		65		

5. What number comes before? ____ 9 ____ 16 ____ 93

6. What number comes after? 13 ____ 65 ____ 99 ____

7. Write the number shown

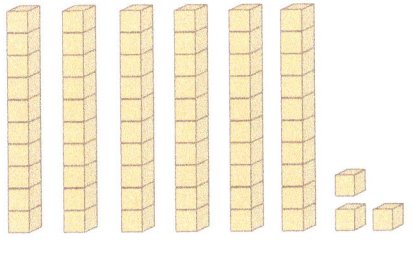   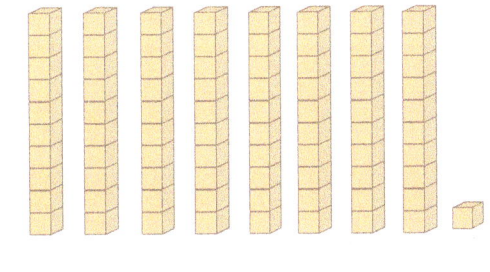

_____   _____

8. Spell 22 _____   Spell 45 _____

9. Write the number that has:

    3 tens and 5 ones? _____
    7 tens and 9 ones _____

10. Order these numbers from smallest to biggest:

15 9 12 20 11 | | | | | |

71 19 99 17 70 | | | | | |

209

ASSESSMENT

YEAR 1 END OF YEAR:

One on One Assessment Sample: Algebra

1. Add these

    4 + 0 = _____ 0 + 15 = _____

2. Subtract these

    7 – 0 = _____ 83 - 0 = _____

3. Draw a picture to solve this problem:

    > There were 10 ladybirds. 6 flew away but then 3 came back. How many now?

4. Use addition strategies to solve these: Tell me what you used:
   (Think big, count small? Count on? Addition to Ten?)

    2 + 43 = _____
    4 + 6 = _____
    13 + 2 = _____

5. Use the hundreds grid to complete these sums

1	2	3	4	5	6	7	8	9	10
11	12	13	14	15	16	17	18	19	20
21	22	23	24	25	26	27	28	29	30
31	32	33	34	35	36	37	38	39	40
41	42	43	44	45	46	47	48	49	50
51	52	53	54	55	56	57	58	59	60
61	62	63	64	65	66	67	68	69	70
71	72	73	74	75	76	77	78	79	80
81	82	83	84	85	86	87	88	89	90
91	92	93	94	95	96	97	98	99	100

(a) 34 + 10 = _____ (b) 12 + 10 = _____
(c) 25 + 20 = _____ (d) 38 + 9 = _____
(e) 77 + 11 = _____ (f) 67 – 10 = _____
(g) 78 – 20 = _____ (h) 42 – 9 = _____

Specialised Edition

YEAR 2 ASSESSMENT OVERVIEW

I can...	Date	Date	Date
Recognise all numbers to 1000.			
Count to 1000, forwards and backwards and from any starting number.			
Order numbers to at least 1000.			
Represent numbers to 1000 in multiple ways.			
Show an understanding of mathematical language, e.g., partition, order, equals, place value, number sentences.			
Continue counting patterns in twos, fives, tens (and threes) forwards and backwards to 1000, from any starting point.			
Represent skip counting patterns on number lines and hundred grids.			
Identify the missing number in a number sequence using counting patterns to 1000.			
Partition numbers into hundreds, tens and ones.			
Group collections of objects into fives or tens to facilitate more efficient counting.			
Solve simple addition and subtraction problems using a range of strategies – both mental and written.			
Recognise the connection between addition and subtraction and use this to solve problems.			
Identify and use halves, quarters, eighths (and thirds) of shapes and collections.			
Complete multiplication problems using repeated addition, arrays and groups.			
Complete division problems by grouping objects into equal sets.			
Order small collections of Australian coins and notes according to their value.			
Count small collections of Australian coins and notes.			

Please note: The following assessment piece is a sample only and does not cover everything that needs to be explored and assessed. Use this to identify areas to focus on during learning sessions.

Teacher For Early Years

YEAR 2 BEGINNING OF YEAR:

One on One Assessment Sample: Number

1. Count forwards to 100 _____   Count backwards from 100 _____

2. Count to 100 in twos _____ fives _____ tens _____

3. Count back from 100 in twos _____ fives _____ tens _____

4. Write numerals correctly (adult to call out two-digit numbers – 35, 68, 73, 52, 49)
   _____

5. Circle the SMALLEST number in each rectangle

56	28	41	14	22	27
13	30	93	39	61	81

6. Put these numbers in order from smallest to largest

14	40	4	41	44	10

   ____ ____ ____ ____ ____ ____

7. Fill in this 100s grid

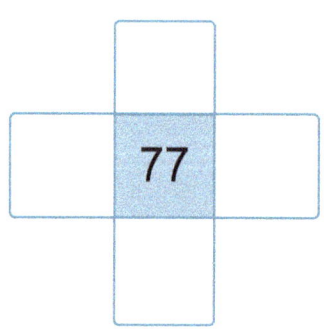

   How do you know the missing numbers?
   _____
   _____
   _____

8. Finish these patterns: Can you write the rule after each pattern?

   6, 8, 10, 12, ___, ___, ___   _____

   45, 55, 65, 75, ___, ___, ___   _____

   95, 90, 85, 80, ___, ___, ___   _____

   42, 39, 36, 33, ___, ___, ___   _____

9. Spell 100 _____

ASSESSMENT

212

Specialised Edition

YEAR 2 BEGINNING OF YEAR:

One on One Assessment Sample: Algebra

1. What do these symbols mean?

   ⓐ + _____

   ⓑ - _____

   ⓒ = _____

2. What is a turnaround? Give an example of a turnaround

   _____

3. **Mental calculations: Doubles**

   | 2 + 2 = ____ | 3 + 3 = ____ | 6 + 6 = ____ | 7 + 7 = ____ |

   | 10 + 10 = ____ | 25 + 25 = ____ | 4 + 4 = ____ | 5 + 5 = ____ |

   | 8 + 8 = ____ | 9 + 9 = ____ | 40 + 40 = ____ |

4. **Mental calculations: Addition to 10** (Use turnarounds to find eleven possible answers). <u>The answer is 10</u>. Write as many sums as you can with the answer being 10.

   ___ + ___ = ___   ___ + ___ = ___   ___ + ___ = ___

   ___ + ___ = ___   ___ + ___ = ___   ___ + ___ = ___

   ___ + ___ = ___   ___ + ___ = ___

   ___ + ___ = ___   ___ + ___ = ___

5. Mark had $10 and then he found $14 more. How much does he have now? How did you work it out?

   _____

6. Use the number line to show **14 + 4**

   1 _____ 20

7. Complete these sums using 'Counting On' or 'Finding Friendly Pairs'

   ⓐ 25 + 1 = _____   ⓑ 44 + 2 = _____

   ⓒ 7 + 1 + 3 = _____   ⓓ 6 + 2 + 4 = _____

   ⓔ 5 + 8 + 8 = _____   ⓕ 25 + 1 + 1 = _____

Teacher For Early Years

YEAR 2 END OF YEAR:

One on One Assessment Sample: Number

1. Count forwards from 500 to 600 _____ Count backwards from 600 to 500 _____

2. Count from 700 to 800 in twos _____ fives _____ tens _____

3. Count back from 200 in twos _____ fives _____ tens _____

4. Write the numbers shown in the boxes below

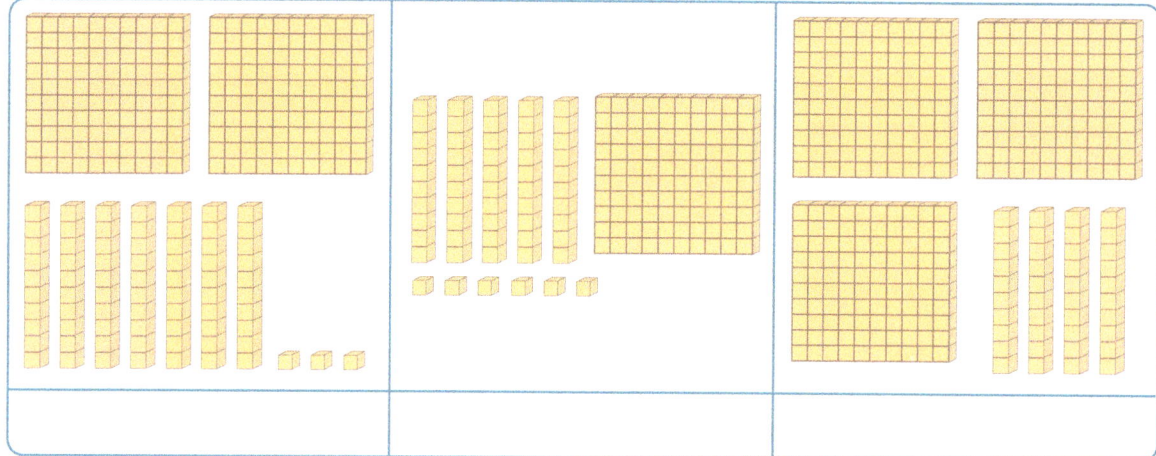

5. What number comes before and after?

_____ 58 _____   _____ 400 _____
_____ 644 _____   _____ 898 _____

6. Write these numbers in words:

175 _____
413 _____
560 _____

7. Continue the counting pattern:

765, 770, 775, _____, _____, _____
100, 110, 120, _____, _____, _____
303, 306, 309, _____, _____, _____

8. Order these numbers from smallest to biggest:

678 680 702 _____
999 546 103 _____
456 389 22 _____

9. Circle three numbers between **585 – 620**

617   426   591   311   595   569

Specialised Edition

YEAR 2 END OF THE YEAR:

One on One Assessment Sample: Algebra

1. Work out these sums – **use the grids** to show your working out

    ⓐ 38 people were on a bus and then 24 more got on. How many people are on the bus altogether? _____

    ⓑ Lucy scored 46 points and Abbey scored 37. How many points did they score altogether? ___

    ⓒ Mikhayla had 42 lollies but then she gave 28 to her friends. How many did she have left? _____

2. Write the sum **4 x 5** using repeated addition _____

3. Draw an array to show the sum **3 x 7 =**

4. Answer these sums – What strategy did you use? Colour to match the strategy to the sum and show your working out under each strategy

Amelia has 22 mosquito bites. Myla has 10. How many more mosquito bites does Amelia have than Myla?	Split strategy
64 + 25 =	Doubles +1
7+3+5=	Compensation strategy
25 + 9 =	Finding the difference
8 + 9 =	Look For friendly pairs

Appendix

Teacher For Early Years

A	C
a	c
B	D
b	d

Specialised Edition

F	H
f	h
E	G
e	g

APPENDIX: ENGLISH

219

Teacher For Early Years

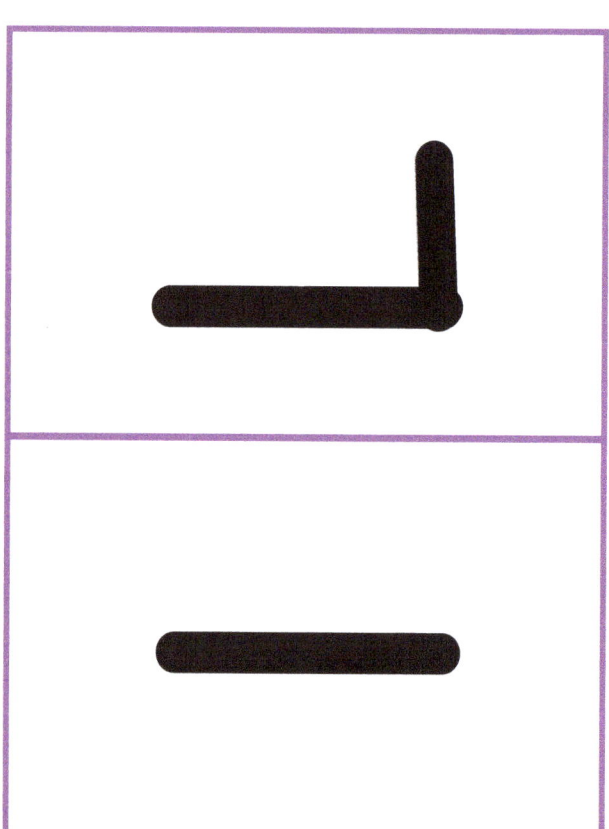
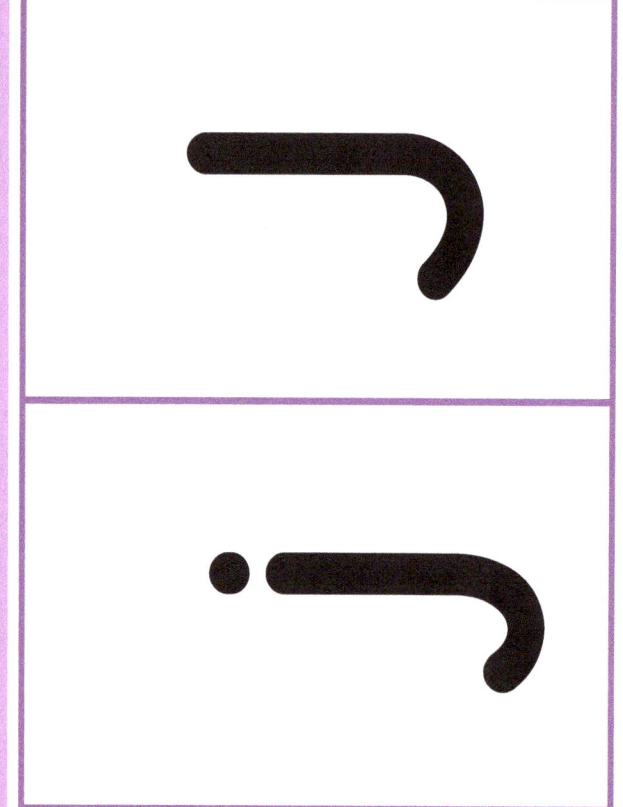

Specialised Edition

N	P p
n	p
M	O
m	o

APPENDIX: ENGLISH

Teacher For Early Years

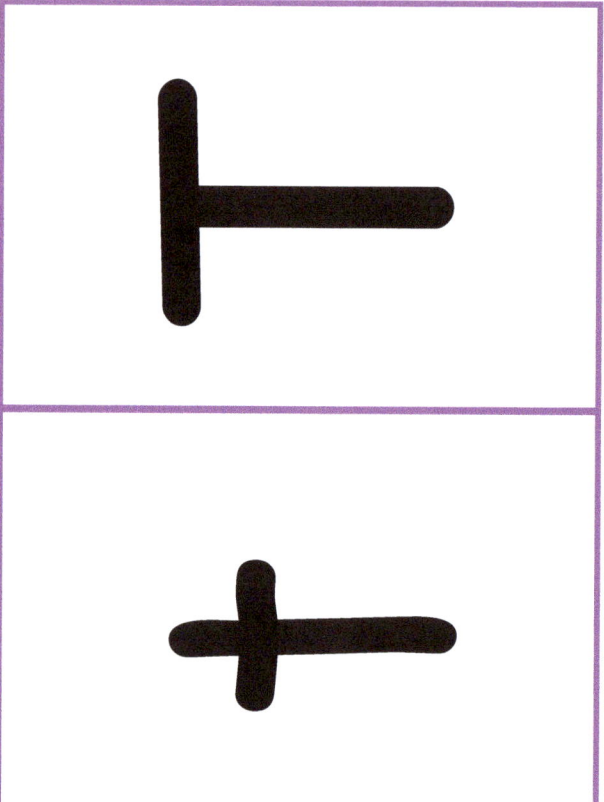
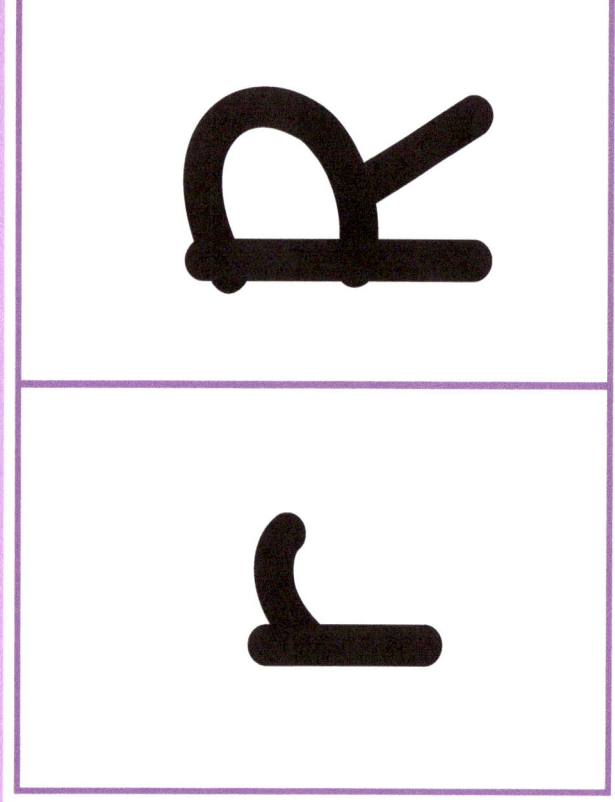

APPENDIX: ENGLISH   222

Specialised Edition

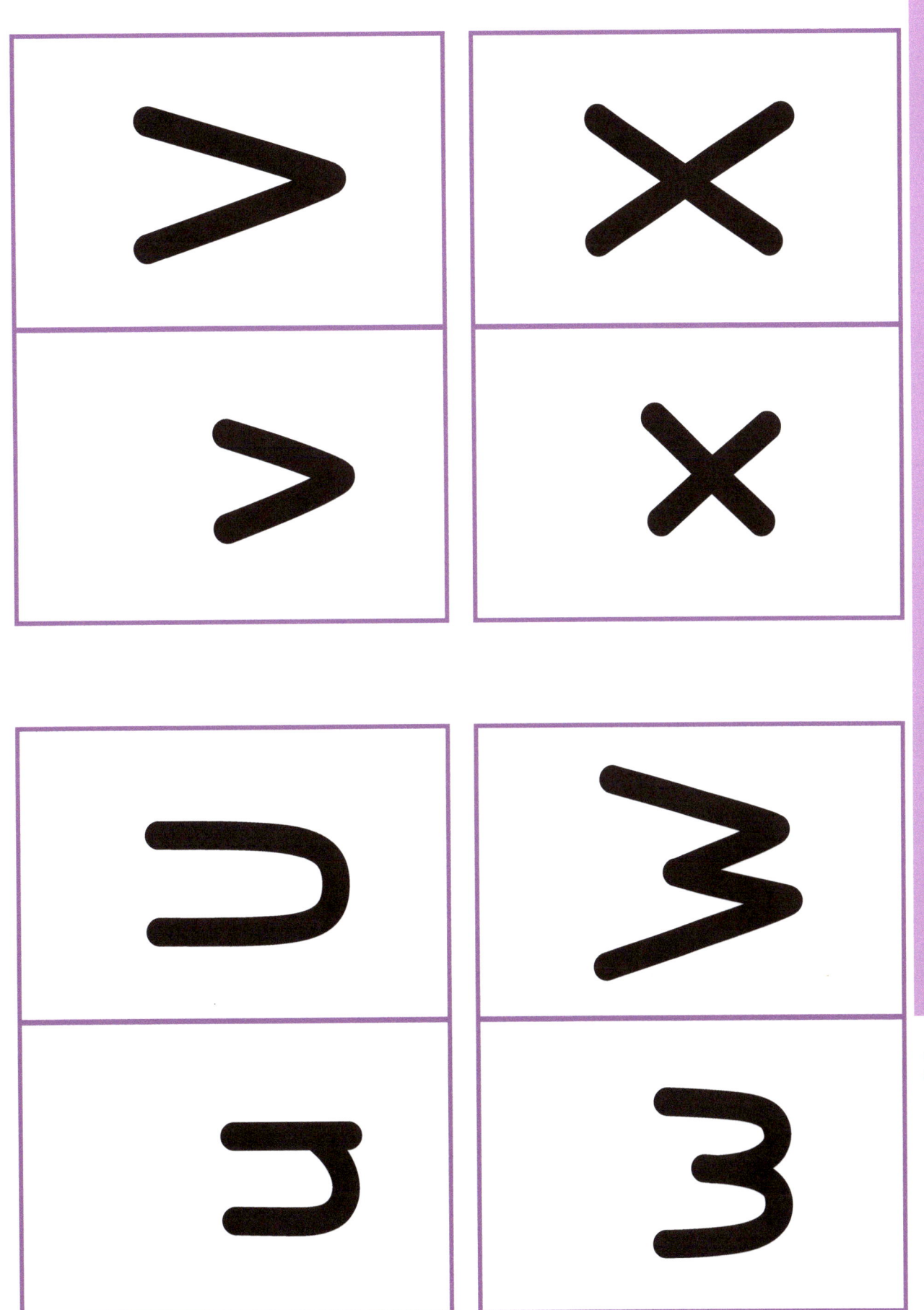

APPENDIX: ENGLISH

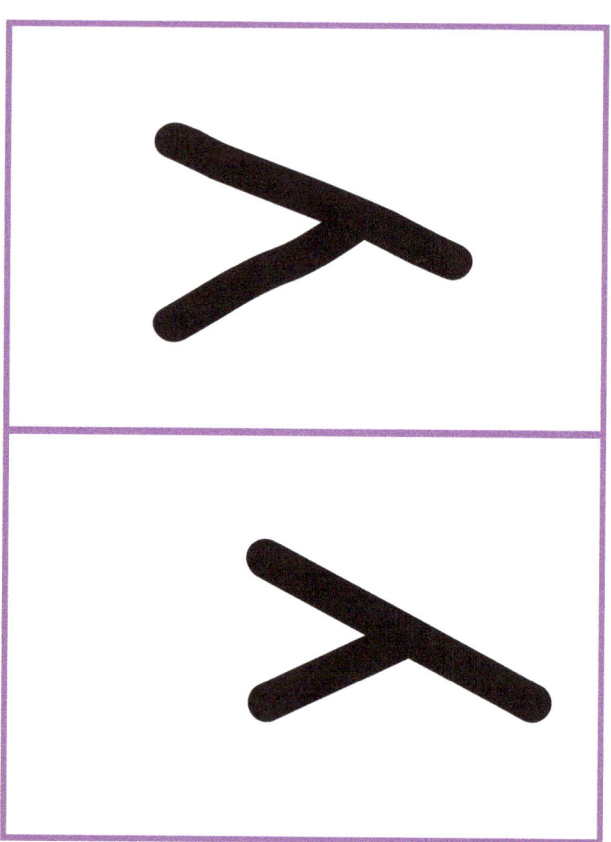

Concepts of Print – Tell me about the book

Can you show me the front of the book? Back of the book?	
Can you find the spine?	
Where is the blurb?	
Can you point to the title?	
Can you point to where the author's name is written?	
(open book) Can you show me where to start reading?	
Which way do the words go?	
Can you point to the words as I read them?	
Where do I go when I finish reading the top line?	
How do I turn the pages?	
(Next page) Can you point to the first word on this page?	
Can you point to the last word on this page?	
Can you point to a lowercase letter on this page?	
Can you point to an uppercase/capital letter on this page?	
Can you find a number on this page?	
Can you point to one word on this page?	
Can you point to two words on this page?	
Can you point to a picture/illustration?	

Specialised Edition

LETTER/SOUND CHECKLIST

Copy and cut the upper and lowercase letter flashcards on **pages 218-224**. Show children cards out of sequence and use this checklist as an assessment tool to identify letters they know and letters they need to learn.

	Name	Sound	Word
a			
b			
c			
d			
e			
f			
g			
h			
i			
j			
k			
l			
m			
n			
o			
p			
q			
r			
s			
t			
u			
v			
w			
x			
y			
z			
Total			

	Name	Sound
A		
B		
C		
D		
E		
F		
G		
H		
I		
J		
K		
L		
M		
N		
O		
P		
Q		
R		
S		
T		
U		
V		
W		
X		
Y		
Z		
Total		

Teacher For Early Years

Children need to be explicitly taught the difference between letters, words, and sentences. Remind students of the rules for a complete sentence (see checklist page 77). Re-write each white box below, under the correct heading.

I can identify letters, words and sentences.

m	I like playing at the beach.	The girl	Can you help me?
teacher	Santa	We sat under a tree.	butterfly
j	w	Rabbit in box.	pink towel

Letter/Word/Sentence sort

Letter	Word/s	Sentence

Specialised Edition

EDITING A SENTENCE

Read the following rules to your child.

We use a **capital letter** to show the start of a sentence. We use a **full stop (.)** to mark the end of a **complete** sentence, when it is a statement.

ABCDEFGHIJKLMNOPQRSTUVWXYZ

I can use full stops and capital letters.

1) i will ride my bike today
_____

2) this is my sister
_____

3) zebras are black and white
_____

4) i am going outside
_____

5) come and play with me
_____

SENTENCE BOUNDARIES

Read the following rules to your child.
We use a **full stop (.)** to mark the end of a complete sentence.
We use a **question mark (?)** when a question has been asked.
We use an **exclamation mark (!)** to show emotion.

I can edit sentences: What mark do I need?

.   ?   !

How are you today

My name is _____

A snake slithered through the grass

Stop hurting me

Are you coming to the disco

My dad is so funny

What time is it

Here is the letter you asked for

Can I please have a drink

Specialised Edition

I can use Adjectives.

Use at least **five interesting adjectives** to describe each of these characters.

Extension: Write a descriptive paragraph about each character. What do you imagine they are like? What might they do?

I can write Noun Groups.

We can make our sentences more descriptive using a cluster of words to describe the noun. **Number, size, colour, taste, temperature, personality and appearance** would be the most commonly used noun descriptors (adjectives) used in the Early Years.

Three tiny, red birds

Write your own noun groups using the following pictures:

____ ____ ____   ____ ____ ____

I can identify Conjunctions.

Conjunctions in their simplest form, are words that join sentences together to make a sentence more interesting. Some examples are:

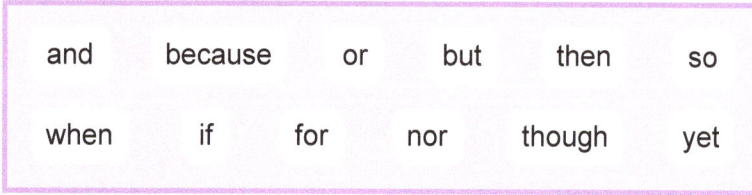

Join these sentences using a different conjunction for each one.

1. I like lions. I like zebras.

2. I did not eat my dinner. I don't like pasta.

3. The boy was lost in the woods. His mum called emergency services.

I can use Adverbs.

Adverbs are words that describe verbs, adjectives or other adverbs (but never nouns). They tell how, when, where and by how much. **In the Early Years,** we begin by learning that adverbs describe verbs ('how' something is being done). Some adverbs that children in the Early Years should be exposed to include:

To describe **speed and volume** – quickly, slowly, quietly, loudly, silently, noisily

To describe **actions** – bravely, busily, excitedly, oddly, wildly, cleverly, politely, selfishly, wisely, foolishly, happily, sadly

To describe **effort** – easily, sloppily, simply, messily, carelessly, lazily, beautifully

Sample List of Adverbs

How	When	Where	How much/ often
cheerfully	always	there	often
worriedly	occasionally	here	never
accidentally	yesterday	anywhere	always
secretly	today	everywhere	everyday
carefully	tomorrow	home	sometimes
well	now	inside	once/twice
gladly	soon	outside	rarely
eagerly	before/after	away	usually

Add an adverb to support the verb

ran _____
ate _____
nodded _____
worked _____
whispered _____
attacked _____

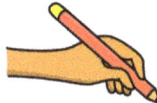

I can write Bump it Up sentences.

Children are encouraged to enhance basic sentences by adding in adjectives, adverbs, conjunctions and events.

The girl jumped.   The boy laughed.
The man coughed.   The witch cackled.
The baby cried.   The pig built.

Add in adjectives, adverbs, a conjunction and an event.

E.g. The boy jumped.

The small, skinny boy jumped quickly over the barrel because he was trying to escape the charging bull.

231

I can Compare and Contrast.

Use a Venn diagram to compare two characters/texts/events/numbers/settings. What is similar/different about them?

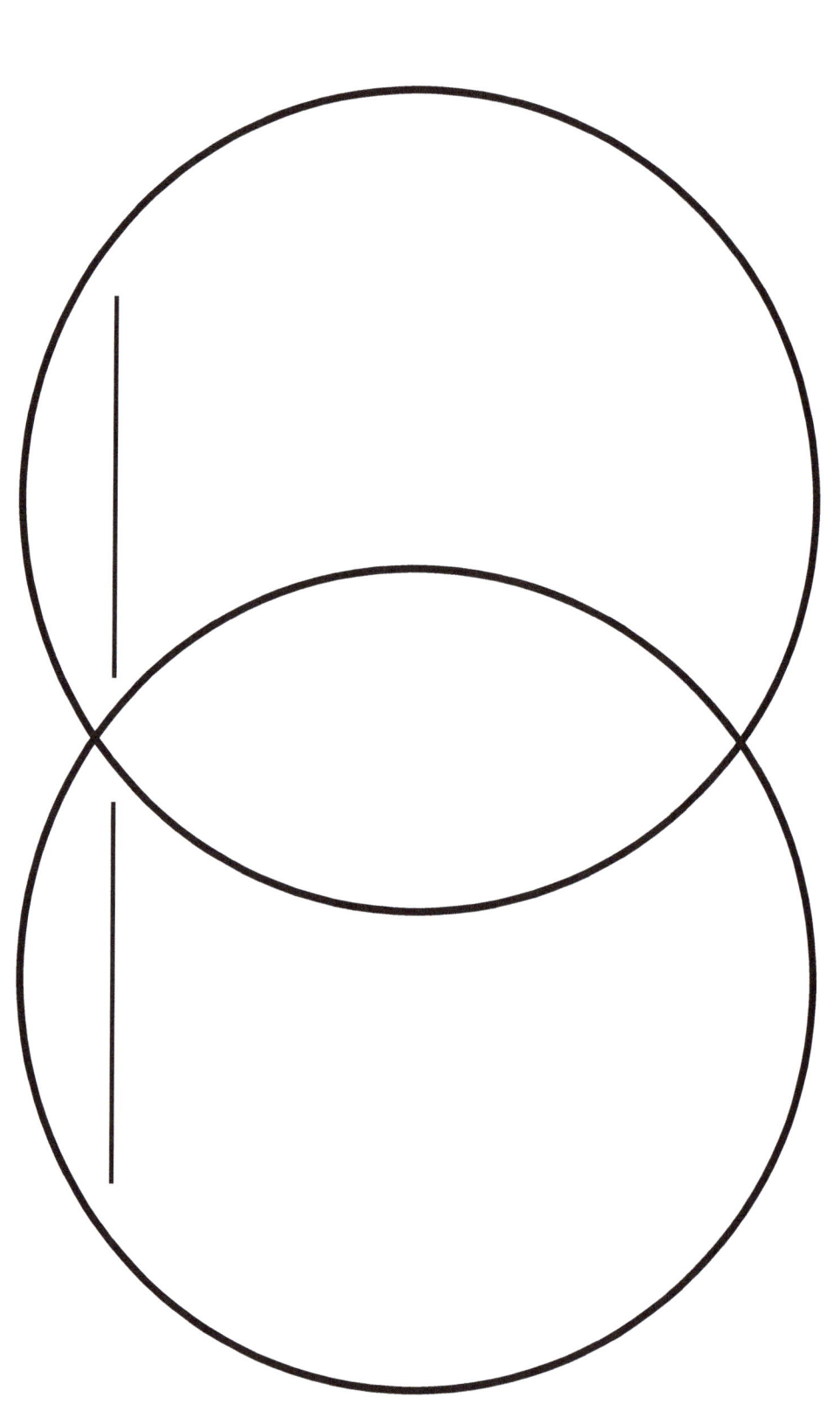

Specialised Edition

I can Illustrate my sentence.

APPENDIX: ENGLISH

233

I can use Commas to separate list items within a sentence (Year 2).

RULE: We use **commas** to separate the items in a list in our sentences. Put a comma between all items except for the last two. Between the last two items write the word 'and'.

Helen likes dogs cats elephants giraffes koalas.

Peter plays football soccer tennis hockey.

Aaron likes Star Wars Harry Potter Xbox Minecraft Roblox.

Caroline shops at Big W Coles Target K-Mart.

Can you write some of your own sentences?

_____
_____
_____
_____
_____
_____
_____

Specialised Edition

> **I can use Quotation (speech) Marks.**

Remind students that they need <u>four parts</u> – **opening speech marks ("")**, **closing speech marks ("")**, **a capital letter** and an **end mark (. or , or ? or !)**

we've lost our class pet   exclaimed Terry.

it's your fault   yelled Karen.

no, it's yours   shouted Julie.

let's look under the table   Adam suggested.

oh yes, maybe it fell under there   said Lisa.

found it   yelled Monica.

The rest of the class cheered.

fantastic   smiled Ms Margaret.

Can you write some of your own sentences?

_____
_____
_____
_____
_____
_____

Mnemonic Spelling Tricks

because
big elephants can always understand small elephants

people
people eat omelettes, people like eggs

come
can't open my eyes

does
dogs only eat sausages

laugh
laugh and u get happy

rhythm
rhythm helps your two hips move

eight
even I got hot tonight

ocean
ogres can eat any nail

said
spiders and insects dance

Mnemonic Posters

there, their or they're?
there
their
they're (are)

right or write?
right
write

your or you're?
your
you're (are)

friends
Friday always ends with friends

believe
Never believe a lie

together
to-get-her

forty
Naughty forty doesn't play with letter u

desert or dessert?
A desert is full of sand (one s) and a dessert is full of sweet stuff (two s's).

island
An island is land with water around it.

Teacher For Early Years

STRUCTURE AND FEATURES

The following pages will explore the basic structure and features of some commonly used text types for the Early Years. Even in the foundational years, children should be exposed to a range of text types and start exploring the purpose and intended audience of a range of texts. The following pages will support children to begin to explore and replicate the generic structure of a variety of texts.

TYPE OF TEXT: Children need to know that there are many different text types and that they have identifiable text structures and language features that help the text to serve its purpose.

PURPOSE: Why was it written? Who was it written for?
▸ Refers to a specific reason for writing and intended audience.

STRUCTURE: How is the text built? What is the format?
▸ Refers to the way the text is organised.

🔥 When using the words *'text structure'* in front of children, use closed fists to mimic stacking hands one on top of the other – to make the link with *'building'* the text.

FEATURES: What language would I hear? What punctuation marks would I see?
▸ Refers to the components of the text.

🔥 When discussing *'features'* of a text, make hands into binoculars to make the links with language and devices they will see and hear in particular texts.

Specialised Edition

THE WRITING PROCESS

Before beginning any writing, children need to be immersed in a range of mentor texts to comprehend and de-construct, focusing on the structure and language features of each text.

The structure and language features should be modelled explicitly, so that children understand expectations before beginning writing. Please see the posters in appendix on **page 238-259** to support this. Children also need to know that their writing will be shaped depending on its purpose and audience. Remember, the writing process is huge! Writers have to think about letter formation, writing conventions (top to bottom, left to right), spaces between words, neatness, punctuation, etc., when they just want to get their ideas down on paper.

 It is helpful for children to physically move an object, each time they move to the next stage of the writing process, such as a small drawing of themselves onto posters labelled with each stage.

 PLANNING

 FIRST DRAFT

 PROOFREADING and EDITING

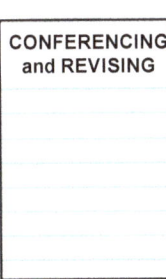 CONFERENCING and REVISING

GOOD COPY

1. PLANNING:

- **Talk** about what they are going to write! Children can't write it, if they can't say it.
- Discuss the intended **audience and purpose** of the piece of writing.
- Explore **structure and features** of the text type. See posters in the appendix, **pages 240-259**.
- List **learning goals and success criteria** – Today I am looking for... **See page 17**.
- Start getting ideas on paper, by brainstorming with **mind maps** or using visuals such as **story maps or planning templates**. See appendix for templates on **pages 240-259**.

 This stage is a chance to support children to orally or visually represent their ideas before beginning the writing process. It is the time to immerse children in rich vocabulary, activate prior knowledge and explore punctuation marks, as well as providing a scaffold of the generic structure and features of the text type they will be writing.

2. FIRST DRAFT:

- Should be **guided** and **co-constructed** using think alouds.
- Encourage children to refer to ideas created during the **planning** phase.
- Support them to write in sentences and remind them that **mistakes can be corrected** in the **next two stages.**

3. PROOFREADING and EDITING:

- Children **read their writing aloud** and **fix mistakes they see and hear**, listening for intonation and checking that they have punctuation marks as well as ensuring that their writing is in sequence and makes sense. **Make changes** to the text, considering sentence structure, punctuation, and descriptive language.
- Give them the **Check Your Sentence** check list on **page 77**.

4. CONFERENCING and REVISING:

- Children have fixed as many mistakes as they can and are **ready to share** their writing.
- **Adult should quickly skim the text** and identify the main areas of focus, before going through the text with them. Correct remaining mistakes together. Focus on spelling, grammatical structure, detail, cohesive devices (linking words) and punctuation.
- Check that it meets the needs of **audience** and **purpose**.
- Go through the **Working Together to Check Your Writing** questions on **page 78**.

5. FINAL COPY:

- **Publish their final copy** – using their best work with corrections. It could be typed and printed, neatly rewritten, or presented on a poster or app.
- Use the **Writing Goal Checklist** on **page 79** to identify future goals.

Recount/Journal

Features

- Can be fiction or non-fiction
- Written in past tense
- Descriptive language
- Write using all of the senses
- Time words – First, then, after that, later on, last, finally, secondly
- Emotive words
- Proper nouns, pronouns
- Year Two students should be encouraged to incorporate figurative language (see page 86)

Purpose: To retell events

Structure

Title

- Introductory paragraph to orientate the reader. Should include who, what, when, where and why information.
- Sequential paragraphs about different events.
- A personal evaluation which refers back to the beginning of the recount.

RECOUNT WRITING

Use descriptive language (adjectives, noun groups and adverbs – see **pages 229-231**), figurative language for Year Two students (see **page 86**), time words (see **page 240**), the five senses (seeing, hearing, smelling, tasting and touching) and the five W's + H questions (who, what, when, where, why + how), to enhance child's writing from this:

> On my holiday, I went to the pool.
> Then I had lunch.
> Then I went to the shop.
> Finally, I went home.

To this:

> On my amazing holiday, I went to the sparkling, blue pool to have a swim with my best friend Nicole. My mum drove us in our white Subaru. When we arrived, we went straight to the plastic table to put our towels in our favourite spot. After we put on our sunscreen, we jumped into the refreshing water. We played and played until our skin went wrinkly and then we hopped out to dry off before eating a delicious ice-cream.
>
> After the pool, we went to the shops to get afternoon tea. We went to McDonald's and we each got a tasty Happy Meal, even my mum. The toy was a little figurine of Ronald McDonald on a swing and when I pushed the button he went around and around. Next, we went to get some food from the grocery shop for lunches, including fruit and cupcakes. Nicole bought some Vegemite to put on her sandwiches.
>
> Finally, we left the busy shops and started the long drive home. We had one of the pink cupcakes from the grocery store while we were driving. After that, it was time to drop Nicole back at her house and go home and hang our wet towels and togs on the line. It was a long day of swimming, eating and having fun in the sun. At home, we fell asleep in our comfortable beds.

Letter/Email

Features

- Can be formal or informal
- Who it is to and from
- Email can be sent to multiple recipients
- Information/messages
- Digital safety – emails last forever

Purpose: A message: to give someone information

Structure (Informal)

- Greeting: Dear ---, (leave next line blank).
- Message (leave next line blank).
- Salutation: From --

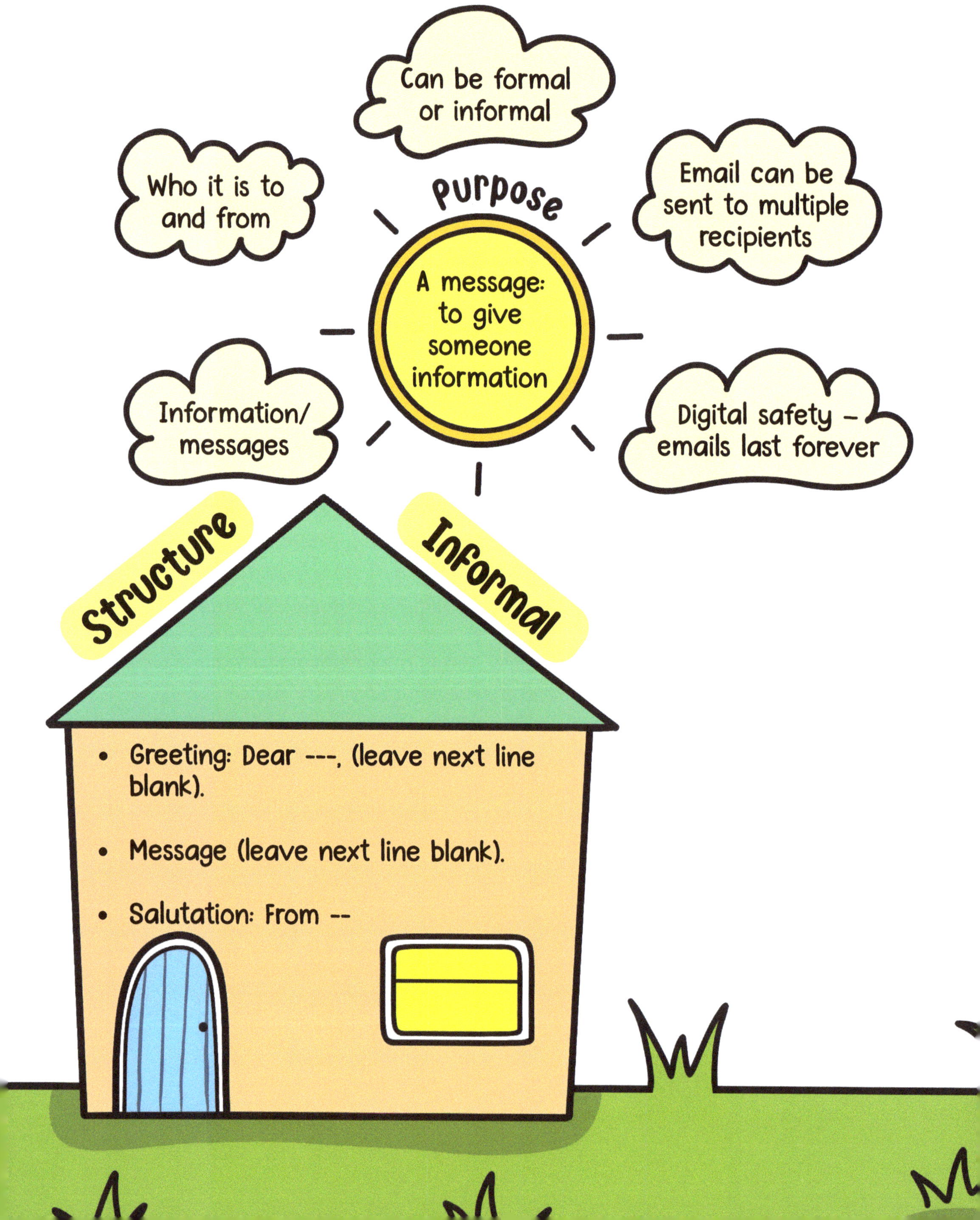

Specialised Edition

Letter writing template for the Early Years

Dear _____ ,

_____

_____

_____

_____

_____

From _____

Procedure

Features

- Measurements
- Verbs, adverbs and adjectives
- List – one item per line
- No characters or dialogue
- Steps in numerical order, each step beginning with an imperative verb or an adverb
- Labelled diagrams or photographs to show process or finished product
- Written in present tense

Purpose
Gives instructions on how to make or do something

Structure

Title

Headings and subheadings

- Goal (for Year Two students).
- List of materials/ingredients.
- Numbered steps/clear instructions, each step on a new line.

Specialised Edition

Procedural writing template for the Early years

Title:
(must match what is being made)

Goal/Explanation:

(This section could be used as an extension activity; it explains the task and should make the reader want to make it)
E.g., Use this recipe to make the best chocolate brownies in the world.

Ingredients/Materials/What you need
(A list - one item per line, no text connectives or joining words).

- _____
- _____
- _____

Steps/Method/Instructions
(Steps should be numbered and each step should start with a verb or adverb).

1. _____
2. _____
3. _____
4. _____

Narrative – A story

Features

- Organised into paragraphs according to sequence of events
- Can be fiction or non-fiction
- A myriad of descriptive language including adjectives, verbs, adverbs as well as proper nouns, time words and exciting punctuation marks
- Dialogue using direct and indirect speech
- Year Two students should be encouraged to incorporate figurative language (see page 86)
- Written in past or present tense

Purpose: To entertain

Structure

Title

- Beginning or Orientation (introduces who, when, where).
- Build Up – leading up to the problem.
- Problem or Complication.
- Solution or Resolution (The characters solve the problem).
- Ending or Conclusion (describes lessons learnt or how things have changed since the beginning).

Narrative Planning Template for the Early Years

Beginning - Orientation		
<u>Who</u> is in the story? Characters Goodies/Baddies	<u>When</u> did it happen?	<u>Where</u> did it happen? Setting

Problem – Complication **USE EXCITING WORDS**

_____
_____
_____
_____
_____

Solution - Resolution

_____
_____
_____
_____

Ending - Conclusion

_____
_____
_____

APPENDIX: ENGLISH

Storyboard to support Retell (Foundation–Year 1)

Beginning	Middle	End

Specialised Edition

Storyboard to support Retell (Year 1-2)

Beginning _____	**Problem** _____
Solution _____	**Ending** _____

APPENDIX: ENGLISH

249

Exposition/Persuasive

Features

Purpose: To convince/persuade someone of something

- High modality words: definitely, certainly must etc.
- Connectives to keep building on the point of view: firstly, secondly, furthermore etc.
- Persuasive devices: rhetorical questions, exaggeration, emotive language, alliteration, rhyme, repetition, descriptive language
- Arguments organised into paragraphs
- Facts (statistics, evidence) and emotive opinions (point of view)
- Personal pronouns such as I, we, our, us to connect with the reader
- Strong sentence starters: In my opinion, It is obvious that, I strongly believe
- Usually written in present tense

Structure

Title – should strongly indicate the author's opinion

- Introduction: introduces the three reasons (arguments) that will be explored and gives some background information.
- Reason (argument) 1 with support examples, explanations facts and opinions.
- Reason (argument) 2 with support examples, explanations facts and opinions.
- Reason (argument) 3 with support examples, explanations facts and opinions.
- Conclusion: restates three reasons identified with a recommendation for moving forwards.

PERSUASIVE/EXPOSITION WRITING

Create three arguments *'for'* or *'against'* a topic – E.g., Kids should/should not have to do homework, weekends should be three days long, dogs should always be kept on a leash.

Explore high modality words such as **definitely, certainly, obviously, clearly, absolutely, wholeheartedly, always etc.** These words help us express how strongly we feel about something.

Explore sentence starters that use high modality words such as

| It is obvious that… | Clearly, we need to… |
| I am absolutely certain that… | I wholeheartedly believe… |

Generic structure of a Persuasive text

Paragraph 1, Introduction	State your opinion and gibe background information. Identify the three reasons/arguments that you will be exploring.
Paragraph 2, Reason 1	State your first argument and back it up with supporting details, examples, evidence.
Paragraph 3, Reason 2	State your second argument and back it up with supporting details, examples, evidence.
Paragraph 4, Reason 3	State your third argument and back it up with supporting details, examples, evidence.
Paragraph 5, Conclusion	Restate your opinion and the three arguments that you identified, with a recommendation for moving forwards. Finish with a bang – *That is why I firmly believe…*

The **OREO** explanation is frequently used to explain argument writing in persuasive texts.

O = Opinion
R = Reason
E = Explanation/examples/evidence
O = Opinion restated

The **triple stuffed OREO** on the next page is a great asset to support Year Two students to see the structure of a persuasive text.

My Oreo Planning Sheet

Topic: _____

Opinion
O

Reason
R

Example
E

Reason
R

Example
E

Reason
R

Example
E

Opinion
O

FOR and AGAINST

Sort the following sentences as a **'For'** or **'Against'** statement for getting a pet horse.

> Horses are expensive to feed and look after.
>
> Horses are quiet, they will not bark and wake up the neighbours.
>
> Horses produce manure which people buy to put on their gardens.
>
> Horses need a lot of land to run around on.
>
> Horses are very hard to look after.
>
> Horses can be trained to race and win money.

FOR	AGAINST
1.	1.
2.	2.
3.	3.

Practise writing <u>three reasons **'For'**</u> and <u>three reasons **'Against'**</u> doing homework.

Children should have to do homework	Children should NOT have to do homework
1.	1.
2.	2.
3.	3.

When writing persuasive texts, it is also beneficial to know the difference between facts and opinions. <u>Zebras are black and white mammals with four legs is a **fact**. I love zebras is an **opinion**.</u> Have a go at writing some facts and opinions.

FACT	OPINION

> The following samples were co-constructed with Year 2 students after reading **Hey Little Ant** by **Hannah Hoose and Phillip Hoose** and following the structure and ideas on **page 250-253**.

Sample demonstrating an 'Against' argument

We Should NOT Squish Ants!

It is very obvious that we should never squish tiny, defenceless ants. They are just trying to live their lives in peace, they are part of nature, and they help to keep the world clean. Ants must be protected, never squashed.

Firstly, I am absolutely certain that ants don't want to die. They just want to mind their own business and live a happy and healthy life in peace. They are not trying to steal, they need food too, just like you. They can not drive to the shops and buy their own chips. We love chips and so do they. One chip could feed their whole town for lunch. They need food or they will not survive. Sometimes, that means they need to borrow food from humans.

Secondly, ants are an extremely important part of nature, they each have a job to do within their colony. Their family and friends rely on them. They must help collect food and build nests for all of the other ants. If they didn't help, the unprotected baby ants would all die and you don't want that to happen, do you?

Thirdly, anyone can clearly see that ants help to keep our world clean. When you dropped your sandwich on the floor the other day, guess who cleaned it up? You got it, ants! They are tiny cleaners who work for free and help to keep the world looking beautiful. Why wouldn't you want a beautiful and clean environment?

In conclusion, it is obvious that it is not ok to kill ants because they help to clean up nature and they need to help keep their family alive. I wholeheartedly believe that they are just trying to mind their own business and live a happy and peaceful life. We need to protect these tiny creatures from monsters who want to hurt them.

Sample demonstrating a 'For' argument

Ants Are the Worst!

You must agree that all ants should be killed because they are tremendously annoying, they always sting us, and they constantly steal our picnic food. All these crazy creatures should be eliminated by the exterminator! The time has come for us to destroy these disgusting thieves!

In my opinion, ants are absolutely the most annoying beasts in the world. They will crawl all over babies and pets and even over your legs if you are sitting near their nest. When these horrible animals are thirsty, they will form a ginormous line of tiny, black crooks to try to get into the sink area of your kitchen. You end up with thousands of thirsty ants crawling everywhere! They even build their houses in your pot plant, spreading dirt all over the place!

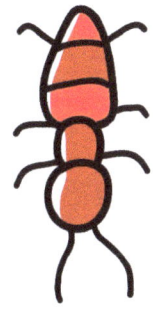

Anyone can see that ants have stingers that they can use to bite or sting us. The bite causes a huge red lump, and you may need ice or cream to stop the pain. If you had a special party, you would not be able to enjoy it because you would be too busy trying to cover your bites with ice packs. If you do not have ice or cream, some people have to put spit on their bite and that is gross! That red lump looks so unsightly, that no-one would like to pay attention to you.

I am absolutely certain that these wicked, rude burglars will come and eat all of your special food and even try to get into your drink! What if you were starving and you found out that all the mean, greedy ants had stolen half of your lunch? You would be so disappointed if they ate all of your dinner too. It would leave you as a hungry, hungry human.

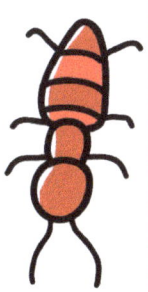

There is no doubt that all ants should be killed at once. Ants are the most annoying creatures in the world. They constantly bite us and they always steal our special things. It is time to sacrifice all of the evil insects so that we can live happily ever after.

Information Report

Features

- Non-fiction
- Formal language
- No characters or dialogue
- No exclamation marks (!) or ellipses (...)
- Headings and subheadings
- May have
  - Index
  - Glossary
  - Contents page
- Photographs, tables, labelled diagrams, keywords, captions
- Topic-specific vocabulary
- Written in present tense

Purpose: To inform about a topic

Structure

Title

- Introduction to explain the subject.
- Heading and subheadings
- Organised into paragraphs with real information, separated according to different features of the topic.

Animal Information Report – Note-taking Template

TITLE:

INTRODUCTION

DESCRIPTION/APPEARANCE
(What does it look like?)

DIET (What does it eat?)

HABITAT (Where does it live?)

INTERESTING INFORMATION (How does it behave? How does it reproduce (have babies)? How does it move?)

Information Report template

Introduction

Habitat

Description

Specialised Edition

Diet

Diagram

Interesting Information

APPENDIX: ENGLISH

NUMBER RHYMES — LEARNING NUMERALS

Number 1 is like a stick,
A straight line down, it's very quick!

For number 2, go right around,
Then make a line across the ground!

Go right around, what will it be?
Go around again to make a 3!

Down and across and down some more,
That is how to make a 4!

Go down and around and then you stop!
Then make a line across the top!

Start up the top, then go right down and then make a loop across the ground.

Across the sky and down from heaven,
That is how to make a 7.

Make a "S" but then don't wait,
Close it up to make an 8!

Make a loop and then a line,
That is how to make a 9!

Make a one and then a zero,
You've made 10 because you're a hero!

1	6
2	7
3	8
4	9
5	10

one	six
two	seven
three	eight
four	nine
five	ten

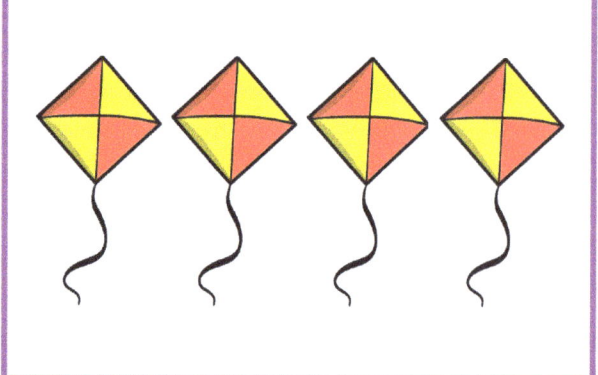 

Cookies for Addition and Subtraction

Five Frame

Ten Frame

Foundation Pattern Assessment

Copy these patterns

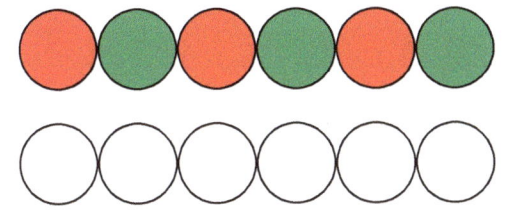   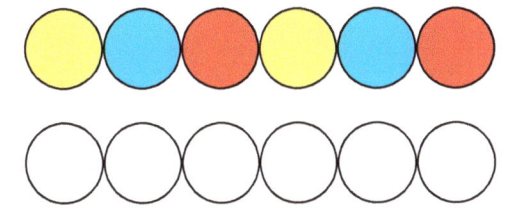

Continue these patterns

1.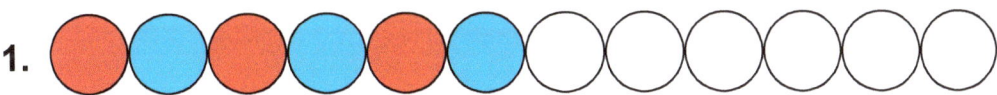

2.

Create your own pattern

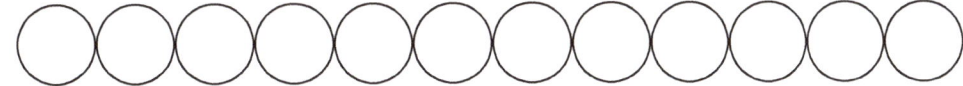

APPENDIX: MATH

NUMBERS to 10 THINKBOARD

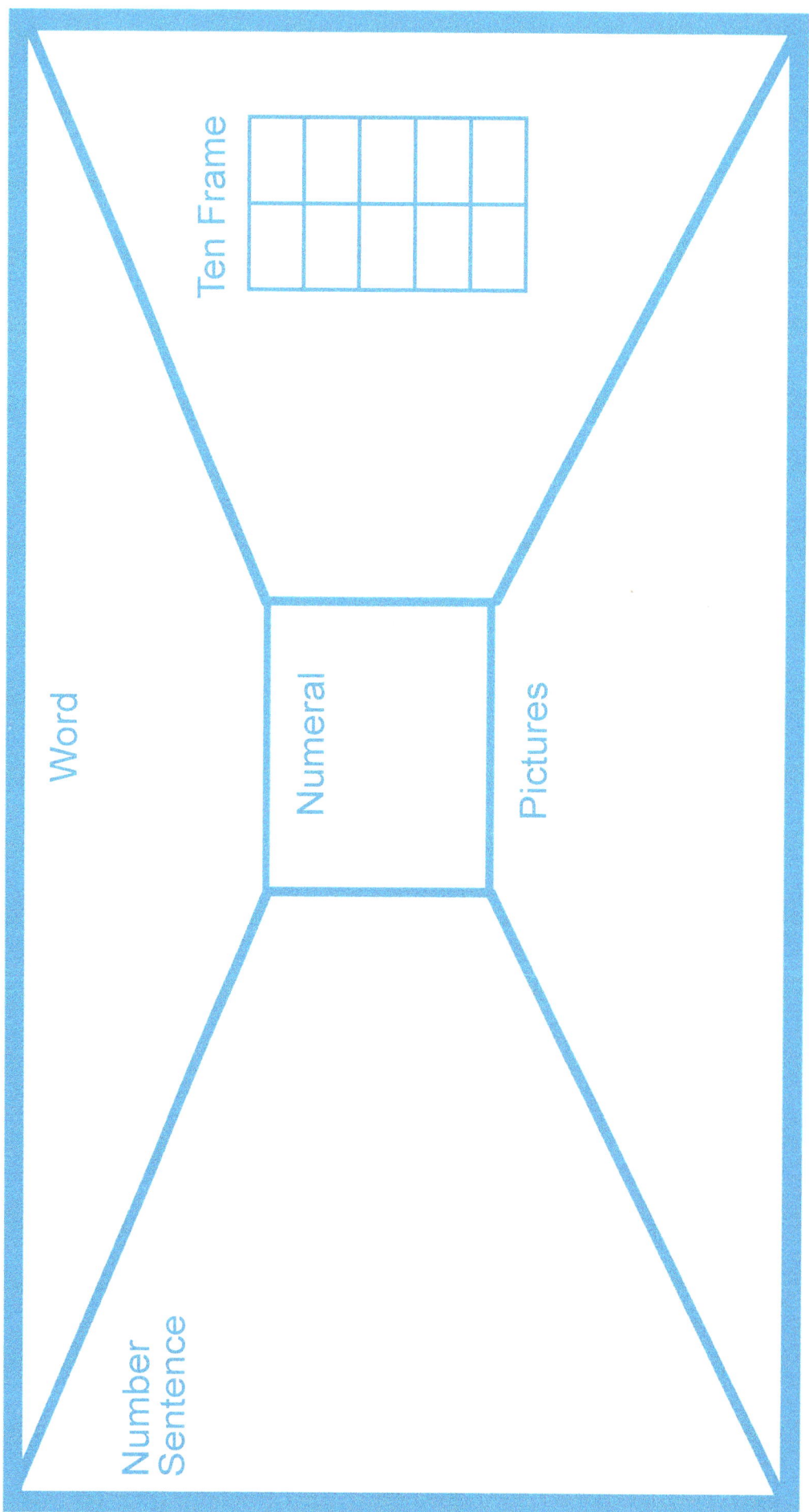

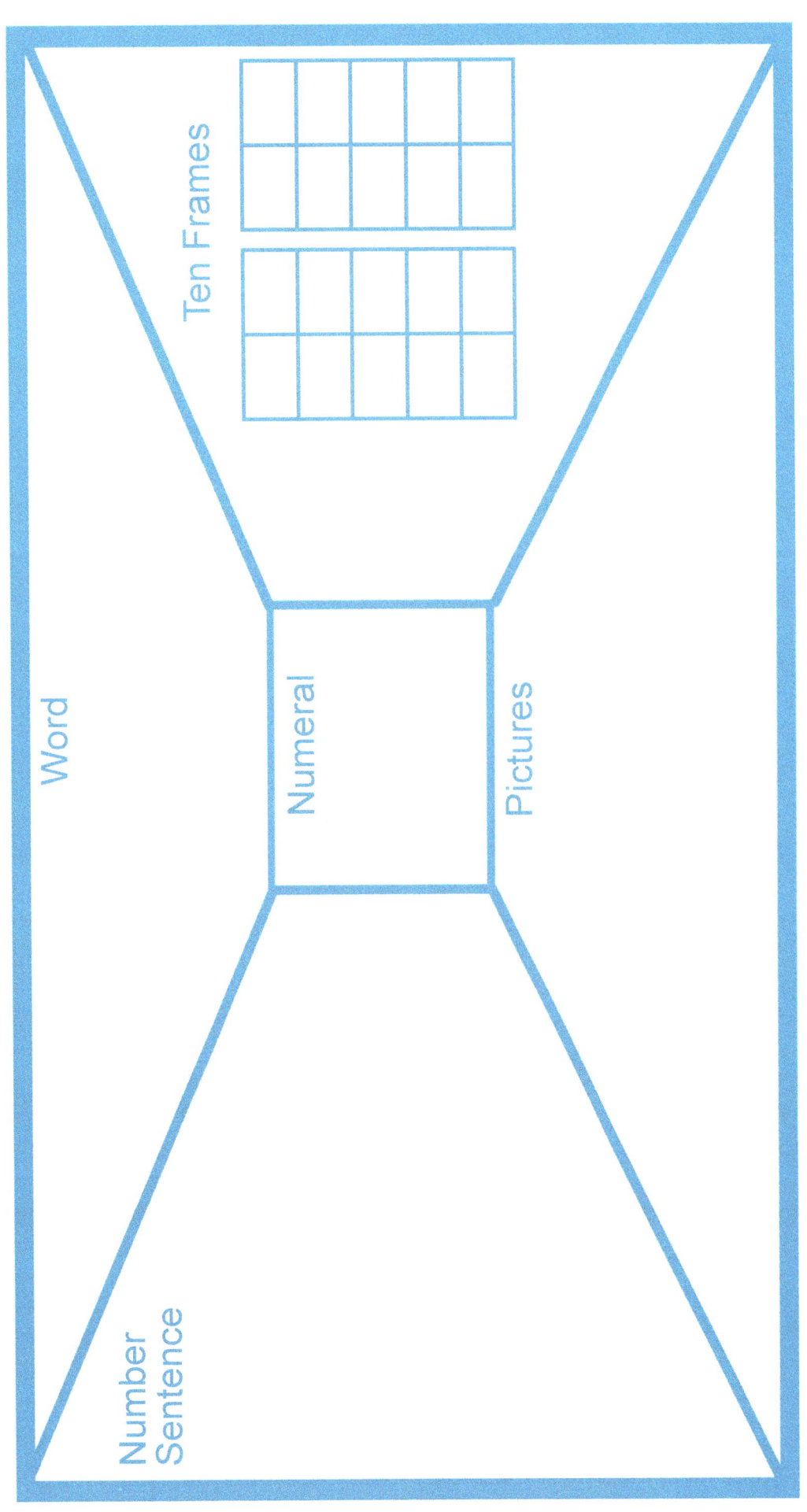

Hundred Grid

1	2	3	4	5	6	7	8	9	10
11	12	13	14	15	16	17	18	19	20
21	22	23	24	25	26	27	28	29	30
31	32	33	34	35	36	37	38	39	40
41	42	43	44	45	46	47	48	49	50
51	52	53	54	55	56	57	58	59	60
61	62	63	64	65	66	67	68	69	70
71	72	73	74	75	76	77	78	79	80
81	82	83	84	85	86	87	88	89	90
91	92	93	94	95	96	97	98	99	100

Blank Hundred Grid

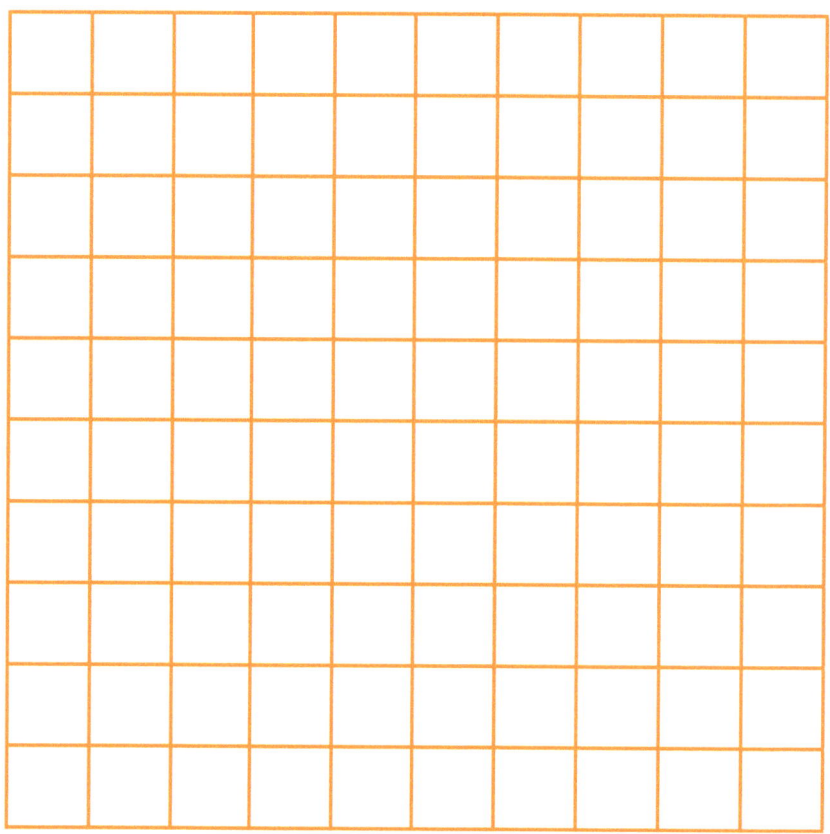

MAB or Base 10 Blocks – copy, laminate and make numbers

Two-Digit Place Value Chart

TENS	ONES

Three-Digit Place Value Chart

HUNDREDS	TENS	ONES

Lily pads and Frogs:
To use when solving multiplication and division problems.

Specialised Edition 275

APPENDIX: MATH

Number of the Day: two-digit

Number

Odd or Even

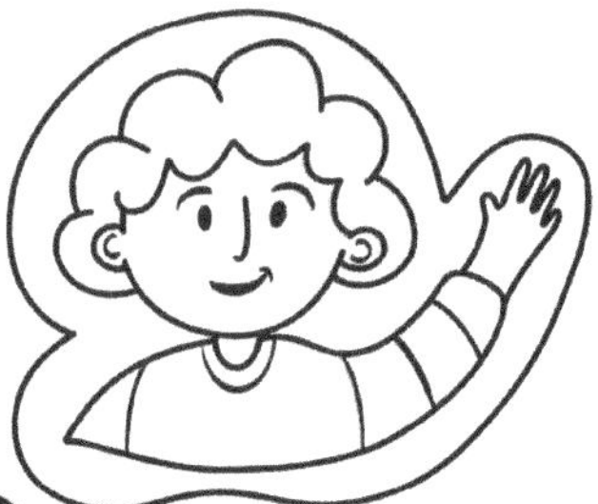

Tally marks

(Spell number)
_____ is the same
as _____ tens
as _____ ones

Where is it? Draw an arrow on the number line:

Fill in the number line
0 10 20 30 40 50 60 70 80 90 100

one more | one less

ten more | ten less

Draw tens and ones

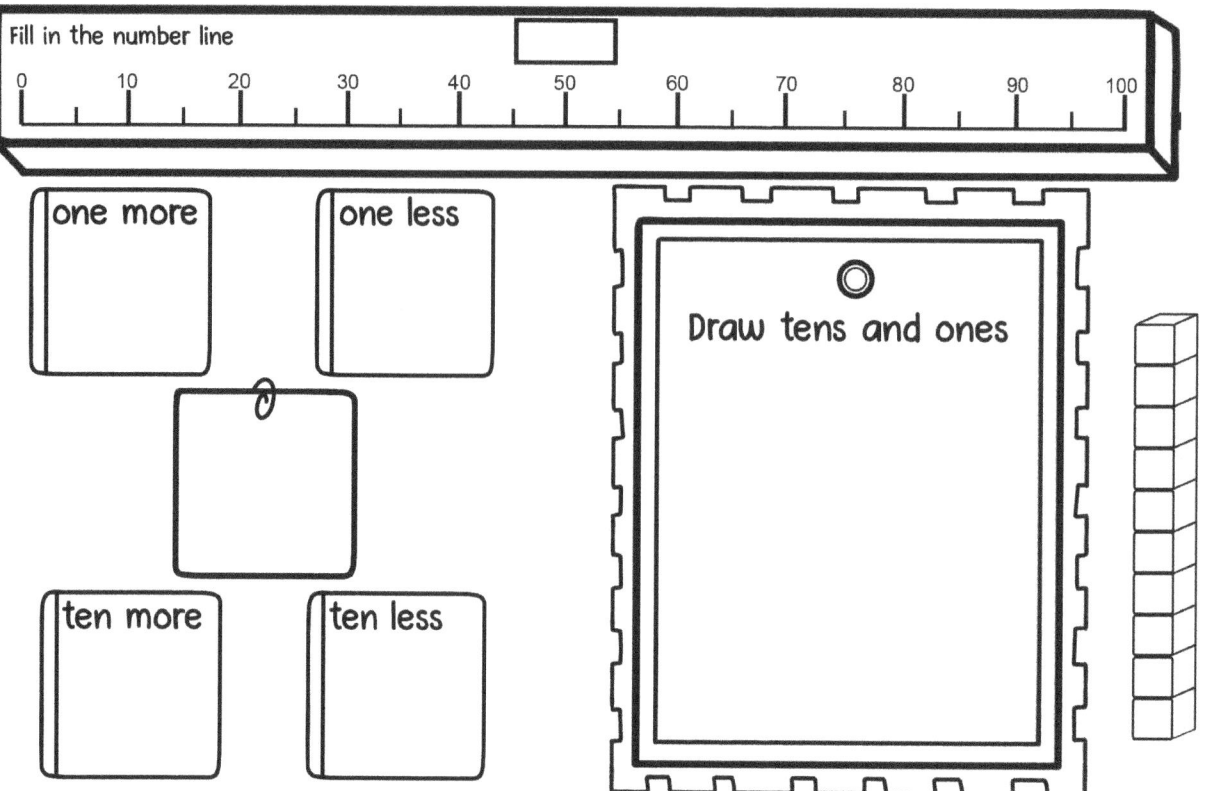

Number of the Day: three-digit

Number

Odd or Even

Round it to the nearest

ten _____

hundred _____

(Spell number)
is the same as ____ hundreds, ____ tens, and ____ ones.

Where is it? Draw an arrow on the number line:

Fill in the number line
0   100   200   300   400   500   600   700   800   900   1000

one more

one less

ten more

ten less

one hundred more

one hundred less

Number in expanded form

_____ +

_____ +

_____

GLOSSARY OF TERMS

Addend	One of the parts in the addition algorithm.
Addition Strategies	Ways to solve addition calculations, explained in detail on **pages 152 -175**.
Adjective	A word used to describe a noun e.g., *beautiful, green, lumpy*.
Adverb	A word that adds to the meaning of the verb. It tells how, when, where and for how long something is happening e.g., *quickly, loudly, weekly*.
Algorithm	A process or formula for solving a problem or completing a task.
Alliteration	Alliteration is the repetition of the same initial letter in successive words for effect e.g., *she sells seashells by the seashore*.
Antonyms	Words opposite in meaning to each other e.g., *long/short, hot/cold*.
Apostrophe	A punctuation mark used to indicate missing letters in words or possession of an object e.g., *do not = don't, is not = isn't / John's hat, Jesus' miracle*.
Array	A pictorial representation using images or shapes arranged in equal rows and columns.
Articulation	The ability to form clear and well-defined sounds in speech.
Base Word/Root Word/ Main Word	A word from which other words are built e.g., *rest, resting, rested, restful*.
Blend	Two or more consonants that together make a blended sound e.g., *bl, fr, dr*.
Bossy/Magic/ Silent E Rule	Adding an 'e' to the end of a word with a short vowel, can change a short vowel sound into a long vowel sound e.g., *mat + e becomes mate, twin + e becomes twine*.
Bundling Sticks	Bundling a concrete object (popsicle sticks, straws, pencils, etc.) into groups of ten to support understanding of counting, calculations and place value.
Comma	A punctuation mark (,) indicating a pause in a sentence, or used to separate items in a list.
Comparing	Noting similarities and differences between objects and things.
Confusing Letters	Also called tricky letters, are letters that often confuse small children. These include b/d, p/q, m/w, n/u, i/j.
Conjunctions	A word used to join or link different parts of the same sentence e.g., *and, so, but*.
Consonants	21 of the 26 letters of the alphabet – all letters excluding a, e, i, o, u.
Compound Word	Two words joined together e.g., *butter + fly = butterfly*.
Contractions	Two words shortened to one, using an apostrophe to show missing letters e.g., *I am = I'm, I have = I've*.
Difference	The result of subtracting one number ftrom another.
Digraphs	A combination of two letters representing one sound. e.g., *sh, ch, th, wh*.
Ellipses	A punctuation mark consisting of three dots, often denoting suspension points or trailing off in thought.
Equation	A number sentence containing numbers and an equals sign (=).
Exclamation Mark	A punctuation mark (!) indicating an exclamation. Also called an 'emotion' mark.

Factors	A number that multiplies with another number to form a product e.g., *the factors of 12 are 2 and 6.*
Figurative Language	Language devices used to enhance writing. In the Early Years, we often use alliteration, onomatopoeia, similes, rhyme, repetition, exaggeration, personification.
Five Frame	A frame with five adjoining squares in one row of five. A useful visual resource to support counting and calculations to five.
Fraction	A part or portion of a whole amount.
Full Stop	A punctuation mark (.) used to indicate the end of a complete sentence.
High-Frequency Words	Words that occur most often in speaking, writing and reading e.g., *and, can, it.*
Homograph	Words that are spelt the same with different meanings e.g., *Feel the wind/wind it up, bow before the king/she wore a bow in her hair.*
Homophone	Words that sound the same but have a different spelling e.g., *tale/tail, know/no.*
Hundred Grid or Hundred Chart	A 10 x 10 table with spaces for one hundred numbers, most commonly 1 – 100.
MAB/Base 10 Blocks	A mathematical manipulative used to support the development of place value. Blocks are represented in ones, tens, hundreds and thousands.
Metaphors	Comparing two items by saying one is the other e.g., *He was a volcano, ready to erupt.*
Modal Words	Used to demonstrate the amount/degree or how definite you are about something. Low modality words are *maybe/possibly* and high modality words are *definitely/certainly.*
Multiples	A number that can be divided by another number, a certain number of times, without a remainder e.g., *12 is a multiple of 2 and 6.*
Nouns	Word used to name a person, place, animal or thing e.g., *girl, park, candle.*
Noun Groups	A group of words based on a noun e.g., *miserable, old cow; dry, windswept desert.*
Number Line	A line on which numbers are marked at intervals. A useful resource for skip counting and completing calculations.
Number Sentence	A sentence using numbers and mathematical symbols (see also, equation).
One to One Correspondence	When counting, saying one number name while touching one object.
Onomatopoeia	Words that sound like the action they represent e.g., *bang/splash/meow.*
Ordering	Placing numbers and objects in sequence.
Paragraphs	Several sentences (usually less than 10), grouped around a single main idea.
Partitioning	The act of breaking numbers into parts (partitions), to make calculations easier.
Patterns	A repeated design or ordered set or numbers arranged according to a rule.
Personification	Giving human qualities to a non-living object or thing e.g., *The trees were dancing in the wind.*

Place Value	Each digit has a value depending on where it is placed in the number.
Prefixes	Letters attached to the beginning of a word to change its meaning e.g., *unhappy, replay, disappear.*
Proper Nouns	The given name of people, places, objects and events e.g., *Peter, Bonds, McDonalds, Falls Festival.*
Pronouns	Referring to the participants; someone or something e.g., *he, she, they, I, you, it, this.*
Punctuation	Marks used when writing to indicate intonation, clarify meaning, separate, and complete sentences.
Question Mark	A punctuation mark (?) which indicates a question.
Quotation Marks	A punctuation mark (" ") used to show direct speech. They must open, close, start with a capital letter and have a punctuation mark at the end. e.g., *"Pick up your shoes!"*
Regrouping/ Trading/Carrying	The act of re-arranging groups in place value. e.g., *swapping ten ones for one ten in addition and subtraction calculations.*
Repetition	A language feature used in storybooks, helps children join in with the story.
Rhyme	Words that have or end with a sound that corresponds with another e.g., *hour/power, wool/full.*
Rounding	To change a number to a more convenient value that is shorter, simpler or easier to represent e.g., *$19 can be rounded up to $20*
Sight Words	Words that occur most often in speaking, writing and reading that are not easily decodable and are learnt by sight e.g., *the, was, come.*
Similes	A phrase that shows the likeness between two things e.g., *As busy as a bee, as loud as a jet.*
Skip Counting	Counting forwards or backwards in multiples of a number other than one.
Subitisation	Instant recognition of the number of objects/dots in a group.
Suffixes	Letters added to the end of a base word e.g., care*less*, care*ful*, car*ing*.
Sum	The product of an addition equation.
Syllables	Breaking words into sound chunks. Each unit has one vowel sound (not necessarily a vowel, but a vowel sound).
Symmetry	Something is symmetrical when it is exactly the same on both sides.
Synonyms	A word that means exactly or nearly the same as another e.g., *large and huge.*
Tally Marks	A counting system useful for when counting with ongoing results.
Ten Frame	A frame with ten adjoining squares in two rows of five. A useful visual resource to support counting and calculations to ten.
Turnaround	Reversing the addends in addition or factors in multiplication algorithms and still reaching the same answer.
Verb	A word of action, speech or thought e.g., *run/yell/believe.*
Vowels	5 of the 26 letters of the alphabet, a,e,i,o,u. (Note: the letter Y can also do the work of the vowel and is sometimes called the sixth vowel).
Word Bank Book	A book for children to write spelling words and new vocabulary in, and use as a personal dictionary. Should be filled with words and referred to frequently, to support students with their writing.

www.ingramcontent.com/pod-product-compliance
Lightning Source LLC
Chambersburg PA
CBHW040950020526
44118CB00045B/2828